D0403467

MECHANICS' INSTITUTE
MECHANICS'.
MERCANTILE LIBRARY

THE WINDSORS

THE WINDSORS

A Dynasty Revealed

Piers Brendon and Phillip Whitehead

Hodder & Stoughton
LONDON SYDNEY AUCKLAND

First published in 1994 by Hodder and Stoughton
a division of Hodder Headline PLC

10 9 8 7 6 5 4 3 2 1

British Library Cataloguing in Publication Data

A CIP catalogue record for this title is available from the
British Library

ISBN 0 340 61013 1

Typeset by Hewer Text Composition Services, Edinburgh
Printed and bound in Great Britain by Mackays of Chatham plc

Hodder and Stoughton Ltd
A division of Hodder Headline PLC
338 Euston Road
London NW1 3BH

ACKNOWLEDGEMENTS

We should like to express our warmest gratitude to the many people who have contributed to the making of this book.

Our prime debt is to those who agreed to be interviewed for the documentary film *The Windsors*, of which this is, so to speak, the printed version. These include: Lady May Abel-Smith, Lord Ardwick, The Archdeacon of York, the Venerable George Austin, Georgina Battiscombe, Tony Benn, Lord Boyd-Carpenter, Lord Brabourne, Sarah Bradford, David Cannadine, Dame Barbara Cartland, Barbara Castle, Lady Elizabeth Cavendish, Lord Charteris, Professor Anthony Clare, the Hon. Alan Clark, Kenneth de Courcy, Susan Crosland, the Earl of Dudley, Robert Edwards, Frau Elbing, Elizabeth Emanuel, William Evans, Michael Fagan, Sir Edward Ford, Sir Dudley Forwood, Malcolm Fraser, Rosina Furze, Frank Giles, John Grigg, George Hadley, Lord Hailsham, Patricia, Viscountess Hambleden, Willie Hamilton, the Earl of Harewood, Bob Hawke, Sir Edward Heath MP, India Hicks, Lady Pamela Hicks, Ian Hislop, Anthony Holden, Maxwell Hutchinson, Hywel Jones, Penny Junor, Richard Kay, Thomas Keneally, Elizabeth, Countess of Longford, the Hon. Lady Veronica Maclean, Michael Mann, Mrs Fiona Maxwell-Stuart, James McClelland, Suzy Menkes, Lady Alexandra Metcalfe, David Metcalfe, Lady Mosley,

Countess Mountbatten, Andrew Neil, Nigel Nicolson, Eileen Parker, Mike Parker, Dr June Patterson-Brown, Marigold Percival, the Rt. Hon. Enoch Powell, Sir Shridath Ramphal, Lady Jane Rayne, Julian Ridsdale, Mary Robson, Kenneth Rose, Alice Rudgley, Sir Steven Runciman, Jon Savage, Michael Shea, Nicholas Soames MP, Reinhard Spitzy, Minnie Spooner, Dr Jean Thin, Sir Michael Thomas, Peter Townsend, Malcolm Turnbull, Andreas Prinz von Coburg, Lloyd Waddy, Dr Michael Willoughby, James Whitaker, Philip Ziegler. To others who gave information and assistance but do not wish to be named, we also extend our thanks.

We have received, in addition, unstinting help from those involved in making the television programmes themselves: Annie Fienburgh, Kathy O'Neil, Stephen White, Austin Hoyt, Sallyann Kleibel, Polly Lansdowne, Sue Davison, Tim Lewis, Rob Wright, Jack Amos, Lil Cranfield, Paul Lashmar, Kate Hawkins, Kate Sheekey and Rosie Brown.

We are grateful to the staff of the Cambridge University Library, the London Library and the Public Record Office.

Finally we must mention the forbearance of our families during the arduous months of research and composition. Although each of us wrote about the period he knew best – Piers Brendon doing the first half of the book and Phillip Whitehead the second – collaboration required constant consultation. For long periods we were closeted together in an anti-social huddle. Our respective wives and children have been supremely tolerant.

ILLUSTRATION CREDITS

Black and white photographs

'Edward VII and family . . .', 'George V, Duke of York and Mary at home', 'George V's well-drilled children', 'Princes Edward and Bertie . . .', 'The Delhi Durbar', 'King George V and Lord Stamfordam', Royal Archives Windsor Castle; 'Prince George and Princess Mary on their honeymoon', 'Four monarchs in succession', 'Edward . . . after falling from his horse', 'Edward Prince of Wales . . . Thelma Furness', 'Royal Cousins King George and the Kaiser', Hulton Deutsch Collection; Investiture of Edward Prince of Wales at Caernarvon', BBC Hulton Picture Library; 'Royal Cousins', Paul Popper Ltd; 'Proclamation', Imperial War Museum; 'Prince "Bertie" Duke of York . . . Elizabeth Bowes-Lyon', Rex Features.

'George V's Silver Jubilee', 'Edward Prince of Wales . . . races', 'Duke of Windsor broadcasting his abdication', 'King George VI and Queen Elizabeth . . . coronation', 'Princess Elizabeth . . . ATS training centre', 'King George . . . founding a "Pig Club" during the war', 'The Queen at "The Times" office with Rupert Murdoch . . .', 'The queens in mourning . . .', Hulton Deutsch Collection; 'King Edward VIII leaving an aircraft . . .', Bundesarchiv; 'King Edward VIII and Mrs Simpson . . . cruise', 'The Duke and Duchess of

Windsor meet Hitler', Popperfoto; 'The Duke and Duchess of Windsor on their wedding day', Camera Press Ltd; 'The Duke of Windsor gives the Nazi salute . . .', Fardergemeinschaft Fur Bergmans Tradition 'King George VI and Queen Elizabeth inspect bomb damage . . .', 'Princess Margaret and Group Captain Peter Townsend . . .', 'A marriage that might have been', Rex Features.

Colour photographs

'Queen Elizabeth II by Cecil Beaton', Camera Press Ltd; 'Princess Margaret and Lord Snowdon', 'Queen Elizabeth opens the Victoria Underground Line', Hulton Deutsch Collection; 'Charles's Investiture as Prince of Wales', Hulton Picture Company; 'Charles with Mountbatten', Syndication International Ltd; 'Lady Diana Spencer pursued by the press', 'The wedding of Prince Charles and Princess Diana', 'Queen Elizabeth II and Prime Minister Margaret Thatcher', 'Australian Prime Minister Paul Keating . . . the Queen', 'Prince Andrew and his wife Sarah . . .', 'Prince Edward engaged in amateur dramatics', 'The marriage of Prince Charles and Princess Diana looks close to collapse', 'Windsor Castle in flames', Rex Features Ltd; 'Prince Charles and his young family on holiday . . .', JS.

'Winterhalter's portrait of Queen Victoria . . .', Royal Collection Enterprises; 'George V: a sailor-king', 'Prince Edward received a naval education', 'Lady Elizabeth Bowes-Lyon on her engagement . . .', Topham Picture Source; 'Lessons at Windsor for Princesses . . .', 'Queen Elizabeth II . . . Princess Anne . . .', 'The Growing Royal Family', 'Majesty on the move: Coronation', 'The balcony tableau', Hulton Deutsch Copyright; 'King Edward VIII by Walter Sickert', Bridgeman Art Library; 'Royal Conversation Piece by James Gunn', National Portrait Gallery; 'Princess Margaret by Cecil Beaton', Camera Press Ltd.

CONTENTS

	Family Tree: The Windsors	x–xi
	Introduction	xiii
1	The Making of a Dynasty	1
2	A Royal Family Business	23
3	The King Versus the Prince	43
4	Edward the Innovator	67
5	Rebuilding the Royal House	87
6	Brothers at War	109
7	The Image of a Queen	129
8	A Maturing Monarchy	151
9	The Critics Gather	175
10	Two Queens in the Hive	193
11	Family Affairs	217
12	After the Fire	239
	Notes	257
	Index	275

The Windsors

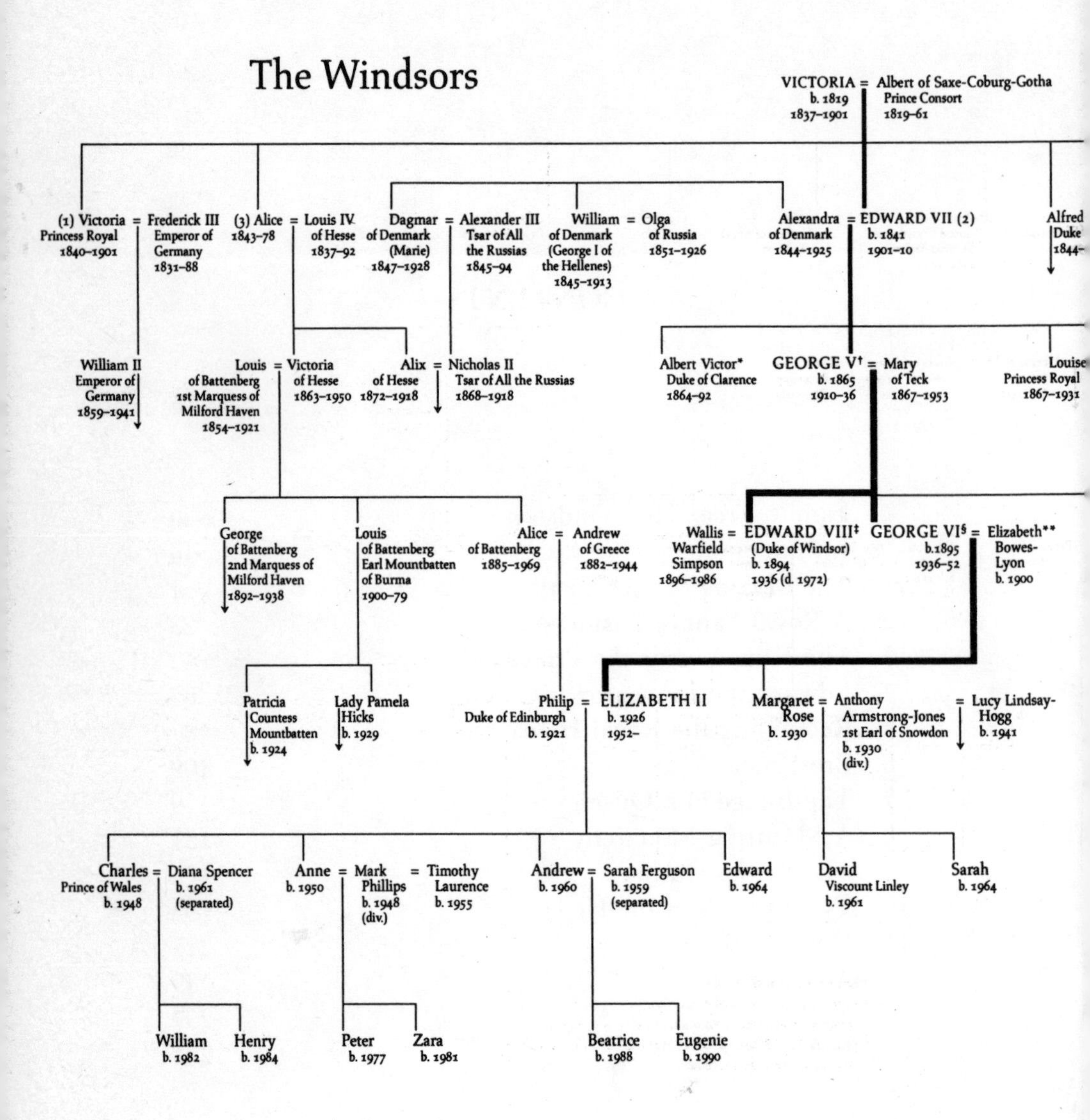

VICTORIA = Albert of Saxe-Coburg-Gotha
b. 1819
1837–1901
Prince Consort
1819–61
(1) Victoria
Princess Royal
1840–1901
= Frederick III
Emperor of Germany
1831–88
(3) Alice
1843–78
= Louis IV
of Hesse
1837–92
Dagmar
of Denmark
(Marie)
1847–1928
= Alexander III
Tsar of All the Russias
1845–94
William
of Denmark
(George I of the Hellenes)
1845–1913
= Olga
of Russia
1851–1926
Alexandra
of Denmark
1844–1925
= EDWARD VII (2)
b. 1841
1901–10
Alfred
Duke
1844–
William II
Emperor of Germany
1859–1941
Louis
of Battenberg
1st Marquess of Milford Haven
1854–1921
= Victoria
of Hesse
1863–1950
Alix
of Hesse
1872–1918
= Nicholas II
Tsar of All the Russias
1868–1918
Albert Victor*
Duke of Clarence
1864–92
GEORGE V† = Mary
b. 1865
1910–36
of Teck
1867–1953
Louise
Princess Royal
1867–1931
George
of Battenberg
2nd Marquess of Milford Haven
1892–1938
Louis
of Battenberg
Earl Mountbatten of Burma
1900–79
Alice
of Battenberg
1885–1969
= Andrew
of Greece
1882–1944
Wallis Warfield Simpson
1896–1986
= EDWARD VIII‡
(Duke of Windsor)
b. 1894
1936 (d. 1972)
GEORGE VI§ = Elizabeth**
b.1895
1936–52
Bowes-Lyon
b. 1900
Patricia
Countess Mountbatten
b. 1924
Lady Pamela
Hicks
b. 1929
Philip
Duke of Edinburgh
b. 1921
= ELIZABETH II
b. 1926
1952–
Margaret Rose
b. 1930
= Anthony
Armstrong-Jones
1st Earl of Snowdon
b. 1930
(div.)
= Lucy Lindsay-Hogg
b. 1941
Charles
Prince of Wales
b. 1948
= Diana Spencer
b. 1961
(separated)
Anne
b. 1950
= Mark
Phillips
b. 1948
(div.)
= Timothy
Laurence
b. 1955
Andrew
b. 1960
= Sarah Ferguson
b. 1959
(separated)
Edward
b. 1964
David
Viscount Linley
b. 1961
Sarah
b. 1964
William
b. 1982
Henry
b. 1984
Peter
b. 1977
Zara
b. 1981
Beatrice
b. 1988
Eugenie
b. 1990

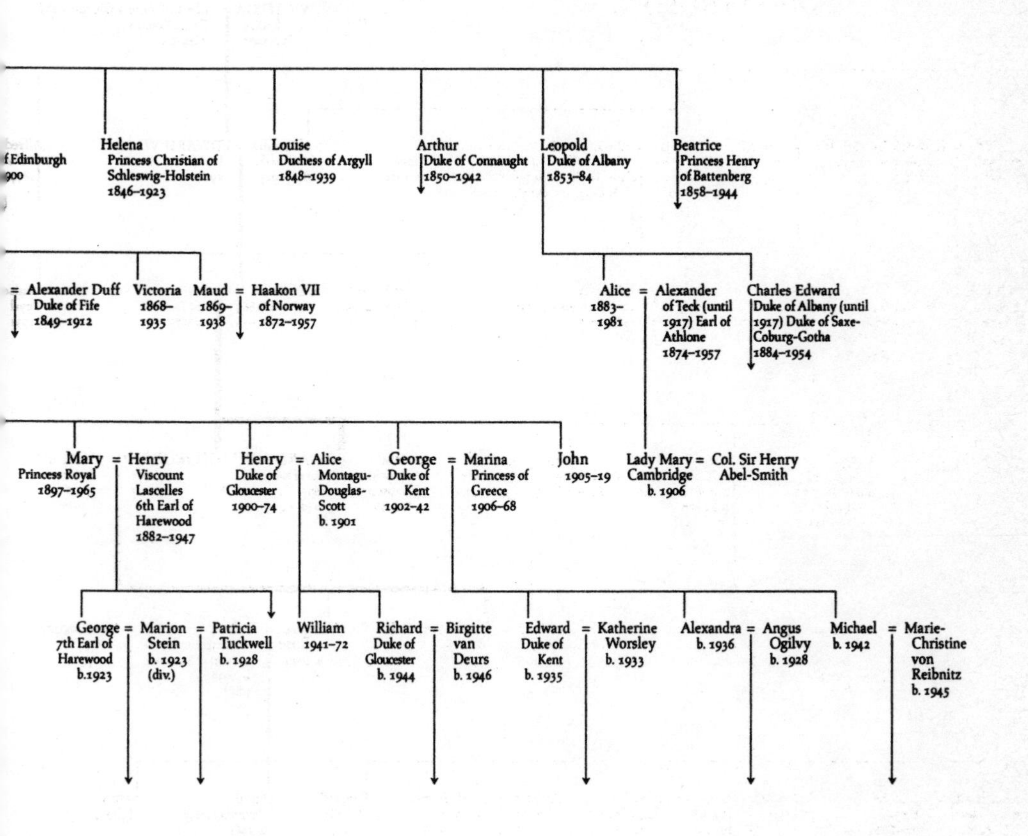

* Known as Eddy to the family.
† Formerly Duke of York and Prince of Wales.
‡ Formerly Prince of Wales. Known as David to the family.
§ Formerly Prince Albert and Duke of York. Known as Bertie to the family.
** Best known as the Queen Mother.

INTRODUCTION

This book, based on research done for a major television series of the same name, is the first serious study of the modern monarchy in the light of recent revelations. It is, so to speak, a post-*glasnost* biography of the House of Windsor from its creation in 1917 to the present day. Although Buckingham Palace remains more tight-lipped than the Kremlin ever was, the rifts within the royal family have let some daylight in upon majesty. Each faction has had its say and a new climate of candour enables us to see the past, as well as the present, more clearly. So this is an account of a dynasty from which the taboo has, to some extent, been lifted.

Nevertheless, secrecy remains the British disease and even in these unbuttoned days reticence about royalty is a conditioned reflex, especially among those admitted to the charmed circle itself. Although television affords unique access, many of the witnesses interviewed were too discreet to tell their whole story on camera. They were, however, less guarded off the record. Sometimes they even supplemented their accounts with documents, letters and photographs long hidden from outside eyes. So this book incorporates many personal testimonies, which help to illuminate the character of individual Windsors and to disperse the fog of mystery which has traditionally surrounded the throne.

Its aim, though, is to be revealing without being prurient, to be frank but not iconoclastic. Britain's peculiar institution deserves objective assessment: royal personages should be subject to unblinking historical scrutiny. This may seem shocking. Past writers have been inclined to regard themselves as literary courtiers, Gold Nibs in Waiting. Following Disraeli's celebrated advice, they have laid flattery on with a trowel. Yet only through incisive analysis can we give a new, vivid and fair picture of a family that has for generations been the symbol of Britain's national life.

As such it has become enveloped in myth as well as incense. In particular, it is represented as the avatar of traditions dating back to an age of chivalry, heraldry and pageantry. Queen Elizabeth II lives in Windsor Castle, fortress of William the Conqueror. At her coronation in Westminster Abbey she sat in Edward I's chair. Among her crown jewels are the sapphire from the ring of Edward the Confessor, the ruby worn by Henry V at the battle of Agincourt and the pearl eardrops of her namesake Elizabeth I. As Supreme Governor of the Church of England she bears the title which Pope Leo X bestowed on Henry VIII before the Reformation, Defender of the Faith. As hereditary head of a democratic state without a written constitution, she reigns through a shadow of the divine right which Charles I tried to exercise. But for George III, she might be sovereign of America. She presides over the ghost of Queen Victoria's empire, the largest ever known.

In reality, far from being the repository of immemorial custom, the monarchy has constantly reinvented itself to meet altered circumstances. Anything but an immutable national emblem, the Crown has adapted, sometimes from grim necessity, sometimes with rare ingenuity, to win the loyalty of the masses. When the horses broke their harness at Queen Victoria's funeral, for example, the gun carriage holding her coffin (shrouded in white, not black, since she was going to rejoin her beloved Albert) had to be pulled by sailors. The innovation proved popular and it became an instant tradition. Similarly the Investiture of Edward (VIII) Prince of Wales at Caernarvon Castle in 1911 was a novel and wholly fabricated ceremony masquerading as part of Britain's antique heritage.

The magnificent Delhi Durbar, later that year, was almost equally artificial, though the Archbishop of Canterbury vetoed the King-Emperor's attempt to crown himself, Napoleon-like, in front of his Indian subjects. Most striking of all was the transformation which George V accomplished in 1917. Bowing to chauvinistic passions stirred up by the First World War, he changed his family name from Saxe-Coburg-Gotha to the resoundingly English Windsor.

This metamorphosis gives the present book its title and its starting point. The emergence of a British butterfly from a German chrysalis was, indeed, an astonishing event. Denying an ancestry writ large in countless genealogies, the King re-created the monarchy in his own image, that of a grizzled old sea dog who had settled down to become a home-loving Norfolk squire. He appeared as a little Englander, albeit with a king-sized empire. Although he had scarcely a drop of English blood in his veins George became what Queen Elizabeth II, as a child, called him: 'Grandpapa England'. Yet this was only the first of many crucial changes – prompted by new challenges – in the ostensibly archaic institution personified by the Windsors.

To present the monarchy to the sovereign people, ever more splendid royal marriages were staged. Other novelties, notably the King's Christmas broadcast and his Silver Jubilee, proved excellent advertisements for the House of Windsor. Golden-haired and fresh-faced, Edward Prince of Wales became the first royal media star. On succeeding to the throne he hankered to be called 'Edward the Innovator', though almost his only innovations were to flirt with Fascism and to allow the Beefeaters to shave off their square beards. But when he abdicated to marry the American divorcée Wallis Simpson, sterling efforts were made (not least by the *Times* and the BBC) to promote slow, stammering George VI as the reincarnation of George V. And no one proved more adept at public relations than Queen Elizabeth, who in 1952 became the Queen Mother. This radiant matriarch always stole the show, but she also stiffened her husband's backbone behind the scenes.

The people's war, the rise of Labour and the loss of empire

imposed fresh strains on George VI, who responded to them with difficulty. But Elizabeth II became Queen with the clear determination to change nothing but her clothes. Calls to modernize the monarchy were dismissed as a contradiction in terms, though some of its more old-fashioned features (such as the presentation of debutantes at court) were gradually discarded. Continuity was the sovereign's *raison d'être*. And the Queen's policy was to secure it through the Georgian combination of public spectacle and private discretion. The former was epitomized by her glittering coronation, transmitted to her subjects through the magic new medium of television. The latter was maintained when Princess Margaret renounced her planned marriage to the divorced Group Captain Peter Townsend.

As Queen Elizabeth's reign progressed, however, it became increasingly hard to combine publicity and privacy. Tentative efforts were made to bridge the widening gap between Crown and people. But endeavours to popularize the monarchy, such as the carefully stage-managed television film *Royal Family* of 1969, tended to erode its mystique. And during the 1980s the media, which had for so long enhanced the appeal of the Windsors, became less deferential and more intrusive. Reacting against the organized silence which had concealed regal peccadilloes – not least Edward VIII's involvement with Wallis Simpson, when it was making headlines all round the world – newspaperdom is now inclined to publish and be damned. The tabloid press, in particular, feeds the mood of public disillusionment by revealing the contrast between fairytale idyll and playboy reality.

So, in the last few years, members of the royal family have lapsed in status from revered icons to latex puppets like those on the satirical TV show *Spitting Image*. Princess Michael of Kent has been branded a plagiarist. Princesses Margaret and Anne have been through awkward divorces, the latter recently marrying again (this time an equerry) in a low-key ceremony. After topless cavortings with her 'financial adviser', the Duchess of York is in disgrace. The estrangement of the Prince and Princess of Wales, together with the tapes of their intimate conversations, have even sullied their superstar glamour. More seriously, they have cast doubt on the succession to the throne, weakened Commonwealth ties and rescued British republicanism from the historical black hole into which it had fallen. Prince Philip's private life is now the subject of curiosity. The Queen herself, after the discovery that royal tax avoidance was also a recently invented tradition, has been forced to beat an embarrassing fiscal retreat. The extent of public disenchantment was made manifest at the height of her *annus horribilis* in 1992 when, with symbolic precision, Windsor Castle caught fire. Far from sympathising, most of her subjects were outraged at being expected to pay the full cost of its renovation.

The old monarchy, the embodiment of traditional British family values, also seems to have gone up in smoke. Many people doubt if it can be restored to its traditional place in public affection. But the Windsor story has not ended with the Windsor fire, even though it provides a dramatic climax to this book. The monarchy still touches hidden areas of the British psyche, those parts which other institutions cannot reach. It retains a prehensile hold on the British imagination, despite developments which threaten to sap its strength: the country's growing involvement in Europe; advancing Commonwealth republicanism, notably in Australia; the Thatcherite attack on vested interests which impede the enterprise economy; widespread aspirations, expressed by Prime Minister John Major himself, to create a classless society; and a steep national decline which makes regal pomp and circumstance seem incongruous.

In their short history the Windsors have exhibited a startling capacity to evolve. The book concludes with a consideration of just how they can create a new image for themselves to face the challenges of the next millennium. For there is little doubt that the dynasty will rise again, like a phoenix, from the ashes of Windsor Castle.

[illegible]
[illegible]
[illegible]
[illegible]
[illegible]
[illegible]
[illegible]
[illegible]
[illegible]
[illegible]
[illegible]
[illegible]
[illegible]
[illegible]
the Duke would show [illegible]
[illegible] Evelyn [illegible]

1

THE MAKING OF A DYNASTY

History does not repeat itself so much as offer suggestive similarities; not least of them is the resemblance between the careers of two Princes of Wales a century apart. Like Prince Charles today, his great-great-grandfather Edward, Queen Victoria's eldest son, was kept waiting an unconscionable time for the throne. As he said in 1897, 'I don't mind praying to an Eternal Father, but I must be the only man in the country afflicted with an eternal mother.'[1] Furthermore, Edward had no proper job to keep him occupied. Constitutionally restless, irritable and butterfly-minded, he was bored by his beautiful but vacuous wife, who eclipsed him in popularity. 'Edward the Caresser' engaged in sexual slumming and still more dangerous liaisons with aristocratic ladies. In the early 1890s the muckraking journalist W. T. Stead recorded that country gentlemen were 'unanimous that the Prince would never rule over them, that he was a wastrel, a gambler and a whoremonger'.[2] In the early 1990s the royal biographer Anthony Holden opined that publication of the tape-recorded telephone conversation between Prince Charles and Camilla Parker-Bowles had 'severely – perhaps terminally – damaged' his chances of becoming king.[3]

The parallels between the two princes are piquant but by no means precise. Edward was a Falstaffian roué, whereas

Charles is a vegetarian Hamlet. Edward was discreet – Buckingham Palace was able to buy back incriminating letters he had written to women such as Giulia Barucci, self-styled 'greatest whore in the world', and Lady ('Babbling') Brooke, Countess of Warwick. Charles has proved as unlucky in love as he has in his electronic eavesdroppers. The confident Edward enjoyed an increasingly servile press, while the opposite is true for the diffident Charles. Edward required constant diversion on the merry-go-round of high society. Charles favours solitary introspection in the Hebrides or mystical communion, with his aged Jungian guru Laurens van der Post, in the Kalahari Desert. Edward was obsessed with punctilio, whereas Charles flirts with alternative medicine and organic farming and insists that he has always fought to escape from royal protocol. Edward's wife, Alexandra, was complaisant about her husband's peccadilloes where Princess Diana is not.

Nevertheless, current fears about an interrupted succession seem groundless, for in 1901 Edward duly became king and was hailed as a 'worthy successor'[4] to his mother. It was not that he had reformed, but that he gave such a convincing impersonation of majesty. He also benefited from the restoration of the family fortunes in Queen Victoria's declining years. The flicker of republicanism provoked by her black widowhood was snuffed out after the Prince himself nearly died of typhoid in 1871. When the Queen persuaded Disraeli to make her Empress of India five years later she set her personal seal on an empire that dwarfed all others. Her ingenious Prime Minister gave to 'an ebullition of individual vanity . . . the semblance of deep and organised policy'.[5] He even allowed the new title to be proclaimed at an imperial assemblage more extravagant than any previous durbar – the Viceroy's plans, he said, 'read like the Thousand and One Nights'.[6] The alliance between Crown and Empire lasted for three generations and was of immense importance in stimulating the loyalty of the masses.

So was the pageantry epitomized by Queen Victoria's Golden and Diamond Jubilees, in 1887 and 1897. Actually the Queen herself disliked ostentation and insisted on wearing a bonnet rather than a crown, much to the disappointment of visiting maharajas. Doubtless she feared the kind of criticism voiced by the 3rd Earl of Durham: at a time of widespread destitution the 'damned snobbish fuss of the old woman's jubilee excites my wrath', he expostulated.[7] But the Jubilees, with their processions, parades, services, addresses, memorials, exhibitions, banquets, balls, school treats, village fêtes and firework displays, not to mention their unprecedented shower of honours, had a terrific appeal. They marked the Queen's emergence from her long mourning seclusion and her apotheosis as the mother of the nation as well as the 'Grandmother of Europe'. Commodities like Bovril and Colman's Mustard advertised themselves via the celebrations. Vast amounts of commemorative china found a ready market. So did the patent automatic bustles which played 'God Save the Queen' whenever the wearer sat down. Like the Romans, the British relished circuses. As George Gissing wrote in 1897, the people behaved like 'some huge beast purring to itself in stupid contentment'.[8]

Perhaps their purrs and cheers were a spontaneous outpouring of loyalty to the sovereign who symbolized the state; but there is no doubt that Britain, in common with aspiring rivals such as Germany, Russia, Japan and the United States, was deliberately deploying spectacle to promote patriotism. This was not new. Rulers as remote as Augustus Caesar and Louis XIV had exemplified Montesquieu's maxim that 'The magnificence and splendour which surround kings form part of their power.'[9] However, the peculiar role of the late Victorian monarchy was classically formulated by Walter Bagehot, a brilliant journalist who gave the nation its nearest thing to a written constitution. 'A royal family sweetens politics by the seasonable addition of nice and pretty events', he wrote – events like marriages, coronations, funerals and investitures, which 'speak to "men's bosoms" and employ their thoughts'. A monarchy would not be necessary, Bagehot considered, where education was universal and government could rely on the rationality of the governed. But such was the 'bovine stupidity' of the British masses that they required a totem. Thus royalty must sometimes be 'paraded like a pageant' as well as 'commonly hidden like a mystery'.[10] Only through acts of allegiance to the dynasty, played out upon the national stage, could social cohesion be maintained. Only a quasi-divine monarch, pavilioned in splendour and girded with praise, could keep secular faiths at bay. So, at least, believed the traditional ruling class. After Queen Victoria's Golden Jubilee the Archbishop of Canterbury declared: 'everyone feels that the socialist movement has had a check'.[11]

Unlike his mother, King Edward VII adored the trappings of grandeur. As much as his nephew, Kaiser Wilhelm II of Germany, he loved donning sumptuous uniforms. Squeezed into them, 'Tum Tum' (as he was nicknamed) looked every inch a king, horizontally as well as vertically. Indeed, oblivious of Carlyle's stern admonition that dandies sacrifice the immortal to the perishable, Edward regarded the wearing of correct clothes as a moral duty. Changing them, as his biographer Philip Magnus remarked, had given him, when Prince of Wales, 'an occupation of a kind', helping him to 'invest idleness with dignity'. Breaking the panama hat while making the grey topper, Edward was able to change fashion itself. He spent about four months of each year of his reign abroad, revelling in his position as 'Uncle of Europe' – he had relations in Germany, Greece, Italy, Spain, Russia, Denmark, Norway and Sweden – and keeping his valets busy with his plethora of foreign uniforms and decorations. Edward relaxed in transparent anonymity among the republicans of Paris, where, as the *Dictionary of National Biography* charmingly phrased it, he 'enjoyed varied intercourse with French society'. At home the King appeared before his subjects on state occasions caparisoned in the full panoply of majesty.

Edward had considerable powers of visualizing and arranging ceremonies in which he would play a starring role. He revived the elaborate State Opening of Parliament and began work to create London's grand processional way: widening the Mall, building Admiralty Arch, erecting the Victoria Memorial and refurbishing and refacing Buckingham Palace. It became the backdrop for a perpetual pageant, just as Lutyens was to design New Delhi to be the setting for a perpetual durbar. The King bestowed decorations lavishly, creating new honours such as the Order of Merit, based on the German 'Pour le Mérite'. He taught his son a lesson which the future George V never forgot – 'that pomp, if it is to retain its symbolism and its magic, must be, not magnificent merely, but meticulously ordered and planned'.[12] This rubric Edward applied to his own coronation, which consequently proved less chaotic than his mother's, despite the inclusion of his former mistresses in the so-called 'King's Loose Box' and the infirmity of aged ecclesiastics such as Archbishop Temple. Too blind to read the service properly, he nearly put the consecrated bread on the carpet and collapsed when doing homage to the King, who pulled him to his feet and revived him in the disrobing room with a cup of soup.

After Edward's death, his unprecedented lying-in-state at Westminster Hall was attended by a quarter of a million people. Nine kings rode through London in the funeral procession on 20 May 1910; all but one were related by blood or marriage. The inevitable squabbles about precedence began even before the potentates reached Britain. Crossing the continent on the same train, King 'Foxy' Ferdinand of Bulgaria and the Archduke Franz Ferdinand of Austria had a sharp dispute about whose coach should go next to the engine. The Archduke, whose assassination at Sarajevo was to precipitate the First World War, won. But when he requested permission to pass through the King of Bulgaria's coach to reach the restaurant car it was refused. In London it was the Kaiser's turn to be downgraded, pride of place behind Edward VII's coffin being given to Caesar, His late Majesty's wire-haired terrier.

Still, the royalties following Caesar were a glittering manifestation of the cousinhood of kings and the puissance of the monarchical principle. Even the dispossessed Orleanist princes came before the official envoy of the French Republic, who was furious. He also complained to ex-President Theodore Roosevelt, whose inferior carriage he shared, that the royal coachmen were clad in scarlet liveries whereas their own wore black. Roosevelt replied that he had not noticed, and that for all he cared the coachman could dress in a green coat with yellow splashes.[13] The former President had no conception of how important such distinctions were to status-conscious Europeans. Unlike earlier royal funerals, which had mostly been attended by the defunct monarch's own subjects, that of Edward VII was a cosmopolitan affair designed to enhance Britain's pre-eminent position in the hierarchy of nations. Representatives from countries as remote as Japan, China, Siam (Thailand), Persia (Iran), Egypt, Argentina, Haiti and Mexico took their appointed places according to rank. Royal personages, even if their skins were yellow or black, preceded commoners, and George V and the Kaiser, flanked by the Kings of Spain, Denmark, Portugal, the Hellenes, the Belgians, Norway and Bulgaria, led all the rest. The crowned confraternity appeared almost to transcend the nation state, giving promise of a reign of concord and amity. After all, the monarch whose obsequies they were attending was credited with having secured the Entente Cordiale between Britain and France. He was even saluted as 'Edward the Peacemaker'.

This was largely fantasy. Dynastic marriages might continue but royal diplomacy, insofar as it existed at all, was virtually impotent. Indeed, far from exercising a pacific influence on Europe, the royal extended family of which Queen Victoria had been head was rent by personal quarrels, often stemming from national rivalries. Anglo-German hostility was perennial. Prince Albert himself had been lampooned on his marriage:

> He comes to take 'for better or for worse'
> England's fat Queen and England's fatter purse.[14]

Albert got few thanks for his endeavours to promote science and the arts, and to modernize a Britain whose technology was falling behind that of Germany. What was remembered was Disraeli's quip that if Albert had lived he would have introduced England to the benefits of absolute rule. Perhaps there was just enough truth in this to ensure that the title of Prince Consort was not bestowed upon the husband of Queen Elizabeth. The family of Queen Victoria, needing to marry Protestant royalty from mean little states like Coburg, which Bismarck called 'the stud farm of Europe', came in for further brickbats. In 1882 the *Secular Review* attacked the 'German king-factory' for turning out 'microcephalous mediocrities' whose main characteristic was 'insatiable cupidity'. Albert was not one of these, but there was no disguising his origins. He favoured Balmoral not because it was Scottish but because it seemed German, reminding him of a Thuringian *Schloss*. The attacks he endured in England were returned with interest when his eldest daughter Vicky married Crown Prince Frederick of Prussia. She was accused of being a British spy and plots were hatched to discredit her via sexual scandal. Vicky's son, Kaiser Wilhelm II, reflected the national antagonism by engaging in a series of spats with his uncle Edward VII, whom he called 'a Satan'.[15] Immediately after Edward's funeral luncheon the Kaiser took the French ambassador aside and suggested that France should enter an alliance with him if Germany challenged England. Divided loyalties divided royalties.

Nevertheless, their scintillating international connections doubtless enhanced the British royal family's glamour before the First World War, and the public demonstration of regal solidarity put on in May 1910 was undeniably impressive. Furthermore, it was repeated in June the following year when George V was crowned in the presence of six hundred royal personages. Several rehearsals produced what one patrician witness called 'a stirring spectacle, beautifully staged . . . a masterpiece of organising skill'.[16] But amid the paeans of loyalty the socialist Keir Hardie, who regarded king worship as a form of idolatry, struck a discordant note. The coronation, he said, 'with its pomp and show, the make believe, the glorification of militarism and all its mockeries of the solemnity of religion, is an affront to all that is true and self-respecting in our national life'.[17]

This criticism hit the mark in at least one respect, for among the coronation honours which King George received was the baton of field marshal of the German Army. Unlike his parents, George enjoyed cordial relations with the Kaiser, who became godfather to his third son. George did not share his father's fondness for foreigners but at this time he seemed to regard Wilhelm as an honorary Englishman. The Kaiser's eccentricities could be indulged because he belonged to the most exclusive caste in the world: both cousins regarded themselves as being members of a regal freemasonry. Both believed in the kinship of kingship.

Personally George did not much resemble William. True, they were both men voluble to the point of rashness, fond of lavatorial humour and practical jokes, sentimental, anti-Semitic[18] and obscurantist. But the Kaiser was vain, brutal, volatile, bombastic and unbalanced. He was also insanely egotistical. The King, on the other hand, was dull, decent, orderly, uxorious and conventional. He was also preternaturally modest. Not until his Silver Jubilee did he appreciate the true extent of his popularity. True, as Churchill memorably said of Attlee, the King had a good deal to be modest about: his abilities were limited. Wilhelm spoke English fluently, for instance, whereas George made little or no progress with German, despite a stint in 'beastly dull' Heidelberg. In fact, as his official biographer John Gore privately concluded, the King was 'a profoundly ignorant and rather stupid man'.[19]

This was not altogether surprising. Although radiant and adored by the public, his mother was intellectually retarded. She wrote in baby-talk to her son even when he had become a bearded sailor, and Lord Carisbrooke said that she was 'the stupidest woman he'd ever met'.[20] George's father, too, was not 'normally intelligent',[21] and Prince Albert had been obliged to modify Edward's education to suit his low mental capacities. Queen Victoria dreaded the effect that this pairing of small, empty brains would have on their offspring. She knew something about breeding. The eldest child of Edward and Alexandra, Prince Eddy (later Duke of Clarence), had, according to his tutor, an 'abnormally dormant' mind. And the naval school of hard knocks taught him and his rather less backward brother George, who was born in 1865, little more than the virtue of strict discipline. Idle, debauched and erratic, Eddy seemed a throwback to the mad, bad

Hanoverians of yore. Queen Victoria demanded that he should be married off as quickly as possible to a minor German royalty, Princess Mary of Teck; but before the nuptials could be celebrated, Eddy died of pneumonia. Rumours persist to this day that he was poisoned because he was unfit to occupy the throne.

George, having sown a few wild oats of his own, took over Eddy's role not only as heir presumptive but as husband of Princess Mary. This blatantly dynastic alliance, consummated in 1893, worked surprisingly well – because the royal couple were as much devoted to duty as to each other. Although considerably cleverer than her husband, Mary deferred to him in everything, right down to the old-fashioned cut of her clothes. She was interested in *objets d'art* and was delighted to have access to what one German ambassador's wife, awed by the golden splendour of Buckingham Palace, called the 'real treasure of the Niebelungen'.[22] But Mary endured without complaint their marital home of York Cottage, darkly embowered in the Sandringham estate, which George furnished with deplorable taste from Maple's store in London's Tottenham Court Road and decorated with reproductions from the Royal Academy and homely proverbs like 'A Stitch in Time Saves Nine'. York Cottage was not grand: commenting on its size, George himself supposed that his servants must sleep in the trees. But it was still a substantial 'gentleman's residence' which hardly merited the snobbish denigration of their relations, one of whom described it as 'a poky and inconvenient place, architecturally repulsive and always full of the smell of cooking'.[23]

Whatever its shortcomings, George adored York Cottage and was quite happy to stay there after he became King. Its great merit in his eyes was that it abutted the fields and heaths of Sandringham, alive with pheasants, partridges and woodcock, as were the lakes and marshes with wildfowl. Shooting, transformed by Prince Albert from an active English field sport to a static German holocaust, was the passion of George's life. Through sedulous practice he became one of the finest shots in the kingdom. He liked a big bag but after one shoot, at which nearly four thousand birds had been slaughtered, he wondered whether they had overdone it. On another occasion he wept at the sight of a dead garden bird. Sport apart, George's chief hobby was collecting stamps, many of which bore the heads of his relations. Philately was a form of genealogy, a subject that tends to interest royalty and one which fascinated his wife.

George's whole life was ordered with martial precision. Every morning he read the *Times*, specially printed on linen for him, as though it were a military despatch. He treated his children like army recruits and subjected them to regular inspections. Mealtimes were parades, punctual to the minute. Being incorrectly dressed was a cardinal sin. Once, after listening to an important report, he said: 'It's all very interesting, Sir Henry, but you should never wear a coloured tie with a frock coat.'

Drilling his household like a martinet, George was rigidly obedient to his own superiors. Despite her obtrusive selfishness he worshipped Queen Victoria. With child-like simplicity he doted on his 'darling Motherdear'. He was awed and terrified by his father, who sometimes treated him with impatient brusqueness. At one luncheon, according to a story which the 3rd Earl of Dudley swore to be true, King Edward got his just deserts.

'Father!' said Prince George.

The King, in full spate: 'Shut up.'

'Father, I must talk to you.'

'Shut up, shut up.'

Shortly afterwards the King told his son that he must not interrupt him. George replied: 'I was only trying to say that there was a caterpillar in your salad, but you've eaten it now.'[24] But Edward was generally a fond father and his 'affection for Prince George was due mainly to the fact that the latter was prepared to be his complete slave'.[25] In private George seems to have deplored the unhappiness caused to his mother by King Edward's determination to grow old disgracefully. His famous final infidelity, with Alice Keppel, was particularly wounding. Edward virtually acknowledged this liaison in public by christening one of his horses with an anagram of his mistress's name, Ecila. But when his 'beloved Papa' died George mourned the loss of 'my best friend & the best of fathers'.

However, the new King reacted against the old one by initiating a reign of rectitude. Gone were the ladies of easy virtue, the raffish racing fraternity and the rich Jewish friends. Instead the court became 'stuffy and frumpish',[26] and louche aristocrats laughed at the prudery of the royal couple. In reviving 'Balmorality' George was doubtless following his own virtuous bent, but he rebuilt one of the two great pillars of the modern monarchy – respectability. The other pillar was pageantry, and George went through the motions manfully. He even wore a crown at State Openings of Parliament, where his father had only worn a field marshal's cocked hat. Max Beerbohm painted a vivid picture of the 'little King with the great diamond crown that covered his eyebrows, and with the eyes that showed so tragically much of effort, of the will to please – the will to impress – the will to be all that he isn't and that his Papa *was* (or seems to him to have been) . . . such a piteous, good, feeble, heroic little figure'.[27]

Others were more impressed. The American ambassador, Walter Hines Page, who considered George a 'sagacious and high-minded' King, described the court ceremonial for the benefit of President Woodrow Wilson. Page reckoned that the 'uniforms and jewels make any opera-scene pale into sheer make-believe' and he found the whole performance an

> amazingly interesting study – how far it is all done consciously, as a method of drawing fresh recruits to the royal-aristocratic point-of-view – how far it is consciously staged and managed so as to appeal to the national and historical imagination? Of course, if the Liberal programme is ever carried out – as, of course, it will be in time – there will come a day when royalty will be superfluous. If in the meantime royalty links itself to the splendour of English history and continues its spectacular appeal to every woman of social ambition, the evil day may be postponed – especially for royalty that lead decent lives as these do.[28]

This was a shrewd analysis. The fact was that at resplendent ceremonies like the Prince of Wales's Investiture George learned how to play his part with a measure of majesty.

None was more glittering than the Indian Durbar of 1911, a fabulous piece of imperial myth-making. It was intended to establish George V as the successor of Akbar and Aurangzeb, to say nothing of Richard the Lionheart, the last English monarch to go east of Suez. The central ceremony gave potent expression to the paramountcy of the British sovereign – the only one to inspect the jewel in the imperial crown during his reign. At the durbar camp outside the city, where a quarter of a million people were housed under ten square miles of canvas, the King appeared as 'a semi-divine figure'[29] in his purple velvet robes and his £60,000 crown, paid for by the inhabitants of India. Together with the diademed Queen, he processed to the gold-domed durbar pavilion set in a vast amphitheatre. They were preceded by attendants bearing peacock fans, yak-tails and gilt maces, and followed by turbaned pages, sons of maharajas. They were saluted by 101 guns and trumpeted by over sixteen hundred musicians. They sat on gold-encased, solid silver thrones atop a great marble dais covered with cloth-of-gold carpet and surrounded by the emblems of majesty – the lotus flower, the king cobra and the Tudor crown. Here George received the generous homage of the Indian princes and a spontaneous demonstration of loyalty from the spectators. This is what the pageant, which disguised novelty in the trappings of antiquity, was calculated to provoke. The King's announcement that the seat of government would move from Calcutta to the once-and-future capital of Delhi was also immensely popular. Determined that the spirit of sovereignty should take perpetual form, King George laid the foundation stone of Sir Edwin Lutyens's New Delhi.

If George V learned in India to give an imperial performance that was 'the perfection of dramatic art',[30] he learned during the first four years of his reign in England to be a constitutional king. This was not easy. The nation was dogged by troubles such as reform of the House of Lords, labour disputes, Suffragette violence and Irish Home Rule. George himself overflowed with old-fashioned prejudices: cars should not be allowed to go more than thirty miles an hour, and only bounders rode motor bicycles; 'There are no gentlemen in Cambridgeshire . . . very few pheasants';[31] it was ridiculous to complain that first-class male passengers were given places in the *Titanic*'s lifeboats rather than steerage women – 'if a man pays first-class fare he is entitled to preference'.[32] Heedless of who heard, the King damned radical ministers such as David Lloyd George. The Welshman in turn complained that both King and Queen were 'hostile to the bone to all who are working to lift the workmen out of the mire'.[33] Another radical, Arthur Ponsonby, who thought King George a well-meaning but 'very undistinguished and uneducated little nonentity', was concerned about his being surrounded by reactionary courtiers.[34] One of these was George V's private secretary, Lord Stamfordham, though even he complained that no sovereign he had served, except Queen Victoria, understood the British constitution. However, the Liberal Prime Minister, H. H. Asquith, took several opportunities to instruct the King in his duties. Over the deeply divisive issue of Home Rule, for example, he told his sovereign 'rudimentary truths in plain language' about the necessity for the Crown to abstain entirely from party quarrels. This lecture had a very 'marked effect'.[35]

By the time war broke out, at the beginning of August 1914, the King had learned that in order to survive he must keep his head below the political parapet. He was slower to realize that using his influence behind the scenes was also fraught with peril, and it took him some time to grasp that Armageddon had smashed the international concert of kings for good. A few days before the war began George told Prince Henry of Prussia (Wilhelm's brother) that he hoped Britain would remain neutral, a message which became garbled in translation and which briefly convinced the Kaiser that he had got a royal pledge, 'the word of a King'. Wilhelm was soon denouncing his cousin as a liar, but George wanted if possible to conduct a gentlemen's war and to preserve friendly relations with his enemy relations. He sent his distant cousin, Count Mensdorff, the Austro-Hungarian ambassador, a warm letter only an hour after

Britain had declared war on his country. He was somewhat intimidated by the chauvinist witch-hunt against Prince Louis of Battenberg, who found himself driven from office as First Sea Lord and whose son, later Lord Mountbatten of Burma, had a 'rotten time' at Osborne when fellow naval cadets accused him of being a German spy. George agreed to the removal of royal foes from the British Army list and permitted Britons who had received German and Austrian decorations to cease wearing them. But in 1915 he tried, and failed, to prevent the removal of the richly embroidered Garter banners of Wilhelm and his ilk from St George's Chapel, Windsor.

The King did not go as far as the Kaiser, who as late as 1916 told the American ambassador in Berlin: 'I and my cousins George and Nicholas [the Tsar] shall make peace when the proper time has come.'[36] But the British monarch did connive at the clandestine contacts which continued, via intermediary royalties in neutral countries, between members of his family on opposite sides. In 1916 the King and Queen were 'deeply moved', at the golden wedding celebration of Princess Helena (Queen Victoria's eldest surviving daughter) and Prince Christian of Schleswig-Holstein, when a telegram arrived from Stockholm conveying the 'loyal and devoted good wishes' of 'William' to his uncle and aunt. Probably George and Mary had more German relations than any other family in the realm. The King's reluctance to strip them of their English titles caused 'murmurings against His Majesty' in 1916.[37] The royal family even became the targets of wartime spy mania: rumours were rife that lights from Sandringham had been seen flashing signals to Zeppelins.

Of course, the hysteria against 'Germhuns' took bizarre forms such as the boycotting of hock and Handel, Bechsteins and dachshunds. Yet as the casualty lists lengthened the British people had real cause to focus their hatred on Germany, especially as defeat now seemed to stare them in the face. England was threatened from behind by an Ireland embittered after the Easter Rising. The battle of Jutland had been indecisive. On the Somme more British blood had been

Edward (VII) Prince of Wales, Princess Alexandra, Princes Albert Victor ('Eddy') and George

Prince George and Princess Mary on their honeymoon, 1893

George (V), Duke of York, and Mary at home

Four monarchs in succession: Queen Victoria, King Edward VII, King George V, King Edward VIII

George V's well-drilled children: Princes Edward (David), Albert (Bertie, future George VI), Henry, and Princess Mary, 1905

Princes Edward (David) and 'Bertie' on the Isle of Wight, 1905

The Delhi Durbar, greatest imperial pageant, 1911

The Investiture, Edward Prince of Wales at Caernarvon, 1911

Royal Cousins: Prince George (on the right) and Tsar Nicholas II of Russia, at Cowes, 1904

Royal Cousins: King George (on the right) and Emperor William of Germany (the Kaiser), at Potsdam, 1913

'Proclamation': The Windsors King George V and his influential private secretary, Lord Stamfordham (inset: Proclamation)

BY THE KING.

A PROCLAMATION

Declaring that the Name of Windsor is to be borne by His Royal House and Family and relinquishing the use of all German Titles and Dignities.

GEORGE R.I.

WHEREAS WE, having taken into consideration the Name and Title of Our Royal House and Family, have determined that henceforth Our House and Family shall be styled and known as the House and Family of Windsor:

AND WHEREAS We have further determined for Ourselves and for and on behalf of Our descendants and all other the descendants of Our Grandmother Queen Victoria of blessed and glorious memory to relinquish and discontinue the use of all German Titles and Dignities:

AND WHEREAS We have declared these Our determinations in Our Privy Council:

NOW, THEREFORE, We, out of Our Royal Will and Authority, do hereby declare and announce that as from the date of this Our Royal Proclamation Our House and Family shall be styled and known as the House and Family of Windsor, and that all the descendants in the male line of Our said Grandmother Queen Victoria who are subjects of these Realms, other than female descendants who may marry or may have married, shall bear the said Name of Windsor:

And do hereby further declare and announce that We for Ourselves and for and on behalf of Our descendants and all other the descendants of Our said Grandmother Queen Victoria who are subjects of these Realms, relinquish and enjoin the discontinuance of the use of the Degrees, Styles, Dignities, Titles and Honours of Dukes and Duchesses of Saxony and Princes and Princesses of Saxe-Coburg and Gotha, and all other German Degrees, Styles, Dignities, Titles, Honours and Appellations to Us or to them heretofore belonging or appertaining.

Given at Our Court at Buckingham Palace, this Seventeenth day of July, in the year of our Lord One thousand nine hundred and seventeen, and in the Eighth year of Our Reign.

GOD SAVE THE KING.

LONDON: Printed by EYRE and SPOTTISWOODE, Limited, Printers to the King's most Excellent Majesty.

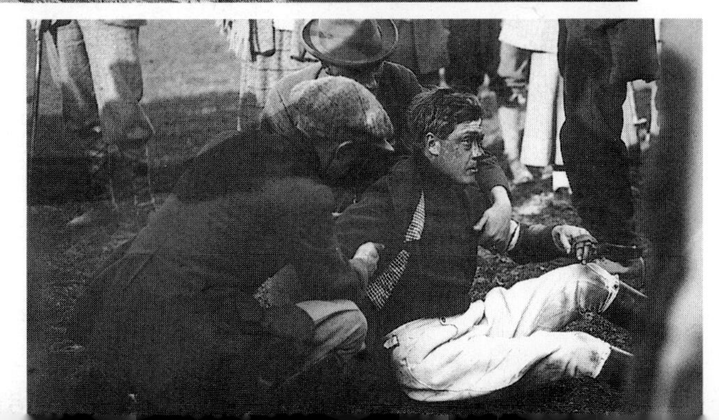

Edward Prince of Wales, after falling from his horse at a point-to-point, 1924

Edward Prince of Wales with his current mistress, Lady Thelma Furness (on the right) and his brother Prince George, 1932

Prince 'Bertie' Duke of York and his new wife Elizabeth, nee Bowes-Lyon

shed to less purpose than ever before. General Sir Douglas Haig had no strategy apart from further attrition, which would result in another disaster at Passchendaele; yet the King supported him with more zeal than was constitutionally proper against the new Prime Minister Lloyd George, whom he referred to contemptuously as '"Thatt Mann", [the King's] Germanic pronunciation becoming very strong'.[38] Paradoxically, however, George himself was 'visibly and increasingly desirous of seeing the war at an end'.[39] The struggle at Verdun had broken the spirit of the French armies, which were close to mutiny. The Italian front was vulnerable, as the catastrophe of Caporetto would prove. Later in 1917 a desperate Britain even sought the aid of international Jewry through the Balfour Declaration, promising Jews a homeland in Palestine. Early in that year the Germans introduced unrestricted submarine warfare, which did their enemies a signal service; for by sinking neutral ships the U-boats brought the United States into the war. But many feared that King George's islands would be starved into submission before American might could be mobilized. The sovereign himself was soon having to tell his subjects to tighten their belts and setting them a royal example. But despite the teetotal pledge, for the duration of the war, that Lloyd George had wheedled out of him, he apparently could not resist a secret tipple of medicinal port after dinner.

Meanwhile, prompted by food riots in Petrograd, the first phase of the Russian Revolution began. On 15 March 1917 Tsar Nicholas II abdicated and a liberal provisional government was established. George's first instinct was to send a message of sympathy to his fallen cousin and to acquiesce in plans to offer him asylum in Britain. He even made secret and successful overtures to the Kaiser to grant the Tsar 'safe conduct'.[40] But during the second half of March the King had a change of heart. Britons had greeted the overthrow of despotism in Russia with euphoria: 'Not since the Bastille fell,' wrote the *Daily News*, 'has there been an event so full of splendid significance for men as the mighty happening of this week in Petrograd.' George himself found the notion of a republican Russia inconceivable and hoped that the socialists would be smashed. But the mood of the moment was expressed by the United States, which became the first nation to recognize the new Russian government. Now Americans could enter with a clear conscience what was plainly a war between democracy and absolutism.

If George gave refuge to Nicholas, Stamfordham advised, he would be associating Britain's constitutional kingship with alien autocracy, and would be giving a lever to 'all the people who are at present clamouring for a republic in England'.[41] At the front there was already 'widespread disrespect for the Crown. When the King was coming to inspect the troops a lot of anti-royal propaganda would go round.'[42] Now it seemed that British libertarians might set up soviets and adopt the creed of Bolshevism. Actually they did little more than waffle and sing 'The Red Flag'; but George was 'greatly disturbed' and cross-questioned a Labour MP, Will Thorne. The people's tribune had expected to meet 'a haughty, stand-offish man with a highly-polished University twang'. He found instead that the King was 'homely and pleasant', and assured him that Britain would never resort to violent revolution.[43]

Still, George was not prepared to provoke domestic socialists by offering sanctuary to the monarch whom their foreign comrades had just ousted. The King of England was already on the defensive about his German cousin. He would not jeopardize his popularity or position on behalf of his Russian cousin. Of course George did not know what the fate of the Romanovs would now be, but he might have guessed; and in fact his role in these events was concealed for a generation. The Prime Minister covered up for the King, while Lord Mountbatten sustained the myth that the blood of his uncle and aunt, the Tsar and Tsarina, was on the hands of Lloyd George. It was too embarrassing to acknowledge that the Russian royal house had fallen so that the British royal house might stand.

Even so, by April 1917 its position was perilously exposed. This was because all Britain's major allies except Italy were now republics, whereas her main enemies were kindred monarchies. A powerful letter in the *Times* emphasized

> the danger to national policy and national liberty of Kings who, in one way or another, are related to the German royal circle. . . . The risk to their people's welfare of monarchs whose spiritual home is Berlin is too great to be borne, and the principle of Monarchy itself has now come to be criticized on that ground.

The writer called for constitutional monarchs to choose mates for their princes from among 'the daughters of their own nobility' and demanded 'a truly national dynasty'.[44] Such appeals were given added point later in the cruellest month of the war, when U-boat sinkings of Allied ships reached their peak.

The novelist H. G. Wells then fired a further *Times* broadside against Britain's 'imported dynasty'.[45] He argued that the nation should show solidarity with republican allies by declaring that its 'ancient trappings of throne and sceptre are at most a mere historical inheritance'. From its leader columns the paper thundered dissent. The Crown was the 'indispensable keystone to the Empire' and Britain's constitutional monarchy had nothing in common with 'the prostrate autocracy' of tsardom or '"militarist" monarchies on the Hohenzollern' model.[46] Nevertheless Wells's assault 'caused much uneasiness at Buckingham Palace', according to the newspaper magnate Lord Riddell, who thought that the King and Queen had been 'badly stage-managed'.

The King, tired from touring industrial areas in an effort to 'induce the thinking working classes', as Lord Stamfordham put it, to regard the Crown as 'a living power for good',[47] was in no mood to be managed at all. He deeply resented Wells's animadversion about his 'alien and uninspiring court', memorably fulminating: 'I may be uninspiring, but I'll be damned if I'm an alien.' Not since George III had gloried in the name of Briton had there been a royal affirmation to compare with this in both sincerity and spuriousness.

Wells returned to the attack in a remarkably seminal and prescient article:

> The European dynastic system, based on intermarriage of a group of mainly German royal families, is dead today. It is freshly dead, but it is as dead as the rule of the Incas. The British Empire is very near the limit of its endurance of a kingly caste of Germans. The choice of British royalty between its peoples and its cousins cannot be [in]definitely delayed. Were it made now, publicly and boldly, there can be no doubt the decision would mean a renascence of monarchy and a tremendous outbreak of royalist enthusiasm in the empire.[48]

Here, ironically, an avowed republican showed the British monarchy the way forward: he revealed that the trump in the royal pack was the patriotic card.

Stamfordham, at any rate, realized what his master must do. Only by changing his surname, as the Prime Minister proposed and as so many of his subjects of German extraction had already done, could George slough off the Teutonic taint. Quite what the King's surname was, no one knew. Probably it was that of Prince Albert, Saxe-Coburg-Gotha – though this was particularly unfortunate since in June 1917 the first mass air raid on London was carried out by aeroplanes called Gothas. But none of the English alternatives suggested was quite satisfactory – among them were York, Lancaster, Plantagenet, Tudor-Stewart and even Fitzroy. It was Stamfordham who finally came up with the perfect solution: the private secretary not only taught George to be a king but also christened his dynasty.

The name Windsor was as English as John Bull. It had been intimately connected with royalty since the reign of the Saxon King Egbert in the Dark Ages, claimed the *Times*, adding loyally that, although Oliver Cromwell had also lived in the castle, he had been 'solicitous for the unkeep of the buildings'. Certainly Windsor Castle had been fortified by William the Conqueror and improved by Henry II. King John had been besieged in it after signing Magna Carta, and Edward III had founded the Order of the Garter there. Edward IV and Henry VIII had added St George's Chapel and they are among fourteen monarchs buried there. Charles II had restored what Samuel Pepys called 'the most romantic castle in the world'. George IV had tacked on mock-medieval machicolations, portcullis-grooves and other embellishments. Kipling had dubbed Queen Victoria the 'Widow of Windsor'. Windsor was as much a symbol of England as St George himself. Now the castle became 'the home of an eponymous House'. Such was the magic of the name that it conferred a new legitimacy on the dynasty.

The *Times* pontificated that it was not wisdom but folly to ignore the masses, who had instinctively disliked Teutonism at least since the beginning of Queen Victoria's reign. Moreover, the change was a 'democratic step',[49] for the continental perpetuation of princehood was also brought to an end. Outside the line of succession, the descendants of sovereigns would be commoners in the third generation – Mr or Miss Windsor. The title once borne by Queen Mary, Serene Highness, was abolished. Other royal relations in Britain also relinquished their German names and dignities. The Queen's brothers, the Duke of Teck and Prince Alexander of Teck, became respectively the Marquess of Cambridge and the Earl of Athlone. The King's cousins, Prince Louis and Prince Alexander of Battenberg, became the Marquess of Milford Haven and the Marquess of Carisbrooke.

In a further effort to steady the throne, the Titles Deprivation Act punished princes of the United Kingdom fighting for the enemy. Most notable among them were the Duke of Cumberland (and Brunswick) and the Duke of Albany (and Saxe-Coburg-Gotha), who were stripped of their English styles, though not their British citizenship. Even now King George was disinclined to pursue the vendetta. Agitated by the 'heaps of letters abusing' him for his alien kindred, the King had actually tried to maintain to a cynical Asquith that his cousin Prince Albert of Schleswig-Holstein was 'not really fighting on the side of the Germans' because he had been 'put in charge of a camp of English prisoners' near Berlin.[50] But the cutting of these ties and the resoundingly English aliases adopted by his relations at home seemed to win widespread approval. Some, though, considered that the monarchy had made a foolish and defeatist move. Abroad, the transmutation was regarded as a royal loss of face and the Kaiser famously sneered that he was going to the theatre to see *The Merry Wives of Saxe-Coburg-Gotha*.

Certainly the nailing of its patriotic colours to the national masthead did not solve all the monarchy's problems. Nor, in the corrosive atmosphere of racial hatred that prevailed, did hard work by Clive Wigram, the King's assistant private secretary, 'to get Their Majesties a good press'.[51] Nor, in the summer of 1917, did the creation of new, more democratic civilian honours such as the Order of the British Empire. As their theoretical fount, the King should have received a rich reward of loyalty. However their real fount was Lloyd George who, in search of funds and support, distributed them on such a lavish scale (22,000 by 1919) that music hall comedians joked about the 'Order of the Bad Egg'. George V was livid about the devaluation of the currency of kingship, but there was nothing he could do about it. The Welsh Wizard had the power and the guile to get his way, though Arthur Balfour did once ask him, 'Whatever would you do if you had a ruler with brains?'[52] At least the royal hands were clean. Nevertheless, even when the Central Powers collapsed his position did not seem particularly secure. As Lloyd George said, 'Emperors and Kingdoms and Kings and Crowns are falling like withered leaves before a gale.'[53] The Kaiser, the Austrian Emperor and the King of Bulgaria all became fugitives. All over Germany smaller thrones were vacated – in Prussia, Saxony, Bavaria, Württemberg, Mecklenburg, Brunswick and Hesse – while, as often as not, revolutionary frenzy prevailed. The red tide even lapped over British shores.

It was stemmed not by a latter-day Canute but by a combination of luck and judgement. Britain was fortunate in being the only stable constitutional monarchy to emerge on the winning side. George V, in his new incarnation as head of a manifestly national dynasty (whose crown, nevertheless, was the golden link that bound the British Empire together), received the peace dividend and reaped the fruits of victory. After it was signalled by maroons, on the eleventh hour of the eleventh day of the eleventh month of 1918, exultant crowds surged round Buckingham Palace to proclaim their loyalty. Their jubilation was undampened by the drizzle, which the

King and Queen themselves braved, riding through the streets in an open carriage. The American poet Ezra Pound happened to see the sovereign at close quarters and wrote: 'Poor devil was looking happy, I should think, for the first time in his life.'[54]

Back at Buckingham Palace the delirious throng shouted again and again, 'We want King George!' Several times he emerged, wearing the uniform of an admiral of the fleet and accompanied by Queen Mary, to acknowledge their acclaim from a balcony festooned with crimson velvet and, in the evening, theatrically lit by arc lamps. Notwithstanding the difficulties still to be faced, this massive demonstration of enthusiasm boded well for the House of Windsor. After dinner, no longer bound by his pledge, the King ordered that the wine cellars should be unlocked. George V celebrated the end of the Great War with a bottle of brandy laid down by George IV to mark the triumph of Waterloo. The amber liquor proved to be 'very musty'.[55]

2

A ROYAL FAMILY BUSINESS

The armistice did not bring peace of mind to the head of the new House of Windsor. Advisers warned George V that the Crown was in a less secure position in 1918 than it had been in 1914. Lord Esher wrote that 'The monarchy and its cost will have to be justified in the future in the eyes of a war-torn and hungry proletariat endowed with a huge preponderance of voting power.'[1] Like every British sovereign from Queen Victoria to Queen Elizabeth II, King George sometimes feared that he would be the last of his line to occupy the throne, yet surely the defeat of his foreign enemies made him invulnerable at home. 'Why should our people have a revolution?' he asked plaintively. 'We are the victors, we are the Top Dog.'[2]

Just three days after the victory celebrations, however, the Labour Party held its first election rally, in the Albert Hall. At it the tub-thumping leader of the Transport Workers' Union threatened to employ 'extra-constitutional means' to achieve his ends and hoped 'to see the Red Flag flying over Buckingham Palace'. Until that hope was realized, his supporters contented themselves by cheering the Bolsheviks and draping a red flag over the crown in the royal box. The Albert Hall authorities refused to accommodate future Labour meetings, but were forced to back down when the Electrical

Trade Union put out their lights. Meanwhile, the socialist *Herald* gave its entire front page to the headline CROWNS AND CORONETS THREE A PENNY. Inside, it quoted Kant's dictum that 'the first condition of perpetual peace was that every Government should be a Republic'.[3]

In fact only a small minority of British socialists wanted to abolish the monarchy. However, the Labour Party was violently opposed to Allied attempts to turn the revolutionary clock back in Russia and it aspired to get rid of the capitalist social order in Britain. The election, in which six million new voters took part, two-thirds of them women, effectively made Labour the main opposition party. Equally worrying for the King were post-war problems of dislocation and demobilization which resulted in strikes and mutinies. He was most horrified, though, by popular demands to 'Hang the Kaiser'.

Even when inveighing against Hun atrocities King George would not condemn his cousin in so many words. To Franklin D. Roosevelt he simply said: 'You know, I have a number of relations in Germany, but I can tell you frankly that in all my life, I have never seen a German gentleman.'[4] The King was content to ostracize the Kaiser, who bitterly resented the treatment, declaring that 'monarchs should not allow a mere war to affect their personal relationship after it is over'.[5] Other German relatives appealed to George to oppose plans to extradite the Kaiser from the Netherlands and arraign him before a war crimes tribunal. They warned 'Your Majesty, whose family originated among us' that such a trial threatens 'every throne (including the English throne)'.[6] King George agreed, but was unable to formulate a response. Then he discovered – from the newspapers – that Lloyd George proposed to put his cousin on trial in England, which appalled him. Would it not put the King in 'a very delicate and invidious position', said Lord Curzon, if the Kaiser were brought 'to the country the most famous Sovereign of which was his Grandmother; where his Mother was born; and from which she was married; where he has constantly stayed as a Royal Guest; and where his cousin is at the present moment on the Throne?'[7] As it happened, the Dutch government refused extradition and the Kaiser lived on in mellow exile at Doorn.

In the aftermath of the First World War in Britain King George concluded that the Communist contagion was as virulent as the pandemic of Spanish flu, which killed more people than the war itself. In December 1918 the King vainly tried to persuade President Woodron Wilson to send his fresh army to 'Russia to protect the country from Bolshevism', promising 'that the Admiralty would arrange transport and defray the cost'.[8] George had a real fright when disabled veterans crowded menacingly around his horse during a parade at Hyde Park; but they merely wanted to register their grievance about Lloyd George's failure to conjure up a land fit for heroes to live in. Dining at the Palace, Asquith was subjected to what he dismissed as 'a lot of man-in-the-bus nonsense' about Bolsheviks. In fact the entire royal family was infected with an obsession which almost matched that of Winston Churchill who, having mastered the Hun 'tigers', now wanted to beat the Bolshevik 'baboons'.[9]

Scarcely a hint of regal dread reached the outside world or ruffled the ordered serenity of Buckingham Palace. Even in the dark year of 1917 what chiefly seemed to preoccupy courtiers was whether peers should have to wear robes at the Opening of Parliament, or whether munitions workers should remove their gloves before shaking hands with the Queen. The rule was that no one should do anything that had never been done before. Rare exceptions were made, such as the institution of regular garden parties so that a wider spectrum of society could come into contact with royalty. But in general archaic customs such as the ban on wearing glasses at court continued, however absurd they might seem. Behind their backs Lord Esher described the King as obstinate and feeble and the Queen as virtuous and unimaginative. Likening Buckingham Palace to Tsarskoe Selo before the revolution, he considered it 'wonderful that the whole edifice [of the monarchy] has not crumbled under an avalanche of ridicule'.[10]

In fact the spectacle remained as impressive as ever, especially on state occasions. Then the great gilded apartments became vivid with life and fragrant with incense, which

Queen Mary thought would kill germs. Around the royal family there formed a living frieze; the Gentlemen at Arms in their scarlet and gold jackets and burnished helmets with white plumes; the Yeomen of the Guard wearing velvet caps, red tunics and the Elizabethan ruffs revived by George IV; the liveried footmen with their white breeches, buckled shoes and flour-powdered hair, who were ranged in matching pairs and paid according to height. The Lord Chamberlain, his rich court dress emblazoned with the symbolic gold key of his office, walked backwards before the King and Queen, who invested the whole picture with magic. Hollywood, as one upper servant observed, could never match it.

Visitors to Buckingham Palace felt that they were watching an Arabian Nights entertainment set in an Aladdin's cave. They were dazzled by the profusion of gold plate, porcelain, gilt thrones, tapestries and sumptuous paintings, to say nothing of the three hundred clocks that kept two men in full-time employment. If the trappings of grandeur gave enchantment to monarchy, the retainers helped to keep it on its pedestal. Their titles seem to echo down the ages – the Master of Horse and the Mistress of Robes, the Yeoman Bed Hanger and the Lord High Almoner, the Gold Stick in Waiting and the Poet Laureate. Later, during the Depression, Queen Mary feared that all this might provoke resentment among their suffering subjects and efforts were made to avoid ostentation. But after the First World War, as the Countess of Airlie wrote, 'The old formula of pageantry as a panacea for discontent was revived.'[11]

In particular the monarchy demonstrably associated itself with the sacrifices made during the war and with the new hopes engendered by the peace. The King honoured Empire troops who paraded through London. When Lloyd George returned from Versailles, the King created a precedent by meeting him at Victoria Station. As they drove back to the Palace people threw flowers into the carriage, and when a laurel wreath landed in the King's lap he gave it to his Prime Minister (who subsequently passed it on to his mistress). The King took a prominent part in celebrating Peace Day and Victory Day. He also inaugurated the Two Minutes' Silence, and on the second anniversary of the armistice unveiled the Cenotaph in Whitehall, a poignant monument to 'The Glorious Dead'.

Even more moving was the funeral of the Unknown Warrior in Westminster Abbey, an overwhelming act of national catharsis. In the presence of a hundred winners of the Victoria Cross the King walked behind the coffin at the service which the *Times* called 'the most beautiful, the most touching and the most impressive . . . this island has ever seen'.[12] His wreath bore a card written in his own schoolboy hand. But these obsequies were also an assertion that 'nothing had changed, heroes were still heroes, the Big Words retained their authority'.[13] The funeral was a consecration of chivalry whose apotheosis was the Crown. The identification of King and Country was spelled out on the tomb itself. The inscription concluded: THEY BURIED HIM AMONG THE KINGS BECAUSE HE HAD DONE GOOD TOWARD GOD AND TOWARD HIS HOUSE.

The King engaged with equal solemnity in secular ceremonies. Queen Victoria had been hissed at Royal Ascot; King Edward had been cheered; King George was revered. Under his aegis the formalities became stricter. The white badges giving entry to the Royal Enclosure became harder to obtain. As at country houses visited by the King, women could never appear twice in the same attire, and buying a whole set of new outfits for Ascot cost £2,000 – perhaps £60,000 at today's values. Queen Mary, who seldom laughed because she thought it made her look like a horse, once expelled a sporting peeress for wearing a sailor's cap inscribed in gold lettering 'HMS Good Ship Venus'. While the roads round about were choked by motor traffic, the royal party still processed through Windsor Great Park in polished landaus managed by bewigged postillions. Nothing angered the King more than the imputation that his public performances were 'good propaganda' – he once exploded with wrath when the Prince of Wales used those words. But there is no doubt that George much enhanced his popularity by grand patronage of a sport that appealed to all classes of his subjects.

Even more calculated to win him their devotion was the fact that he seemed to be the head of a happy family. Where

George IV had been, in Bagehot's phrase, 'a model of family demerit', George V burned many of his more incriminating letters. Where the newspapers had lampooned Edward VII as Prince of Wales, remarking for example that there was nothing between him and Lillie Langtry, 'not even a sheet', they were astonishingly deferential towards his son – even the cartoonists treated him with respect. King George appeared to pull the throne nearer the hearth: he made it the Windsor chair of the paterfamilias as well as the seat of majesty.

Thus, at a time when almost every family in the land had been ravaged by the war, the royal family was presented as the *beau idéal* beloved by the Victorians. Family prayers, shared joys and sorrows, the sweet discipline of loving, honouring and obeying – all made domesticity seem the finest, the most wholesome, the truly natural form of existence. To those outside the walls Windsor seemed everything a home ought to be – a school of morality, a temple of felicity, a bastion of security. But to its younger inmates it was more of a prison house. This was because the royal happy family was a myth. As Lord Hardinge said, the King behaved towards his children like a 'brute'.[14] He set traps in matters of costume and punctilio into which his children naturally fell, whereupon the King would roar at them like a latter-day Captain Bligh, his rough beard twitching, his blue eyes blazing. As the royal librarian said, the Windsors made bad parents: like ducks, they trampled on their young. When Lord Derby remonstrated with the King about this treatment he famously replied: 'My father was frightened of his mother; I was frightened of my father; and I am damned well going to see to it that my children are frightened of me.'[15]

Queen Mary was, as her eldest son remarked, equally frightened of her husband. Because she was larger than him it was often thought that she ruled the royal roost. Jokes were made about 'George's Dragon' and 'George the Fifth and Mary the Four-Fifths'. Ample-bosomed as a ship's figurehead, she was nicknamed 'Soutien-Georges' by the French (a pun on their word for a brassière). In fact, for all her imposing looks the Queen was cripplingly shy and utterly subservient. Tongue-tied as a girl, she had placidly transferred her affections from the late Prince Eddy to Prince George. While courting she remained stiff and inhibited, never flirting or holding hands or showing warmth. Without question Mary became genuinely fond of George, and vice versa, but there seems to have been little passion in her feeling for him. She obeyed George as a husband but venerated him as a king. Being the product of a morganatic marriage, a mere Serene Highness, Mary was painfully conscious that she herself was not wholly royal; but to others she seemed so regal, so decorated and gem-encrusted, as to be scarcely human. The socialite MP Sir Henry 'Chips' Channon described her as sparkling like the Jungfrau. At Lord Harewood's wedding a myopic E. M. Forster bowed to the iced and many-tiered cake under the impression that it was Queen Mary.[16]

Perfectly poised, the Queen carried out an exhausting schedule of ceremonial functions as though she had been programmed to the task. Even by George's exacting standards Mary dressed impeccably, although English aristocrats, who were inclined to regard the royal family as middle-class, deplored her habit of preening herself in her finery and having her servants 'parade round her as if she were a model'.[17] But Queen Mary embodied majesty in a fashion that compelled attention and demanded admiration. Driving past a school for the Orphan Daughters of Officers and finding that the children responded to her waves with vacant stares, she muttered under her breath: '*Cheer*, little idiots, can't you?'[18] Capable of freezing upstarts with a glacial *hauteur*, she did occasionally unbend towards ordinary people, though she was apt in the process to reveal the great gulf between them. Viewing London slums with horror and amazement, she once asked a group of East Enders, 'Why, why do you live here?'[19]

But Queen did not entirely sublimate her personality in that of the King. While he pored over his stamps, she liked to read. However, the Queen was not interested in general culture: she approved of her children's tutor burning an 'indecent' novel by Balzac, and she may even have sympathised with her husband's comment on Margot Asquith's indiscreet memoirs: 'People who write books ought to be shut up.'[20] The sort of books the Queen liked dealt with her own relations, and she studied the European royal family tree, root and branch and twig. Similarly she preferred chocolate-box portraits of obscure archdukes to paintings of merit on other subjects.

Her taste in precious stones, however, was catholic. The Queen had 'an emotional lurch of the heart when she saw beautiful jewels,' and, as Suzy Menkes has said, she was 'avaricious'[21] to the point of 'mania'. Perhaps as a result of her relative poor childhood, she hated paying for them; despite being conscience-stricken about the fate of the Russian royal family, during the Depression she bought some of its emigré members' finest gems for 'a fraction' of their true worth.[22] Wearing jewellery was an acknowledged way of defining status at the time, especially in Germany, so displaying it was a duty as well as a pleasure. When Countess Mountbatten's young husband, greatly daring, admired the Queen's amethyst brooch, she replied, 'Ah, but you haven't seen the best one.' Drawing herself upright, she revealed beneath her 'marvellous bosom an enormous amethyst stomacher, simply vast'.[23] By comprehensively out-dazzling the aristocrats around her, Queen Mary projected a peerless image of majesty.

The Queen also had an insatiable appetite for all other kinds of costly bric-à-brac, spending much of her leisure sorting and cataloguing the immense hoard of the House of Windsor. Indeed, she so loved domestic organization that she occasionally turned up at friends' houses when they were out and started to cut down their ivy or rearrange their furniture. The Queen adored Fabergé animals, jewelled watches and gold musical boxes, and she never missed an opportunity of adding to her hoard. This was one reason why she had such a passion for India, where the maharajas handed out jewels like blackberries.

The Queen also acquired goods by means ranging from extortion to outright theft, and many stories are told of her begging and kleptomania. Warned of her impending arrival, antique dealers, jewellers and stately home owners locked away their more prized possessions. When the owner of one country house forgot to hide a valuable piece of Georgian china Queen Mary said, 'It's so kind of you to give me that; it's just what I want for my collection. I'll tell the chauffeur to put it in the car.'[24] Taking tea with old Lady Hudson, the Queen admired a set of chairs painted by Angelica Kauffmann and said that they would go well with a Kauffmann table which she owned. Lady Hudson held out valiantly, but by nine o'clock 'the chairs went off in the royal Daimler'.[25] According to Sir Steven Runciman, where the owners or their heirs can be identified the present Queen has sent back items thus acquired by her grandmother.

Busy collecting as well as carrying out her duties, Queen Mary had no time for motherhood but enough for procreation; indeed, Admiral Fisher nicknamed George and Mary 'Futile and Fertile'. Her first child, the future King Edward VIII (known to family and friends by the last of his seven Christian names, David), was born in 1894. A year later came Albert; called Bertie by his intimates, he was created Duke of York in 1920 and crowned King George VI after his elder brother's abdication. Then followed Mary (later the Princess Royal) in 1897, Henry (later Duke of Gloucester) in 1900, George (later Duke of Kent) in 1902, and finally John in 1905. This last child was mentally handicapped and epileptic. When it became clear that 'he was never going to be able to play a full part in life' his parents secreted him in a cottage with his own little entourage, 'rather like the Monster of Glamis'.[26] After his death in 1919 he was buried at Sandringham beside Queen Alexandra's youngest son, who had lived only for a day.

Queen Mary had none of her mother-in-law's maternal instincts. Like others who could afford to do so, she consigned her children to the care of servants. But even when they were brought downstairs, neat and tidy for their early evening inspection, the Queen did not kiss, cuddle or hug them. Partly she must have been reacting against Queen Alexandra, who often descended on York Cottage, accompanied by some of the seventy-five Sandringham dogs, to carry off her grandchildren to play canasta, do jigsaw puzzles or race slices of buttered toast down the seams of King Edward VII's trousers. But mainly, it seems, Mary was incapable of radiating warmth even towards her own flesh and blood. Sometimes, it is true, the Queen did achieve a certain intimacy with her children, playing and laughing with them. And during the war David often told her what a joy it was to have a fond mother in whom he could confide. But when she died in 1953 he remarked, 'I somehow feel that the fluids in her veins must always have been as icy-cold as they now are in death.'

Certainly the Queen was never capable of protecting her brood from their irascible father. Starved of love in infancy, they were treated like midshipmen from the age of reason. Bertie, nervous and prone to ill health, suffered worst. Although he was naturally left-handed, he was made to write with his right hand. This may have prompted or accentuated his stammer, a condition not helped, when he was stuck for a word, by his father's impatient 'Get it out!' Furthermore, like his brother Harry, Bertie was made to wear splints in bed to correct his knock knees.

If the royal children were subjected to a regime calculated to produce psychological cripples, they were given an education designed to ensure that they remained intellectual pygmies. To preserve their exclusiveness George appointed a tutor – an undistinguished prep school master; they thus lacked the stimulus and companionship of other boys. Arthur Ponsonby, a radical member of the courtier family, likened their condition to that of servants, 'shut off from natural intercourse with ordinary human beings. They use funny old fashioned rather ungrammatical language and have the same love of funerals and diseases and are touching and fussy.'[27] Queen Mary's contribution was to instruct them in genealogy and needlepoint. Then, before the age of puberty, the two older boys were packed off to the Royal Naval College at Osborne. George V had decided that what had been good enough for him was good enough for his sons.

More emphasis has traditionally been placed on forming the characters of princes than on developing their minds. Probably that emphasis should be reversed. There is no evidence that the narrow curriculum and brutal regime at Osborne and at the senior naval institution, Dartmouth, had good effects on either prince, though David did somewhat better than Bertie, who was also bullied mercilessly. Nicknamed 'Bat Lugs' because of his big ears, he was pricked with pins to see if his blood was blue. Certainly the royal cadets ended up knowing the ropes

– but they knew almost nothing of history, literature, foreign languages and general culture.

Nevertheless, as they grew towards maturity all the royal children betrayed signs of their repressive and limited upbringing. David was almost pathologically restless, ate like an anorexic, suffered from alternating bouts of high and low self-esteem, and longed to abase himself before a woman he could truly love. Bertie was tongue-tied, a prey to rage and frustration, and grovellingly subservient towards his parents. Princess Mary, kept in royal purdah, was abnormally shy and withdrawn. This was doubtless because the King could never temper the real affection he felt for his favourite child with tact – at her first *accouchement* he paced up and down, recalling the wives of his acquaintances who had died in childbirth. Henry, the first of his family to go to Eton, punctuated his discourse with a whinnying laugh and did much, especially in the way of dull and deep potations, to earn the nickname 'Potty'. George, though bright and handsome, was also wild and volatile; he later experimented with sex and drugs. In short, the royal family was anything but happy.

Edward Prince of Wales, as David became in 1910, was the unhappiest of the lot. Quite against his instincts, he was obliged to sustain the old-fashioned image of royalty. He particularly hated the extravagant charade of his investiture, not least because he feared that his naval friends would laugh at his effeminate costume. Edward was never allowed to escape from the parental realm. His career at Magdalen College, Oxford, devoted to slow reading and fast living, was subjected to minute scrutiny. His taste in clothes, which ran to large, bright checks and soft, comfortable tweeds, produced frequent explosions of paternal wrath.

During the First World War the Prince of Wales wanted to fight but was appointed instead to safe staff jobs behind the lines. He railed incessantly against his fate, falling into moods of paranoid self-pity and suicidal depression. He also filled his diaries with obscene abuse of 'the fucking Boche', talking 'in terms of genocide, of the need to exterminate this race for ever'.[28] But he also exercised his mesmeric charm on Allied troops, often rejecting his Daimler in favour of a green army bicycle. He saw himself as a progressive, even a populist, Prince. Certainly he understood the sufferings of men in the trenches in a way that his father never could – on an early morning visit to the Somme battlefield the King sniffed appreciatively and, not recognizing the pervasive odour of death, remarked: 'Ah! this is the smell that gives one an appetite for breakfast.'[29] Of course, in most ways the Prince remained, like his father, assertively orthodox and took the privileges of royalty for granted. He loathed conscientious objectors and striking miners, despised foreigners and continued to detest 'Huns' for some time. In occupied Germany after the armistice he was billeted with the Kaiser's sister, who infuriated him by having framed photographs of his family all over the house and by calling him 'dear'. 'I feel so ashamed, however one is consoled by the thought that we've "cut them *right* out" for ever!!'[30]

Armageddon also increased Edward's alienation from his parents' generation, making him ever more impatient with artificial conventions. And it sharpened his appetite for playboy pleasures: anathema to his father, this was a world of lipstick and painted fingernails, cocktails and jazz, short skirts and nightclubs. Yet even in the smoky atmosphere of the Embassy Club the Prince's studied informality caused outrage. When he appeared in a dinner jacket, the kind of thing a bandleader might wear, while all the other men were creaking inside the armour of respectability – white tie and tails – the members exclaimed, 'The cad, the swine – how disgraceful when ladies are here.'[31] A cause of scandal in high society was Edward's infatuation with the steely-chic Mrs Freda Dudley Ward. Like Wallis Simpson after her, she both vamped and mothered the Prince, quickly reducing him to a state of mewling dependence. In every sense the integrity of the royal family was threatened.

Shivers of apprehension spread through Buckingham Palace. In the spirit of Bagehot, the aged courtier Sir Frederick Ponsonby warned the Prince of Wales about the risks of making himself too accessible: 'The Monarchy must always retain an element of mystery. A Prince must not show himself too much. The Monarchy should remain on a pedestal.'[32]

Edward considered that, on the contrary, royalty should retain the common touch, demonstrate its humanity and get on terms with democracy. Somewhere between these polar opposites the Windsors have always sought a golden mean, and a brilliant solution, apparently suggested by Lloyd George, was found to the current problem. The Prince should become a roving ambassador for Britain, particularly in far-flung corners of the Empire, and thus overcome the most serious difficulty of his office – the lack of a proper occupation.

Edward's role would be to strengthen imperial ties: loyalty to the Crown had helped to bring the dominions into the First World War on Britain's side and, thanks in part to the expressions of gratitude which Edward was commissioned to utter on his tours, it would help to bring them into the Second. George V appreciated the importance of Greater Britain overseas and had begun his reign by proposing to do for the Empire what Edward VII had done for the peace of Europe, but he was now increasingly averse to leaving home. That Edward should take on this responsibility and exile himself to the colonies, where his clothes would cause less affront and his liaisons would be less dangerous, was a huge bonus.

The Prince proved an immediate success in 1919 on a tour of the New World. Adulated by the press, he became the first royal 'media star', a tricky position in view of his capacity to generate bad publicity as well as good. Everyone in Canada greeted him rapturously, including (despite their French allegiance) the inhabitants of Quebec. In New York he was given a ticker-tape welcome and his 'frank democracy' was said to have 'a strong appeal in Washington'.[33] However, on his return, Edward's constant whistling of the Ziegfeld Follies song 'A Pretty Girl Is Like a Melody' infuriated the King. Although privately proud of his son, he showed little appreciation of his efforts abroad. Edward felt that his triumph had been hollow and that his life was a sham; he dreaded the prospect of being parted from Freda during another planned long tour, this time of the Antipodes. Even Edward's official biographer does not reveal the full depths of his self-loathing and despair. On Christmas Day 1919 the

Prince wrote pathetically to his private secretary, Sir Godfrey Thomas:

> . . . a sort of hopelessly lost feeling has come over me, I think I'm going kind of mad . . . [and] feel incapable of pulling myself together. . . . Christ, how I loathe my job now and all the press 'puffed' empty 'succés'. I feel I'm through with it and long to die. For God's sake don't breathe a word of this to a *soul.* No one else must know how I feel about my life, and everything. . . . You probably think from this that I ought to be in the madhouse already. . . . I do feel such a bloody little shit.[34]

It was a cloacal *cri de coeur* which might be echoed by the present Prince of Wales.

The royal private secretaries sought to avert a repetition of earlier damaging Hanoverian feuds; the new image of a united royal family had to be preserved at all costs. Stamfordham believed that this could only be achieved by compromise: 'His Majesty should try to avoid hypercriticism of HRH's ways, habits, dress', for the world had moved on since 1914, making young people more independent. On the other hand, the King and Queen were 'gravely anxious about the abnormal life' that Edward led. His steeplechasing was not only dangerous but made him the butt of music hall jokes because he fell off his horse so often. His parents were also worried about Edward's 'late hours, lack of food, excess of smoking, restlessness and dislike of reading or any salutary occupation'. If he could reform in these respects, 'play the game', be more punctual, tell the King something of his plans and manage him more tactfully, Stamfordham felt, all would be well.[35]

All was not well, but few outside the charmed circle realized it. The Prince of Wales's tours were, on the whole, outstandingly successful. He had a 'fantastic gift' for making off-the-cuff speeches and of talking to people in a way that 'made them feel like a million dollars',[36] and was usually greeted with an enthusiasm sometimes akin to ecstasy. He reciprocated by driving himself to the point of exhaustion, even nervous breakdown.

To all appearances his oriental venture in 1922 was yet

another triumphal progress. In India, to be sure, the Prince resented the artificiality and the artifice and found it difficult to hide his prejudice against the black and brown races: this was so pronounced that he was even offended when the Theosophist Annie Besant declared that he was the reincarnation of the great Emperor Akbar. Nevertheless, the Prince took a starring role in 'the elaborate display and pageantry' which were designed to impress 'the Oriental mind'.[37] Similarly he did his best to cement good relations with Japan. Indeed, he came like a breath of fresh air into the theocratic court of Hirohito, newly created Prince Regent on account of his father's madness.

The Imperial Palace in Tokyo was such a monument to clotted formality that it seemed like a Mikadoesque parody of Windsor. Japanese courtiers bowed like marionettes, rubbing their knees together as a gesture of further humility and hanging their heads. This was inevitable, for the direct descendant of the Sun Goddess was the focus of an intense national cult – although his power was in inverse proportion to the awe in which he was held.

Nevertheless Edward, who was inclined to patronize Hirohito, would have done well to study him. For, unlike vanquished European sovereigns in 1918, the Emperor of Japan kept his throne in 1945. Even after the shock of defeat he managed to sustain the make-believe world in which royalty wins privilege and respect as a reward for transcendent superiority. By contrast the Prince of Wales, during the 1920s, let his humanity show. It is true that he was exposed to almost unbearable strains – not just the duty to smile interminably at the crowds but the duty not to laugh at dignitaries like the King of Egypt, who barked like a dog. Similarly, the temptations to which he was subjected might have ruined a less susceptible character.

Women threw themselves at him and, despite his callow devotion to Freda, he was anything but averse to casual liaisons. Possibly the Prince's 'frantic promiscuity' was encouraged by his 'sense that he was infertile'[38] owing to an adolescent attack of mumps – his body always remained strikingly hairless. Edward was less abstemious with drink than with food and wore himself out in the relentless pursuit of late-night pleasure, strumming his ukelele into the small hours. Sometimes he looked sulky at official functions that bored him, or sent offensively transparent excuses for his absences. If he had ever heard of Gibbon's maxim, he never accepted that 'The time of a prince is the property of his people.' He swore like a trooper in a curious Cockney-American accent that he developed because 'I determined *not* to speak like Mama and Papa.'[39] Edward felt, in short, unsuited to the role of being a King-in-waiting. As he acknowledged to his private secretary when bemoaning the 'misfortune' of being his father's son, 'I am a misfit.'[40]

Most of the Prince's peccadilloes were kept out of the British press. Furthermore, the Prince deflected criticism by performing brilliantly on occasions. He could even keep the King up to the mark, telling him, for example, that the unveiling of an imperial war memorial in Westminster was not a task for the Prime Minister but 'absolutely a stunt for *you*'.[41] However, as the 1920s progressed the Prince's staff grew ever more worried about his erratic and irresponsible behaviour, and his doomed insistence that he could keep his private and public lives in separate compartments. One member of his retinue grumbled that he was a 'maddening man' because 'you couldn't get him to read anything at all', not even half a sheet of paper.[42] His assistant private secretary, Alan 'Tommy' Lascelles, felt like 'an actor-manager, whose Hamlet persists in interrupting the play by balancing the furniture on the end of his nose'.[43] The warning of Lloyd George, who had himself courted scandal all his life, was pertinent: if Edward was to be a constitutional king he must first be a constitutional Prince of Wales. The King warned the Prince that his double life would be exposed, and continued to nag him with letters which might have been sent, said Lord Louis Mountbatten, the Prince's ADC, from 'a Director to his Assistant Manager'.[44] One courtier went so far as to say that the Prince of Wales had a 'real loathing' for his parents.[45] Comforting a tearful Mountbatten on the death of his father, the Prince remarked: 'I envy you a father whom you could love. If my father had died, we should have felt nothing but relief.'

George recognized that the House of Windsor could not stand if it was divided against itself: it must present a united front to the world. But behind the facade all his sons were ranged in a timorous alliance against the reign of tradition. They resented the fact that in royal doings the past invariably governed the present, and objected to their father's attempts to make them lead sheltered lives – at Cambridge, after the war, Bertie and Henry had to live together in a big house outside college, where the latter spent most of his time catching mice. Prince George wanted to join the Foreign Office rather than the Navy, for which he was unsuited, and complained that the King's only reason for refusing was that such a thing had never been done before. And after the rigours of their upbringing, the royal young men also wanted to have fun.

They engaged in much clandestine junketing, though their hope that news of it would not reach their father was vain. He was furious, for example, to hear that all four princes had attended a riotous party organized by Lord Curzon's youngest daughter, Alexandra, while he was away from his Carlton House Terrace mansion; at this affair Henry managed to break the dining-room table. Prince George was a royal 'tearaway', according to that particular party-giver. She taught him to drive on the Ascot–Bagshot road when he should have been studying at Dartmouth; they were mortified when an 'enormous Daimler' bowled past containing the unmistakable figure of Queen Mary.[46]

The weakest link in the fraternal chain was Bertie. Bashful and dutiful by nature, he was flattened into submission by his parents and detailed to become 'the Industrial Prince'. His task was to visit factories and mines to demonstrate the royal family's concern for the working class. One memorable way in which he tried to do this was at camps designed to integrate public schoolboys and proletarian youths. Khaki shorts, straw palliasses, energetic games, camp fires and community singing would, the Palace hoped, help to inoculate the masses against the contagion of Communism. However, the social divide was typified by the discovery which one lad made when peeking into Prince Bertie's tent – it contained a four-poster bed.

Like his brothers, Bertie got few thanks from his parents

and many rebukes. On returning from one journey the Prince received a wire from his father saying, 'Do not embrace me in public and when you kiss your mother take your hat off.'[47] When Bertie proposed to Helen 'Poppy' Baring, a fast young society lady who apparently had affairs with at least three of the four royal brothers, Queen Mary sent him a telegram which read: 'On no account will we permit your proposed marriage. Mama.'[48] The Queen then set about finding her gauche, immature boy a suitable bride – one who would make a man of him.

Queen Mary's own preferences lay with Protestant princesses of the traditional type, but they were now scarce. Bowing to popular feeling on the subject in 1917, the King had told the Privy Council that his sons could wed commoners; and subsequently Lloyd George had advised that the people would not tolerate foreign marriage partners. In 1922 Princess Mary married Viscount Lascelles. A rich Yorkshire landowner many years her senior, he was rumoured to have proposed to the inhibited Mary as a result of a bet in his club. But the match proved popular. As it happened, Bertie's wife would become the first native-born Queen since Henry VIII's sixth wife, Catherine Parr. The beautiful Lady Elizabeth Bowes-Lyon was Queen Mary's choice. She was the youngest daughter of the 14th Earl of Strathmore, whose family was descended from Scottish kings and had owned Glamis Castle (home of the ghostly 'Monster') for six hundred years.

Vivacious and self-confident, but comfortingly old-fashioned, Elizabeth had many admirers including Bertie himself. At first she refused to take on this twitching, inarticulate Prince, who was prone to tantrums and consumed by self-doubt. Yet Bertie's very vulnerability must have been as much of an attraction as his royal rank and his grand old title, Duke of York. So on to the royal stage stepped the kind of dominant woman for whom all George V's children were searching, for under Elizabeth's smiling exterior there was a determined character. She wore a 'velvet glove', as Peter Townsend has said, but it concealed a 'steely hand'. Her strength compensated for Bertie's frailty. She radiated grace at their wedding in April 1923, which was designed to be exactly what Bagehot had described – 'the brilliant edition of a universal fact'.[49]

Before the war royal marriages had been celebrated without ostentation, mainly because extravagance might provoke hostility. *Reynolds' News*, for example, had compared the wedding of Edward (VII) Prince of Wales to that of George (IV), the Prince Regent: 'Then, as now, the theatres were opened freely to the public, mobs shouted, bonfires blazed, corporations crouched, bishops blessed, and the people's gold poured forth in floods to glorify a royal swine.'[50] But after the war the royal advisers hoped that nuptial pageantry and publicity would appeal to the masses. Bertie became the first Prince to marry in Westminster Abbey for five hundred years, and the wedding procession was watched by a million people. The ceremony was also filmed – though not broadcast, because the Archbishop of Canterbury feared that people might listen to it in disrespectful circumstances. Elizabeth, wearing her royalty like an aureole, was the star of this splendid show.

She also brought Bertie domestic happiness beyond his wildest dreams. Despite her unpunctuality Elizabeth even charmed his father, though she privately hated 'being always under the eye of a narrow-minded autocrat'.[51] Under her emollient influence the King grew more indulgent towards Bertie, whose willingness to conform contrasted so agreeably with the maverick wilfulness of David. Together the Duke and Duchess of York represented all that had made the reign of George V and his consort such a success. Perhaps success would lead to succession: as Chips Channon recorded, many of the Prince of Wales's friends believed that he was far from eager to inherit the throne. Edward himself encouraged Elizabeth to marry Bertie and, he added, eventually 'go to Buck House'.[52]

3

THE KING VERSUS THE PRINCE

If King George V's failures as a paterfamilias were concealed, his successes as the father of his people were trumpeted. This was understandable for, as the historian A. J. P. Taylor has said, George 'had a better record as a constitutional sovereign than any monarch since William III'.[1] Lord Esher complained that virtue dominated the royal household but not wisdom, while Harold Nicolson despised the King for having the intellectual capacities of a railway porter. Yet King George's great strength was that he was the common man writ large, that he embodied the Orwellian ideal of common decency. Following the prescription of Bagehot, whom he had studied, George attempted to advise, to encourage and to warn impartially.

Thus the King wished to maintain the powers of the Lords, but bowed to the will of the Commons. He detested the Suffragettes, but disapproved of feeding them by force. He feared striking workers, but pitied their poverty. He had the usual colour prejudice of his time, but did not think his black subjects should be victimized or treated with condescension. He wanted Ireland to remain within the British Empire, but opposed the Black and Tans' campaign of violence against the nationalists. His courageous visit to Belfast in June 1921, when he called for reconciliation and forbearance, prepared the way for the Anglo-Irish agreement partitioning the country. It was an historic achievement. In a letter to the Palace Lloyd George expressed his gratitude: 'None but the King could have made that appeal; none but the King could have evoked so instantaneous a response.'[2]

That tribute came from a Prime Minister who had less respect for the monarchy than any other twentieth-century occupant of 10 Downing Street. Lloyd George was not a republican, as many thought, but he felt hostile to the whole ambience of royalty – the pomp, the Philistinism and the Toryism. He was embarrassed when the King, assuming that he was conferring an honour, invited him to bear the sword of state in a parliamentary procession. 'I won't be a flunkey,' vociferated the Prime Minister. Fond of hymn-singing himself, Lloyd George was irritated by a royal family who 'don't know the difference between the "Hallelujah Chorus" and "Tommy make room for your uncle"'.[3] If this was an exaggeration, there is no denying the cultural poverty of a monarch who tried to avoid appointing a new Master of the King's Musick and a new Poet Laureate, who thought Turner mad and Impressionism a joke, who confused Lamb with lamb and highbrow with eyebrow. Lloyd George was also bored by royal harangues, remarking that the King 'talks incessantly, but without point or judgement, just like a boy'.[4] Above all, the Prime Minister resented the King's automatic endorsement of the established order, bosses against workers in peacetime, soldiers against civilians during the war.

Lloyd George acknowledged that he treated the King abominably. He neglected to answer royal letters. He failed to consult or even to inform the sovereign about senior appointments or dismissals. Having bamboozled the King into taking the wartime pledge, he lent a sympathetic ear to the rackety Prince of Wales. The Premier brought the honours system into disrepute by using what he considered to be the baubles of rank as counters in the political game. Only with difficulty was Lloyd George persuaded to send the King news that he had signed the Treaty of Versailles.

The King deeply resented this cavalier behaviour and disliked Lloyd George. He complained to Woodrow Wilson's *eminence grise*, Colonel House, about the Prime Minister's 'assumption of autocratic powers'.[5] The King also intrigued against him in secret. General Sir Douglas Haig, commander of the British armies in France recorded in his diary that the King promised he would 'support him through thick and thin', provided that he did not push Lloyd George to the point of resignation. This was a judicious caveat. Having supplanted Asquith without gaining the leadership of the Liberal Party, Lloyd George was in a vulnerable position and the King had more scope than usual to employ backstairs influence. But he could not risk provoking a general election by overtly backing 'brass-hats' against 'frocks'. Still less could the King do anything to promote a military government, as certain officers suggested in 1918. Their 'talk of the king turning out the Prime Minister and putting in soldiers and sailors to run the show' annoyed his assistant private secretary, Clive Wigram. 'The people, the press and parliament would not for a moment stand for such an act.'[6]

But the fact that a military government was even discussed showed how profoundly the elite feared revolution after 1917 – it was a fear which helped to reconcile the King to Lloyd George. For all his faults the Prime Minister was a radical, not a revolutionary; indeed, it was his very radicalism which seemed to guarantee that revolution would be averted. Lloyd George was a 'lightning conductor'.[7] His liberal measures were calculated to take the sting out of socialist agitation.

On a personal level, too, there was something of a rapprochement between monarch and first minister. Lloyd George, who considered his sovereign decent and reliable as well as weak and stupid, learned to relax at Windsor. The King in turn grew to appreciate his Premier's sardonic humour. In 1922 he asked gloomily whether Lloyd George would be meeting Lenin and Trotsky at the Genoa Conference (which aimed to sort out post-war European problems) – then roared with laughter when the Prime Minister replied that he was obliged to shake hands with many men in the sovereign's service, including, recently, a Turkish envoy hot from an East End sodomy house.

Fearful that continuing high unemployment would foster discontent, riot and perhaps revolt, the King clung to Lloyd

George for fear of getting something worse. Better the devil one knew, especially as the Prime Minister was prevented from going too far since the coalition was dominated by Tories. He told Stamfordham to pass on his opinion that the Prime Minister 'is now more necessary to this country than he ever was', that the King had 'complete confidence' in him and that he would 'do everything in my power to help him'.[8]

No power on earth, however, could help Lloyd George once his Conservative allies repudiated him, as they did over his mishandling of the Turkish crisis in 1922. Bonar Law briefly succeeded him before cancer of the throat forced his resignation in May 1923. Then the King exercised one of his few remaining prerogatives – the selection of a new leader. The choice lay between Lord Curzon, former Viceroy of India and Foreign Secretary, and Stanley Baldwin, a relatively inexperienced Chancellor of the Exchequer. Acting on what seemed to be the advice of Law (whose private secretary in fact misrepresented his views) and of the elder statesman Arthur Balfour, the King invited Baldwin to form a government. The King had in fact shown considerable shrewdness. Curzon was a superior person in his own and other eyes but he could not renounce his peerage, whereas Baldwin was an elected Member of Parliament. 'Perturbed at the Labour men having sung the "Red Flag" in the Commons',[9] the King deemed it essential to have a democratic Prime Minister.

Baldwin, however, proved rather a disappointment to King George. Both men were 'one-nation' Tories, favouring 'unity between all classes of our people' under the Crown.[10] Both indulged in rustic nostalgia and espoused the roast-beef virtues of old England. Both disliked foreigners and intellectuals. But Baldwin was reflective and bookish, whereas the King was talkative and read little for pleasure except (as Queen Mary told John Buchan) 'rubbish'. Baldwin was a theoretical countryman; the King was a practical one. Moreover, Baldwin failed his first and most crucial test, which was to keep the socialists out of office. When he called a snap general election at the end of 1923 the result was a hung Parliament, but it was clear that he would be defeated once the Commons met. However, the King advised him to stay in office over Christmas in the hope that he could 'reach some working arrangement with the Liberals'.[11]

George had been brought up to regard socialism as something between a bad joke and a form of blasphemy. In 1917 he had seen what resulted when political blasphemy became orthodoxy in Russia. Since then he had bemoaned every Labour advance, regretting that 'The right people are always too lazy to go and vote.'[12] Later, when giving a reception for the Prime Minister of Australia, he had pointed out the guest of honour to the art historian Kenneth Clark, Director of the National Gallery: 'See that fellow over there? He's a socialist. Give him a good kick in the arse for me.'[13] Now he obviously heeded hysterical voices in the City and the press calling for a last-ditch coalition to avert the 'horrors of Socialism'.[14] These included the confiscation of savings and the nationalization of women, the desecration of churches and the abolition of the monarchy.

Since the constitution is unwritten no one can say that the King's Fabian tactics were in breach of it, but when faced with a similar situation six years later he responded promptly to the decision of the electorate. King George was sensitive to the charge that, in a democratic age, he was attempting to frustrate the will of the people. Labour MPs openly warned that they might be kept out by 'backstairs influence';[15] most outspoken was the pacifist George Lansbury, who viewed the King as 'a short-tempered, narrow-minded, out-of-date Tory, with a tendency to interfere in matters in which the Crown had had no business for 200 years'.[16] He reminded George V of the fate of Charles I.

The King was most upset, but he could not avoid inviting Ramsay MacDonald to form a government when Baldwin duly lost a Commons vote of confidence. Times had changed and, he remarked, 'I suppose I have changed with them'.[17] Actually he had stayed the same. As always he treated his new ministers with 'courtesy, sympathy and helpfulness'.[18] Behind the scenes, though, he remained an 'absolutely dyed-in-the-wool conservative' whose paramount aim was to preserve the status quo. The King, according to the astute analysis of the Tory insider J. C. C. Davidson,

> was very right-wing and he knew where his friends really lay, and [that] the Conservative Party was the King's Party and a radical party was not. But he managed to persuade the Labour Party that he was entirely neutral. This must have required a very great deal of self-discipline. His attitude was very much that of the quarterdeck; anyone who questioned the Captain was next door to being a rebel; but he managed to keep his relations with Ramsay MacDonald and the rest of them so well that they became – and particularly some, like Jimmy Thomas – more royalist than the King. I always felt that this was the most extraordinary *tour de force*, but of course it was mainly because of his character.[19]

This paradox lies at the heart of the King's stewardship. Never was there a less Machiavellian monarch than George V. Yet he had 'a kind of common-sense canniness'[20] which kept him in tune with his people.

MacDonald and his colleagues, many of whom were captivated by the romance of royalty, proved surprisingly amenable. According to Malcolm Muggeridge, the Prime Minister even aped what he took to be sovereign style – 'shook hands by extending two fingers, made conversation by asking fatuous questions, and engaged in little playfulnesses almost like royalty'.[21] George, who responded warmly to his Scottish courtliness, made him feel like a friend and invited him to Windsor where, said MacDonald, 'the homeliness was that of a cottage and sat well in gilt halls'.[22] Other members of the Labour Cabinet were equally awed: in the royal presence their 'knees trembled and they confined their conversation entirely to "Yes, Sir," or to "No, Sir."'[23] Jimmy Thomas, the forthright ex-railwayman, was an exception: he famously told the King that Balmoral was 'a bloody dull 'ouse'.

Puritans such as the Fabian Beatrice Webb disapproved of the way in which soft-brained socialists allowed themselves to be seduced by the social prestige of the court: 'It stimulates the unutterable snobbishness of the lower type of Labour representatives like Jimmy [Thomas], it wiles away the integrity of aesthetes like J. R. M[acDonald], while it gobbles up arrivistes like Ethel Snowden and it even deteriorates decent folk like the Alexanders and Clynes.'[24] However, as the Chancellor,

Philip Snowden, said, critics of this 'submission to flunkeyism' were in the minority.[25] Most Labour voters basked in the reflected glow when newspapers published pictures of their representatives dressing up to take part in royal ceremonies from which they had earlier been contemptuously excluded.

Minor irritations marred King George's relationship with the socialists. He deplored their tendency to sing 'The Red Flag'. Occasionally the *Daily Herald* (which the Bolsheviks subsidized by selling tsarist diamonds) would dilate on the 'degrading sham' of monarchy.[26] Left-wingers also condemned as a costly 'joy ride' the Duke of York's Australian tour. Most of all the King disapproved of the recognition of the Soviet Union, though this was designed to promote trade rather than to denote solidarity. In general, however, the King's relations with MacDonald's ministry remained more cordial than those with right-wing governments. Since the latter could take a strong line with the monarch, having no need to refute the imputation of republicanism, this became an almost invariable pattern.

Thus the Prime Minister made no difficulties about tax concessions which the royal family had recently negotiated. He also agreed that the King should personally fill vacancies to certain court offices. This was intended to relieve Labour men of the embarrassment of occupying such archaic posts, but it also ensured that the Crown would be surrounded by 'persons drawn from a narrow and privileged class' – something that socialists deprecated in theory. They similarly deprecated imperialism, but their attempt to 'replace jingoistic parrot-cries with a more logical colonial outlook'[27] made no appreciable difference to imperial policies. MacDonald and his colleagues showed their gratifying loyalty to Greater Britain overseas at the British Empire Exhibition at Wembley. Intended to boost imperial trade and unity, this extravagant affair indicated that, as Britain's empire grew more hollow, its drumbeat sounded louder. At the opening on St George's Day, 23 April 1924, there were 'scenes of pomp and majesty': a dazzling royal carriage procession round the stadium, a monster choir singing 'Land of Hope and Glory', marches, salutes, obeisances. It was on this occasion that the King broadcast for the first time: with his deep, gruff voice he made an effective communicator. Although believing that the new medium smacked of showbusiness, he was aware of the need to burnish the royal public image: he destroyed an official portrait by Charles Sims because he thought it made him look like a ballet dancer, and he censored films about Queen Victoria. George also took part in other 'aural pageants'.

What most Britons remembered about the Empire Exhibition, however, was not the broadcasting or ritual, not the royal telegram sent round the world in eighty seconds, not displays like the gorgeous Indian palace or the huge Canadian panoramas – not even the sight of Queen Mary riding on the miniature railway. It was the equestrian statue of the Prince of Wales carved in butter. This was an apt substance, for already his popularity was in danger of melting. By 1925 reports of his dancing 'every night & most of the night too' had become so frequent that, the King told the Queen, 'people who don't know will begin to think that he is either mad or the biggest rake in Europe . . .!'[28]

The difference between the unostentations sovereign and his pleasure-loving eldest son was well illustrated in the General Strike of 1926, the greatest industrial dispute in Britain's history. Baldwin, now back in power, warned that Britain was 'nearer to civil war than we have been for centuries'.[29] Actually the outstanding feature of the strike was its peacefulness; but there were extremists on both sides – revolutionary dreamers like A. J. Cook, the miners' leader, and reactionary schemers like Winston Churchill, who wielded his pen like a sword. Privately King George urged the Tory government to show 'positive sympathy for volunteer strike-breakers' and suggested that some strikers' leaders should be arrested. He wanted the suppression of 'genuinely revolutionary elements' and anticipated, even if he did not urge, 'the imposition of martial law'.[30] But the Cabinet did not want class war, and the King's secret advice was ignored while his overt advocacy of conciliation was praised. His plea for national unity, once the nine-day strike came to an end, set the seal on his neutrality.

The Prince of Wales shared the King's attitude towards the

strike, but ignored his father's sensible injunction to stay out of sight for its duration. Edward lent his chauffeur to help distribute copies of Churchill's pugnacious propaganda sheet the *British Gazette*, which referred to strikers as 'the enemy', and he rode round London with 'friends in the Metropolitan Police'.[31] Abroad, the Prince of Wales's conduct was even more imprudent. Taking advantage of the informality of the dominions and colonies, he abandoned self-restraint. On a visit to Canada in 1927 with Stanley Baldwin and his wife, Edward's conduct was almost more than his prim private secretary, Alan Lascelles, could bear. On the surface relations between the tour members remained pleasant, lubricated by the Prince's bewitching charm and the Prime Minister's lazy amiability. But Baldwin considered Edward 'erratic' and 'radical', and wondered 'how he's going to become king'.[32] His views were confirmed at a 'secret colloquy' in Ottawa's Government House, when the private secretary poured out his heart to the Premier: '. . . the Heir Apparent, in his unbridled pursuit of wine and women, and whatever selfish whim occupied him at the moment, was rapidly going to the devil, and unless he mended his ways, would soon become no fit wearer of the British Crown'. Baldwin completely agreed. When Lascelles added that he sometimes felt that the best thing would be for the Prince to break his neck in a point-to-point, the Prime Minister responded: 'God forgive me, I have often thought the same.'[33]

The Prince of Wales's behaviour was even more scandalous in East Africa, where he went to hunt big game the following year. He and his brother Henry seemed determined to indulge in the 'white mischief' which made Kenya's Happy Valley a byword for licentiousness. They played a prominent part in revels at the Muthaiga Club in Nairobi, whose members took cocaine like snuff, drank sundowners until sun-up and swapped wives so often that it was hardly worth trying to remember the ladies' surnames. Prince Edward's most outrageous exploit was to dally at an adulterous rendezvous, arrive late at an official cocktail party, leave early, shin down a Government House drainpipe, get himself arrested by a vigilant *askari* and finally reach the Muthaiga Club, where he was bombarded with pieces of bread and rolled on the floor by the amorous Lady Delamere.

His most celebrated liaison was with Beryl Markham, the sexually voracious aviatrix who in 1936 became the first woman to fly solo from England to America. She had a simultaneous affair with his brother Henry, who afterwards set her up in a suite at the Grosvenor Hotel in London. This was conveniently close to Buckingham Palace, where she allegedly ran around the corridors barefoot and hid in a cupboard to avoid the gimlet eye of Queen Mary. When Beryl's husband threatened legal proceedings in which the Duke would be named as co-respondent, the Queen pronounced firmly: 'One simply could not cite a Prince of the Blood in a divorce petition.'[34] The case was silently dropped and Henry was despatched on far-flung missions to Ethiopia and Japan before being married off to Lady Alice Montagu-Douglas-Scott, daughter of the Duke of Buccleuch. A trust fund was set up which paid Beryl an annuity until her death some sixty years later.

Back in East Africa in 1930, chasing women did not distract Henry's brother the Prince of Wales from the even more energetic sport of chasing animals. Indeed, Edward displayed extraordinary powers of endurance, trekking over rough terrain with experienced hunters such as Denys Finch-Hatton and Baron Blixen, who admired his contempt for 'all effeminate softness' and thought him one of the 'toughest sportsmen' they had ever encountered.[35] The violent physical exertion probably gave him a psychological release from the pent-up frustrations of his position. It also seemed to stimulate him to new excesses of recklessness: he argued about who would shoot a charging elephant until it was almost on top of them. And on a later safari he bet Finch-Hatton and a game warden that they could not attach a picture of his father to the buttocks of a rhinoceros: they crept up on a pachyderm during its siesta and stuck on a couple of British postage stamps.

At the end of November 1928 Edward's pleasures were interrupted by news that his father was gravely ill with septicaemia. This caused deep concern throughout the country and at Westminster. Tory alarmists such as Churchill forecast that, if the King died, a Labour government coming to power at the impending general election would abolish the monarchy; while socialists such as G. D. H. Cole said that Conservative exploitation of the Prince of Wales's popularity could cost them fifty seats. The Prince initially dismissed the report of the King's condition as a Baldwinite election dodge. Lascelles was outraged: 'Sir, the King of England is dying; and if that means nothing to you, it means a great deal to us.' Edward went off without a word to complete the seduction of the wife of a District Commissioner, and Lascelles became still more determined to resign.[36] But after further telegrams the royal party returned home at high speed.

Once the immediate crisis was over, Lascelles duly left the royal service. He did so tactfully enough to remain friends with the Prince, who gave him a motor car as a leaving present. But Lascelles also conveyed his disapproval of a way of life which would, he prophesied, lose Edward the throne. The Prince of Wales replied pathetically that he was the wrong man for the job; this was the conclusion which all his staff had reached, and several felt like following Lascelles's example. In a long memorandum Godfrey Thomas recorded that his own loyalty was 'getting strained – a Private Secretary is more than a clerk. I have covered up for him and told lies for years.' His further jottings shrewdly anatomized the situation.

> If the monarchy is to continue a certain amount of aloofness and mystery – call it what you like – must hedge a king. The Duke of York, with half HRH's charm, is daily gaining popularity at his expense. The King and Queen lead what some people are pleased to consider a humdrum, old-fashioned life. And that's why they're so popular. It is what people want of their sovereign. [There is an] almost universal feeling of dismay at the prospect of the Prince of Wales coming to the throne at the present moment. Overseas there is a deplorable decline in HRH's stock. One of the most serious aspects of the whole affair is the accepted fact that the Dominions are all held together by their common loyalty to the Crown. What will happen if they find their sole link is in the person of a sovereign for whom they have little respect?[37]

To raise such questions in private was one thing, but even such a high Tory journal as the *Sphere* hinted at the same criticisms. The Prince, it said, was naturally 'instinct with fine and kingly qualities', but his upbringing had 'not steeled him to bear the Crown untimely'. Only by undergoing 'a severe novitiate', without nightclubs and 'cosmopolitan' companions, could he be a worthy successor to his father.[38]

The royal secretariat, bound by affection and loyalty, closed ranks. In spite of their conviction that 'HRH is riding for a fall', their reluctance to 'stay and watch him chuck everything away' and their inability to 'put the brake on', its members remained at their posts.[39] Their minds had been concentrated by the sudden prospect of Edward's accession, but as the King made a slow and painful recovery they heaved a collective sigh of relief.

The royal yoke, however, was less easy than before. George V's temper grew more explosive with age. At the best of times, according to Lord Crewe, his language would have brought a blush to the cheek of a Smithfield meat porter; at worst his outbursts were vile. 'Shut the door!' he shouted to a courtier who was ushering out King Amanullah of Afghanistan. 'I can smell that damned nigger from here!'[40] Now, lacking intellectual resources, the convalescent King became testier than ever. His outburst are well illustrated by a royal tirade directed at Anthony Eden one Sunday in January 1934, after the socialist politician Sir Stafford Cripps had criticized 'Buckingham Palace influence' while exonerating the King personally.

> 'What does he mean by saying that Buckingham Palace is not me? Who else is there, I should like to know? Does he mean the footmen? D'you see the fellow says there is going to be a General Election in August? Who is he to decide that? D——d cheek I call it. I have seen moreover in one of his earlier speeches he says that if Labour gets back with a clear majority (which please God it never will) then a Trade Union Congress is to tell *me* who is to be Prime Minister. I'll see them d——d first. That is my business and I'll send for whom I like' etc.[41]

If nothing else, this diatribe is a useful reminder that the ubiquitous, anonymous 'Buckingham Palace spokesman' is a royal ventriloquist's dummy.

The King waxed particularly furious if anything, even official business, interrupted an existence punctuated by Ascot, Goodwood, Cowes, Balmoral, Sandringham and Windsor. He refused to go abroad even on state visits and, when forced to do so for his health, laughed at foreign culture and customs. Breaches of decorum kindled incandescent ire: male MPs lounging on Commons benches in the presence of ladies; the Lord Chancellor failing to wear a silk hat; women walking past Windsor Castle in short skirts – the King bellowed at them from a window. He insisted that his speech at the Opening of Parliament must be kept short because reading it made him so nervous – it had to be printed in specially large type because he would not wear spectacles on such a formal occasion, and on specially thick paper since his hands shook violently. The King was reluctant to receive Mahatma Gandhi, with whom the government was trying to negotiate over the future of India. Not only was Gandhi a 'rebel fakir', he was improperly dressed. In bare feet and dhoti, however, he duly entered Buckingham Palace to meet the frock-coated King-Emperor, who spent much of the interview glowering at his bare knees. Asked about his costume afterwards, the Mahatma said that he thought the King was wearing enough for both of them.

Meanwhile the country had been struck by what Ramsay MacDonald, once again head of a minority Labour government after Baldwin's defeat in 1929, called the 'economic blizzard'. In the wake of the American stock market crash international trade slumped, unemployment rocketed, currencies devalued and capitalist civilization tottered. In 1931 the massive cost of Britain's unemployment benefits unbalanced the budget and precipitated a run on the pound. When the Cabinet split over whether to try to restore confidence in sterling by reducing payments to the jobless, MacDonald declared, 'I'm off to the Palace to throw in my hand.'[42] In the event the King persuaded him that it was his patriotic duty to form a National Government to cope with the crisis. MacDonald knew that he would be signing his own political death warrant, but succumbed to the hypnotic appeal of royalty. Without consulting his party the Prime Minister created a coalition Cabinet of four socialists (including Thomas and Snowden), four Tories (including Baldwin and Chamberlain, but not Churchill) and two Liberals (excluding Lloyd George, who was ill). The King was delighted. His private secretary, Clive Wigram, crowed: 'Our Captain played one of his best innings with a very straight bat. He stopped the rot and saved his side.'[43]

Several socialists charged him with unconstitutional behaviour. Harold Laski, for example, maintained that the Crown's proper part was 'that of dignified emollient rather than of active umpire between conflicting interests' and that a Patriot King was incompatible with parliamentary democracy.[44] Conservatives acknowledged that in getting MacDonald to remain as Premier the King had exerted a 'potent' influence.[45] Certainly his vestigial prerogatives were at their most influential in time of crisis, and he helped to deprive the country of a serious opposition at a fateful moment in its history. But George had merely acted in the spirit of Bagehot, advising and encouraging MacDonald. When Communism and Fascism were widely bruited as the alternatives, the Georgian consensus seemed attractive.

During the Depression, however, the safe, mediocre politicians of the centre had little to offer those at the base of the social pyramid, while the apex trembled in the resulting agitation. During the naval mutiny at Invergordon sailors protesting against pay cuts sang 'The Red Flag' – though they also stood to attention when Marine bands played the National Anthem. Soon afterwards, demonstrators against unemployment shouted 'Up the Reds' and 'Down with Royalty'.[46] And when Prince Bertie visited London's East End in 1932 he was assailed by Cockneys shaking their fists and shouting, 'Food! Give us food! We don't want royal parasites!'[47]

Such manifestations encouraged the King to accept reductions in the Civil List and make cuts in the royal cloth. He dismissed some servants, of whom he had a superfluity. Bertie was obliged to sell his horses, which came as a 'great shock' to him. The King telephoned his eldest son in a nightclub and ordered him to give the Treasury £10,000 a year from the Duchy of Cornwall's revenues. In fact the sacrifices were more apparent than real, though the well-guarded secrets of the royal finances have only recently and partially been penetrated.[48] In 1921 the Prince of Wales had negotiated a tax exemption from the government which by the time of his accession enabled him to build up a private fortune of £1 million (about £30 million at today's values). In 1922 Prince Bertie and his younger siblings were also permitted to treat their allowances as tax-deductible expenses. And in 1932 the King (having for the first time ever secured a tax-free Civil List at the beginning of his reign) pleaded successfully that the Duchy of Lancaster too should be relieved of tax. This brought him £20,000 a year and added substantially to the monarch's income once the Civil List was fully restored in 1935.

All these boons transformed the royal family's financial position at a time when the aristocracy was suffering a sea change. Formerly many landowners had eclipsed the monarchy in wealth and felt 'a certain contempt'[49] for the poor, parvenu Hanoverians. But during Victoria's reign the Crown's situation improved. Edward VII bestowed social prestige on his rich friends in return for stockmarket tips – the Kaiser scorned him as 'a jobber in stocks and shares'.[50] After 1918 one of the few titled folk who could entertain the royal family in the style to which they had become accustomed was Lord Iveagh, a prominent member of the 'beerage'. In 1928 he refurbished his country house at Elveden to receive Their Majesties, decorating Queen Mary's boudoir with Watteau drawings and providing King George with an eighteenth-century painted Venetian bed. The royal party was small, but its luggage arrived in a 25-foot-long van called 'The Lioness'; and among the King's retainers were six chauffeurs, four policemen, a valet, a clothes-brusher, a messenger, a sergeant footman, a groom and a loader. Lord Iveagh was sustained by Guinness, but the fortunes of aristocrats without such stout resources waned dramatically between the wars and many great houses were sold off or fell into terminal disrepair.

The court was thus left in 'splendid isolation';[51] it was

also perilous isolation, for the Crown and the aristocracy needed each other. The sovereign institution gave legitimacy to the hereditary principle and provided the nobility with 'a larger-than-life version of their own hopes and aspirations'.[52] From the King's point of view, lords were lions under the throne, and in the early 1920s he urged reform of the upper House of Parliament for fear that Labour would abolish it altogether. The decline of the aristocracy left the monarchy dangerously exposed, but it became increasingly apparent that the princes, at least, would do little to fulfil 'the vital duty of re-establishing in London a dignified, high-minded Society'.[53] Their father was left perched on a pinnacle with nothing for support but public opinion.

While not courting popularity, the King tried to keep this buttress intact by avoiding ostentation. Although always on parade, the King never flaunted himself; in fact he managed to combine regal splendour and personal simplicity in a manner deeply satisfying to his pinched people. This paradoxical combination was well conveyed in his broadcasts.

During what was called the devil's decade the BBC devoted less time to hunger marches and Fascist aggression than to royal events. Its Director General, Sir John Reith, did his utmost 'to serve the House' of Windsor, and his greatest triumph was to persuade the King to transmit a Christmas message to his subjects.[54] The first such broadcast, written by Rudyard Kipling in 1932, appealed for closer imperial union, stressed the King's dedication to his people and reminded them that this was a day to be celebrated with 'their children and grandchildren'. The BBC's highest recorded audience (91 per cent) heard his words in what the *Daily Mail* called 'one of the most magical moments in the world's history'. Most listeners stood up in their homes afterwards as the National Anthem was played; they had been moved by 'an inspiring, thrilling, deeply impressive experience'.[55]

The King's voice, with its 'gamey' flavour and 'whisky timbre', was 'august but intimate';[56] it conveyed modesty and majesty. As Sir Steven Runciman says, it 'gave a sort of feeling that here was the father of the country talking to us'.[57] Also, of course, King George had managed to associate himself with the quintessential festival of the family and had a new tradition worthy of Dickens, embodying both the spirit of Christmas past and the spirit of Christmas present.

Good cheer, however, was notably absent from the King's final years. Even the unemployment problem at home was overshadowed by the rise of Nazism in Germany. In 1933 King George protested about the persecution of the Jews, though by the following year, after talking to Hitler's Foreign Minister, he took a less 'severe' view of it. The prospect of war, however, grew so ominous that the King threatened personally to wave a red flag for peace in Trafalgar Square.

Less important but more galling anxieties were provided by his own children. The blue-eyed, wavy-haired Prince George became addicted to cocaine, supplied by an attractive American called Kiki Preston (late of Kenya's Happy Valley) who was said to be 'clever with her needle'. Only with the assistance of the closest of his brothers, Edward, was he able to break the habit. Even so, the perfumed Prince George got into endless scrapes. Scotland Yard detectives chased so many of his mistresses out of England, an equerry said, that the Palace stopped counting; and a typical homosexual liaison ended in blackmail and the payment of a large sum for the recovery of incriminating letters. But in November 1934 Prince George, now made Duke of Kent, married the exquisite Princess Marina of Greece, one of the few suitable royalties left. The wedding took place at Westminister Abbey. Few people noticed that during the Greek Orthodox part of the ceremony the Prince of Wales absent-mindedly lit a cigarette on the candle held by a priest. Edward wondered whether his brother's speedily arranged match would last, but reckoned that 'marriage is the only chance of giving him interests outside nightclubs'.[58]

The Prince of Wales himself seemed immune to correction. He was King George's greatest concern, for he held the future of the dynasty in his hand and seemed bent on reshaping the monarchy in his own image. The new model, thought the King, would be informal to the point of decadence. Each man made occasional efforts at reconciliation, and Edward even managed to laugh at some of his father's crustier prejudices. When the Prince said that he had to open a trade exhibition in Glasgow, the King replied doubtfully: 'I've never heard of a gentleman going to Scotland in January.'[59] More often the son was exasperated by the father's continual badgering. At its most trivial this might be a reprimand about the Prince's wearing a jacket that was too light a shade of grey – 'poor narrow-minded man that he is,' sighed Edward, 'oh so stupid.'[60] At its most serious, the King complained about the Prince's pro-German leanings.

Edward believed that Germany had a moral right to adjust the harsh terms imposed at Versailles. He thought Fascism was fashionable and said that England might want a dictator before long. Above all, he favoured the Third Reich as a bulwark against Bolshevism. This was the theme of at least one of the warm messages which Edward received from the Kaiser's Nazi son, Prince August Wilhelm of Prussia, who praised the great leadership of Adolf Hitler and signed himself 'lots of love and Heil Hitler'.[61] The Prince of Wales was critical of the 'too one-sided' British Foreign Office in conversation with the German ambassador, who reported home that the Prince's views about peace corresponded 'word for word with the opinion of our Führer'.[62] When, in a speech to the British Legion, Edward advocated extending 'the hand of friendship' to Germany, the King castigated him for unconstitutional behaviour. If only his eldest son would settle down with a suitable wife, King George thought, such indiscretions might cease. Unfortunately he only seemed attracted by married women such as Mrs Dudley Ward and, later, Lady Furness. Worse still, at the beginning of 1934 he became madly infatuated with Mrs Ernest Simpson.

Born Wallis Warfield in 1896, she came from an impecunious branch of an old Baltimore family and had spent her youth, it was said, 'in much seduced circumstances'. Doubtless rumours about her enslaving the Prince by means of sexual techniques learned in oriental brothels were the 'most terrible nonsense'.[63] But she was certainly a 'good-time girl' who had led a 'fast'[64] life before marrying her second husband, the cigar-smoking, hail-fellow-well-met City businessman Ernest Simpson, in 1928. She shocked Barbara Cartland on first acquaintance by telling 'vulgar stories . . . the sort of rhymes which were made into improper lines'. Wallis was 'aggressively American', raucous in voice and manner, 'very badly dressed' – at least by her later ultra-soignée standards – and embarrassingly gauche. With her straight hair, wide jaw and angular figure, Wallis was not beautiful; indeed, she was 'very unsexy'.[65] But she was 'terribly attractive',[66] feline-sleek and serpentine-svelte. Her skin was smooth as a lotus petal and her wit was brittle as ice. In conversation her huge blue eyes lit up and her face creased into a 'great giglamp smile'.[67] She had 'a wonderful gift for repartee' and was 'marvellously unboring'.[68] In short, Wallis was 'a brilliant man manager'[69] and she did not scruple to manage the Prince of Wales. Ruthless as well as rapacious, she vamped across the 'frozen space' which cut off even the most relaxed of royalties from ordinary mortals.[70] She took an interest in things that interested Edward, such as clothes, gardening, gastronomy and interior decoration. Very soon she had him in thrall. A friend remarked, 'I've never seen one human being so utterly and completely possessed by another.'[71]

When Barbara Cartland saw Mrs Simpson at Claridge's wearing jewelled clips made from Queen Alexandra's earrings, she 'knew it was serious'. These gems were the first drops in a cascade of diamonds, emeralds, rubies and other precious stones with which the Prince smothered her. Her appetite for them was as insatiable as that of Queen Mary herself. 'Wallis had a love affair with her jewels,' said Laura, Duchess of Marlborough. 'She would play with them like a child with toys, laying them out on a table and touching them.'[72] The Prince himself supplied Cartier and other firms with stones and instigated new designs for her gems. They were, as the historian of the royal jewels says, 'Very modern, very daring, quite flashy – and how she enjoyed flaunting them.' But what nobody knew, until the recent sale, was the existence of 'those Squidgy, Camilla-gate messages' on the back of the gems. The inscriptions followed Victorian tradition but were couched in the kind of baby talk which the Prince used in his adoring letters to Mrs Simpson. 'God bless WE' – in other words Wallis and Edward – he wrote. 'Oh!' he exclaimed, 'a boy does miss and want a girl here so terribly tonight.'[73] She responded with the firm parental tenderness for which he had always yearned. Wallis scolded him for his immaturity, made him cut down on smoking and drinking, gave orders at Fort Belvedere (his grace and favour residence near Windsor), let him paint her toenails and criticized his clothes. Sometimes she made him cry. The springs of love are always obscure, but in the Prince of Wales's abject self-abasement there seems to have been at least an element of masochism.

With his help Mrs Simpson shed the last traces of dowdiness. The society photographer Cecil Beaton, whose first impression had been that she was a brawny 'bullock in sapphic blue velvet', now found her 'enormously improved in looks and chic'.[74] Wallis became famous for her lovely clothes, immaculate appearance and perfect taste. She was also renowned for her tact, though Edward himself was anything but discreet and brutally ostracized his former mistresses. The Prince took Mrs Simpson on foreign holidays without her husband, and at the end of 1934 he even smuggled her into Buckingham Palace.

The King was furious, and summoned the head of the Prince's household, Admiral Halsey. It was, said Halsey, a 'terrible interview' in which the King forecast that his son was 'going to wreck the monarchy and the Empire'. Various proposals were discussed, including abdication and getting Cabinet ministers to remonstrate with the Prince.

> HM was *most* outspoken and was really terribly pathetic, especially when the Queen arrived and joined in. There is no doubt HM feels it all most acutely and it is really worrying him. . . . He ended up by saying that he and the Queen had tried to be so punctilious in leading a straight and proper course for the good of his people ever since he came to the throne 25 years before, and how he was on the point of being let down by his eldest son.[75]

It is apparent from this evidence, hitherto unpublished, that Edward really did help to bring down his father's grey hairs with sorrow to the grave. Better than anyone, King George appreciated that heredity is the Achilles heel of monarchy. He realized that attempts to reform the Prince were doomed, at least once expressing the hope that the Crown would pass to his second son, the Duke of York. Halsey and others on his staff did tackle their master again about his behaving 'like a cad'. But as Edward's private secretary said, '. . . if he is determined to go to perdition, either from bravado or infatuation and perhaps conceit, nothing more can be said by his friends'.[76] When he became King, Edward dismissed Halsey, who had served him faithfully for twenty years and had often paid the Prince's bills out of his own pocket without being reimbursed. Only grudgingly was 'the Old Salt' awarded a pension, and when he came to say goodbye the new King did not look up from the book he was reading.

The old King enjoyed a last public triumph which must have added poignancy to his private woes. The first royal Silver Jubilee (and the last imperial one) was held in May 1935. This celebration was a deliberate attempt to muster the nation behind the throne and its revered occupant. Determined to eclipse the barbaric rallies at Nuremberg, the bogus quasi-Roman posturings of Mussolini and the brutal displays of might in Moscow's May Day parades, the government organized a 'pageant unsurpassed in the history of the empire'.[77] In place of Communist tanks and Fascist aeroplanes, the British presented plumed hats, jingling spurs and gilded coaches. It was a triumph of anachronism.

In an address relayed to the cheering multitude through loudspeakers from the Jubilee Service in St Paul's Cathedral, the Archbishop of Canterbury declared that the national spirit of unity had found its centre in the throne and that King George was 'the Father of his People'.[78] That evening the capital was lit up with £250,000 worth of illuminations, and scenes of jubilation not witnessed since the armistice took place in front of Buckingham Palace and all over the Empire. The *New York Times*'s reporter found it hard to convey the 'universality, spontaneousness and genuineness of public enthusiasm'. The Jubilee was good for business, a silver lining to the cloud of the Depression. It augmented the nation's prestige and reflected glory on the National Government. The 'king business' might be discredited elsewhere, but there was no doubting 'the potency of the magic of royalty in Britain'.[79]

The Jubilee festivities continued throughout the icy spring of 1935, with endless royal presentations, inspections, wreath-layings, banquets and balls.[80] Their effect was to exhaust the chain-smoking King George, now plagued by more international and domestic troubles, including the death of his beloved sister Victoria. By January 1936 he himself was dying. His family gathered at Sandringham and even the Kaiser sent a telegram, effecting a death-bed reconciliation which pleased Queen Mary. The old King, clad in a dressing-gown, conducted state business and maintained his dignity to the end. Were his famous last words 'How is the Empire?' (as was reported at the time) or 'Bugger Bognor'? It scarcely matters. But the contradictory legends do reflect both the contemporary and posthumous obfuscation which surrounded George V. Even in death and afterwards, his life had to reflect the image of the monarchy he had created. Harold Nicolson was instructed by Palace officials that royal biography is 'really mythology. You mustn't breathe too heavily upon something of gossamer fragility.'[81] This was one reason for the extraordinary act of euthanasia carried out by the royal doctor, Lord Dawson of Penn, and for the prolonged secrecy surrounding it.

As the King lay in a coma Dawson injected a lethal dose of morphine and cocaine into his jugular vein. The illegal act was executed, with the royal family's approval, to relieve the King's suffering. It was also designed to ensure that his death was reported decorously in the morning papers, notably the *Times* (which Dawson's wife telephoned with a message to hold the first edition), rather than in 'the less appropriate evening journals'.[82] This was 'the supreme example of stage-management'. It made the King's death 'appear as dignified and as well-timed and as perfect as possible, as if it had been a piece of ceremonial like the coronation'.[83] So Dawson's final bulletin, which moved many people to tears, was a sinister fact rather than a poignant forecast: 'The King's life is moving peacefully towards its close.' More prophetic was the old jingle with which Dawson's rivals had long taunted him:

Lord Dawson of Penn
Has killed lots of men.
So that's why we sing
God Save the King.

When his father died, King Edward VIII expressed a frantic, frenzied grief that perturbed his family. He sobbed hysterically and clung to his mother; by contrast she was a model of stoicism, curtseying deeply and solemnly kissing the hand of her new sovereign. Next day Edward went to London by aeroplane, becoming the first English king to fly and arriving, as John Betjeman put it, 'hatless from the air'. A second, more ominous break with tradition occurred the day after that, on 22 January 1936, when Edward VIII's accession was officially proclaimed at St James's Palace. It was a brief, picturesque ceremony – fanfares of silver trumpets and heralds dressed in tabards of azure, gules and gold – which the sovereign was not supposed to witness. Edward ignored precedent and was photographed observing the proceedings from a Palace window. Beside him was the blurred figure of a woman. Few outside the magic circle identified her as Mrs Simpson.

[illegible]

[illegible] Henry VIII [illegible]

[illegible]

[illegible] Edward VI [illegible]

[illegible]

George IV [illegible]

[illegible]

Edward [illegible]

[illegible]

4

EDWARD THE INNOVATOR

Mrs Ernest Simpson was the spectre which haunted the short, unhappy reign of King Edward VIII; but few saw her and fewer realized that she represented an attempt to re-create the monarchy along 'modern' lines. Wallis encouraged her lover to refurbish the institution in the style of American businessmen or populist politicians or Hollywood film stars, all of whom were sustained by the slick apparatus of public relations. They even proposed to bring Buckingham Palace up to date, showing a horrified Barbara Cartland their plans: 'They were going to take away all the wonderful things that had been put in by George IV and make it absolutely modern.'[1] Paradoxically, Mrs Simpson also suggested a return to the past, perhaps even to the Regency, the reign *par excellence* of privilege without responsibility. But 'Edward the Innovator', as he aspired to be called, wanted 'to throw open the windows a little and to let into the venerable institution some of the fresh air that I had become accustomed to breathe as Prince of Wales'.[2] What Edward did not grasp was that this was also to let daylight in upon magic and thus to sin against Bagehot's canon that mystery is the life of royalty. In fact Edward completely failed to understand that a modern monarchy is a contradiction in terms. Enoch Powell makes the point categorically: 'Monarchy is not modern. Monarchy is primeval. Monarchy is ultimate.'[3]

That his father's antique model of the monarchy had unmatched appeal should have been obvious to the new King by the astonishing wave of emotion which swept the country on George V's death. Press, cinema and above all wireless devoted themselves heart and soul to the royal obsequies. The BBC produced an eighty-page policy document entitled *Procedures on the Death of a Sovereign* and broadcast only solemn music, tolling bells, religious services, elegiac poetry and lapidary orations. Even staunch royalists felt that it was unhealthy for British monarchs to be surrounded by an 'odour of ex-officio immortality'. Journalist Philip Gibbs exclaimed: 'I'm beginning to think that the death of the King is the greatest event in human history since the Crucifixion.' However, Gibbs continued blandly, this was a sophisticated response. The masses felt that the national lamentation was appropriate and 'delivered themselves to its emotion'.[4] This may well have been true. But in the absence of public opinion polls the historian can only cite evidence such as the Portsmouth graph showing that 'everyone ceased to use water for cooking, washing etc, while the broadcast of the King's funeral was on'.[5] Probably the official mourning both inspired and expressed popular sorrow. Unquestionably it was orchestrated to promote veneration for the throne and to enhance the spiritual dimension of monarchy.

King George's body was embalmed to prevent a repetition of the explosion which had marred the funeral procession of the Duke of Teck. His coffin, draped in the royal standard and topped by the imperial crown, arrived at King's Cross Station and was escorted by the Household Cavalry to Westminster Hall, where it lay in state for four days. Shops ran out of black and for the first time ever tube trains ran all night, so that his grieving subjects could join the longest queue London had seen and pay their last respects. For twenty minutes on the final evening the late King's four sons replaced the guardsmen around the catafalque, a theatrical gesture widely seen as a soul-stirring valediction.

The next day, under a leaden sky, sailors pulled the King's bier through the purple-bedecked streets. The route was flanked with silent crowds even larger than those which had attended the Jubilee. The beat of muffled drums and the thud of minute guns, the lament of massed pipers and the tramp of marching feet formed part of an aural pageant which became the first truly worldwide broadcast. At St George's Chapel, Windsor, the funeral service was a model of regal dignity. In fact, only a single mishap occurred throughout, though some witnesses regarded it as an evil omen. As the body of the King was being taken to Westminster the apex of the imperial crown, a jewelled Maltese cross containing the legendary sapphire from the ring of the sainted King Edward the Confessor, jolted loose and fell off the gun carriage. A bearskinned Grenadier retrieved it. The new King, 'a figure of great pathos looking half lost'[6] as he plodded forlornly behind the cortège, exclaimed: 'Christ! What will happen next?'[7]

This question was frequently repeated behind the scenes, as Edward set the stamp of his personality on the monarchy. He refused to write letters on black-edged paper as prescribed during court mourning, but continued to use blue stationery, with the scarlet-embossed address of his Surrey home, Fort Belvedere. To his courtiers' distress, he walked short distances, spurning the Daimler. He relaxed sartorial standards at the Palace. He made cuts in the salaries and perquisites of royal staff. These doubtless reflected Edward's anger at his father's will, which left about £750,000 each to his siblings but excluded him because of the fortune he had amassed from the Duchy of Cornwall and the further gains he stood to make from saving on his Civil List. But the new King's meanness was also a consequence of Mrs Simpson's greed for the good things of life. Edward dismissed old retainers who crossed her, and required instant service at irregular hours. His oft-stated anxiety to improve social conditions in his realm did not extend to his own household.

In his official life, too, the King betrayed his contempt for the past. From the first he took no notice of what the Windsor name signified – the importance of being English. Edward not only acknowledged his 'warm sympathy for Germany',[8] he spoke German loudly and well whenever he got the opportunity. The Foreign Office stopped him inviting the Kaiser's Nazi son, Prince William, to King George's funeral; but

Edward's cousin Charles, Duke of Saxe-Coburg, did attend, shocking British sensibilities with his coal-scuttle helmet and his Hitlerian enthusiasms. Nevertheless he still spoke German with an Etonian accent, ate porridge for breakfast and read *Punch.* Capitalizing on his relationship with Edward, the Duke shared with Hitler his opinion that the King had 'resolved to concentrate the business of government on himself', preferred the Nazi Foreign Minister Ribbentrop to the 'oily' ambassador von Hoesch, wanted to meet the Führer personally and had determined 'to bring Germany and England together'.[9] The King certainly irritated the Foreign Office by his initiatives, which were not only unconstitutional but also erratic. For example, he regretted having to shake hands with the Soviet Foreign Minister Maxim Litvinov (who considered him a 'mediocre' character),[10] yet asked him about the possibility of going big-game shooting in Russia.

The King also encouraged the Führer to believe that he could keep on righting what both men saw as German wrongs. In the words of Ribbentrop's private secretary, Reinhard Spitzy, 'Hitler and the people around him believed that King Edward was profoundly pro-German' – both from inclination and by blood. Edward encouraged this view by having at least one secret meeting with Hoesch, in which he said it was a shame that Germany was a political outcast. The King was also 'extraordinarily active'[11] in opposing British intervention when Hitler reoccupied the Rhineland in March 1936. In fact he had no influence on that decision, itself a foregone conclusion, or on any other.

Neither the government nor Baldwin, who had taken over as Premier from the ailing MacDonald in June 1935, trusted the King. Edward had started his reign by reading the official documents in his red boxes carefully but soon treated them as 'mostly bunk'. He left them around at Fort Belvedere where any of his guests could see them; he sent them back stained with wine or charred by cigarettes; he discussed their contents with Mrs Simpson. Few people seriously believed the gossip that she was engaged in an affair with Ribbentrop. It was 'rubbish', as Spitzy says, not least because Ribbentrop was 'a sort of Macbeth', completely under the thumb of his personal

'Lady Macbeth'. Baldwin himself said that Mrs Simpson, who took no interest in politics save as an adjunct to chic, was merely 'a paid agent' of the pro-Nazi Hearst press; but there is nothing in the Hearst archive to support this.

On the other hand there is evidence, not previously published, that she was a genuine security risk. Sir Steven Runciman recalls that his father, then President of the Board of Trade, went to a reception at which Ribbentrop 'started discussing with him what the cabinet had been talking about that morning, Baldwin having reported it to the King, who reported it to Mrs Simpson, who'd been round to the German embassy'.[12] In consequence sensitive papers were withheld from King Edward and for most of his reign he was kept under the surveillance of the security services. Ribbentrop never realized that the King was a political pawn. Ambassador Otto von Bismarck described Ribbentrop as 'such an imbecile he is a freak of nature', but Hitler regarded him as an expert on foreign, and especially British, affairs. Thus the Führer was given cause to hope for some kind of accord whereby 'Britain should rule the waves' as a great imperial power while Germany should have *carte blanche* to expand eastwards.[13]

For Edward even to hint at pandering to German interests was to undermine the great new English pillar of the House of Windsor. But, with the possible exception of Anthony Eden, British politicians regarded their capricious and opinionated new King as more of a nuisance than a danger to the dynasty. Edward was, as his excessively punctilious private secretary Major Alexander Hardinge remarked, 'incapable of transacting the simplest official business'.[14] He read virtually nothing. He spoke first and thought later, if at all. He was, in fact, 'a chatterbox',[15] and his garrulity produced constant gaffes. For instance, he told Mussolini's ambassador that the League of Nations, then imposing economic sanctions on Italy because of her invasion of Ethiopia, was dead and that Italian colonial ambitions should be realized. For the King to advocate appeasement when his government was supporting the League (however half-heartedly) was rash as well as unconstitutional. He showed little wisdom, too, in trying to keep Haile Selassie out of the country and then refusing Eden's request to meet the exiled Emperor, who was immensely popular in England. King George had, after all, received Gandhi.

Yet these were political pinpricks. They were on a par with the new King's insistence that his more handsome profile (the left one) should feature on postage stamps, which necessitated their being redesigned. Similarly, his threat to end the independence of the BBC was mere bombast. Of course the King was right-wing. Diana Mosley, widow of the British Fascist leader Sir Oswald Mosley, maintains that Edward 'was miles to the right of my husband'. With his combination of populism and elitism, says his official biographer, the King was 'in some ways the perfect National Socialist'.[16] Yet Baldwin was surely right in refusing to see this as more than fashionable posturing. The King was a weak man, the Premier thought, who would 'jump on the bandwagon of the most popular cause of the moment'.[17]

In any case, King Edward had little time for politics. He was bound up in a grand passion which, as one aide said, 'bordered on mental uncontrollability'. When the King was with Mrs Simpson he was filled with 'vibrant happiness and joy'.[18] At all times he kept an ear cocked for the sound of his mistress's voice. Alan Lascelles, back in royal service, complained that the King escaped for very long weekends to Fort Belvedere where none of the private secretaries could follow. Even at Buckingham Palace Mrs Simpson restricted their access; and when one did corner him, Edward 'would be too bored to listen to what he was saying'.[19] Once the King climbed out of a window to avoid Wigram and sloped off to see his paramour. He regarded the great grey pile of Windsor as a museum, not a residence, and pillaged the Castle to embellish the Fort with the kind of objets d'art she craved. He borrowed paintings from the National Gallery, removing their frames, labels and numbers and treating them as his own. He smuggled in Paris fashions for her aboard aircraft of the King's Flight. The King settled enough money on Mrs Simpson to make her secure for life – like others, she anticipated that he would eventually grow bored with her. He smothered her in new jewels, especially rubies. By the spring of 1935 the King's infatuation was beginning to sap that other great pillar of the House of Windsor – the integrity of the royal family.

The news that the King was conducting an affair with a married American was spreading from Mayfair salons to country mansions, from *beau monde* to *demi-monde*. Monarchy became the subject of speculation rather than veneration. The motto of the Order of the Garter was disrespectfully scrambled: 'Honi soit qui Wally pense.' The cognoscenti indulged in fascinated conjecture. What was the chemistry between an effeminate man wildly attractive to homosexuals and a mannish woman whom lesbians adored? Did Mrs Simpson have amorous tricks to enhance an allegedly shrivelled virility? Did she, indeed, have a 'sexual hold' over the Prince, as one society lady claimed after quizzing Mrs Simpson's gynaecologist? Or was she more sorceress than seducer? Were the principals even lovers? Edward always denied that he had committed adultery with Wallis, and his official biographer charitably maintains that the case is not proven. Could Mrs Simpson even be a good influence, a matriarch in the making who would wean the King away from drink and stiffen his moral fibre?

Insiders like Chips Channon, who praised Wallis for her great kindness and good sense, answered the last question affirmatively. But she confirmed fears that she was a *femme fatale* in the summer of 1936. The King chartered a luxury yacht, the *Nahlin*, converting the library into a cabin and part of the deck into a golf driving range. Then he invited a small number of raffish patricians to join him and Wallis in a seaborne pleasure hunt in the eastern Mediterranean. It is said in the King's defence that he accomplished valuable political work in the Balkans and Turkey, but such achievements were insignificant and inadvertent. Indeed, he infuriated the Foreign Office. Only with difficulty was he persuaded not to start his voyage from Venice, which would have been interpreted as a conciliatory gesture towards Mussolini. And it took a threat of resignation from the British ambassador in Turkey to induce the King to meet its dictator at all – Edward merely wanted to play golf beside the Bosphorus.

The real importance of the *Nahlin* cruise lay in the fact that it advertised his liaison with Mrs Simpson to the world. He was photographed swimming, driving, walking and talking with her. Sometimes the poses revealed their intimacy, though they were not remotely as compromising as those captured in the recent pictures of Sarah Duchess of York and her 'financial adviser'. However, the King did appear in unconventional attitudes which shocked contemporaries. He went down the Corinth Canal wearing nothing but a pair of shorts. He wandered round Greek villages taking occasional swigs from a bottle of lemonade. He even went about naked in front of other patrons at a Viennese Turkish bath. In fact he displayed a kind of 'corroding frivolity', a 'flippancy of approach' which dented even his monumental popularity.[20] At home the press maintained a discreet silence: the *Daily Telegraph* even omitted Mrs Simpson's name from the guest list of the *Nahlin*. German newspapers and some French ones were equally reticent, as were the more respectable American journals. But popular papers all over the world splashed the story of the *Nahlin* high jinks on their front pages. Englishmen abroad were horrified by this coverage. One wrote that the King's doings, as reported by the American press, had transformed Great Britain 'from a sober and dignified realm into a dizzy Balkan musical comedy attuned to the rhythm of Jazz'.[21]

The *Nahlin* voyage had been a Balkan idyll as far as King Edward was concerned. True, there had been drunken scenes and intermittent sulks. Lady Diana Cooper, herself irritated by Wallis's 'commonness and Becky Sharpishness',[22] reckoned that she was bored to death by the King. But for the most part he and Wallis had behaved like two happy children playing truant. When they returned home Edward said to Lascelles, 'Now Tommy, back to striped trousers and coats again, back to school.'[23] Submitting to discipline, however, was the last thing the King had in mind: what he wanted was to make Wallis his Queen.

It is not clear when he made up his mind about marriage. Edward told his legal adviser, Walter Monckton, that he had decided irrevocably as early as 1934. During the proclamation of his accession, according to Barbara Cartland, the King and Mrs Simpson 'sort of clapped themselves' and 'that was when she was quite sure she was going to be Queen'. Several weeks afterwards, Edward had a meeting with Ernest Simpson in which he supposedly asked this rhetorical question: 'Do you really think that I would be crowned without Wallis at my side?'[24] Ernest, himself engaged in an affair with Wallis's friend Mary Raffray, agreed to a divorce. Everything, Wallis told her Aunt Bessie on 4 May 1936, was on 'a most friendly and arranged basis'. But she was worried that the marriage about which Edward was so sanguine might 'hurt the country and help the socialists'.[25]

The King displayed an extraordinary blend of boldness and naiveté. He was proud of Wallis and wanted others to acknowledge her as the perfect woman; so he declined to insinuate her into his life by the back stairs while sustaining a hypocritical charade of propriety before the world. Edward seemed to assume, moreover, that he could get away with anything, and that the divorce laws could be accommodated to his needs. Despite his loose living, the chorus of public and private adulation had scarcely faltered; it would surely continue when he revealed his grand matrimonial design. Modern marriage, he thought, was a matter of love rather than duty even for a king. Only old-fashioned people would expect him to sacrifice personal happiness to dynastic obligation. In any case there were, as Mrs Simpson said, only a few 'mangy foreign princesses left'. King George himself had widened the catchment area from which royal brides could be chosen, and now King Edward was bent on pushing the principle to its logical conclusion. But Mrs Simpson, a divorced American whom other members of the royal family considered 'a two-bit trollop',[26] was the *reductio ad absurdum* of that principle. Just how absurd, an American newspaper would demonstrate with five photographs: Wallis's first husband; Ernest Simpson; the King; the Archbishop of Canterbury; and the Prime Minister. These were captioned respectively: First Mate; Second Mate; Third Mate; Primate; Checkmate.

Even when it became known in the autumn of 1936 that Mrs Simpson was seeking a divorce, English newspapermen printed nothing about her. Their transatlantic colleagues were astonished by this 'voluntary surrender of the freedom of the press',[27] regarding the 'widespread attitude among Cabinet

Ministers and newspaper publishers that the public should know what is good for it' as 'another sign of the deterioration of British democracy'.[28] But few in Fleet Street believed that their prime obligation was to inform the electorate so that it could properly exercise its vote; rather, their duty was to assist the established order to maintain stability. Of course, British newspapers supported different political parties and even Queen Victoria had tried to influence their policies, though she maintained that editors should be banished from polite society. But towards the Crown and even the aristocracy there was a deferential consensus among newspapermen, who were conscious of their low degree.

Thus in Edward VII's reign Lord Northcliffe, founder of the popular press, wrote to the King's private secretary asking for 'any hint as to what or what not to publish'.[29] For over a generation newspapers presented the sovereign's family as 'a devoted, diligent, correct, thoroughly decent bunch of people'. Journalists completely ignored 'their imperfections, their derelictions, their drunkenness, their drugging' and so, as Philip Ziegler says, 'they got away with it'.[30] The *Times* claimed to live 'by disclosures',[31] but its editor Geoffrey Dawson asked Baldwin 'what he wished done'[32] about reporting the case of Mrs Simpson. At the Prime Minister's request Dawson kept quiet; he boasted that he was as proud of what he withheld from his readers as of what he published. Dawson shared R. A. Butler's view that 'good government flourishes in the dark'. But the culture of secrecy was not just a political matter, a reflection of the ruling class's determination to resist raw incursions of democracy. It was also a product of English inhibition about talking freely in front of children, servants and social inferiors. Was this intolerable humbug or decent reserve? Whatever the case, it largely accounts for the astonishing public silence which enveloped the King and Mrs Simpson.

More positive action was needed to control the licentious foreign press, and offending articles were literally torn out of American journals. The New York *World-Telegram* retaliated with a cartoon showing an Englishman (complete with monocle, walrus moustache and tweed jacket) reading a paper full of holes and saying, 'My word, His Highness must be having a ripping time.' In mid-October 1936 the sale of certain American publications was banned altogether when they trumpeted news of the imminent divorce and announced 'King to Wed Mrs Simpson at Any Cost'.[33] This obliteration of news seems to have been a spontaneous act by wholesalers and retailers who feared libel actions or 'public displeasure'.[34] However, King Edward concluded that it was only a matter of time before the British too would be told the secret.

Accordingly the King called in the leading figure in Fleet Street, Lord Beaverbrook, who was not immune to the enchantment of royalty. When talking to the King on the telephone he rose to his feet and called him 'Sire'.[35] Beaverbrook agreed to help by 'suppressing all advance publicity of the Simpson divorce, and in limiting publicity after the event'.[36] He operated through the Newspaper Proprietors' Association, which was accustomed to killing news of scandals affecting its own members and happily entered into a 'gentlemen's agreement' to protect the Crown. Even supposedly radical journals such as the socialist *New Statesman* and the Communist *Daily Worker* toed the line. John Gunther said that the British ruling class habitually stooped to 'censorship not by ukase but by voluntary conspiracy' and he asserted that this kind of propaganda was 'far more artful than any ever dreamed of by Dr Goebbels'.[37] As a result foreign journalists blazed the Simpson divorce story abroad while Britain remained in the dark.

Both Baldwin and Churchill were later to regret that the news had not broken earlier. And historians have condemned 'the deformities of pre-war journalism',[38] declaring that the country was 'ill-served'[39] by its secretive press. Even Edward was not appreciative. As Chips Channon said, 'The King is at his worst with Fleet Street, off-hand, angry and ungracious; he never treats them in the right way, or realizes that his popularity largely depends on them.'[40] The first royal media star had yet to learn the bitter lesson which the press would teach his successors – that it was a two-edged weapon. It could extol royal public life, but it could also expose royal private life. It could raise up idols and endow them with feet of clay, create myths and destroy them. In the words of Baldwin's confidant Thomas Jones, 'We invest our rulers with qualities which they do not possess and we connive at the illusion – those of us who know better – because monarchy is an illusion that works.'[41]

By October 1936 the illusion was in real danger of being shattered. Sometimes the King was hissed in cinemas and audiences refused to stand for the National Anthem. Baldwin was so worried that he had asked Eden not to trouble him much with foreign affairs; later it was charged that the King's matter had diverted government attention from the Spanish Civil War. But British leaders were no more distracted than the French masses: the Madrid correspondent of *Paris-Soir* complained that his readers found 'the massacre of a hundred Spanish children' less interesting than a sigh from Mrs Simpson.[42]

A week before the decree nisi was granted, Baldwin held the first of his interviews with the King, at Fort Belvedere. Baldwin warned that respect for the monarchy depended on its integrity, and that this could soon be irreparably damaged by public criticism over Mrs Simpson. This argument failed to move the King, for whom she was the reality and, as Walter Monckton observed, all others were shadows. Soon afterwards Edward told Monckton of his intention to marry her.

In the course of their conversation the Prime Minister assured the King that he had performed his public duties with dignity, though they were evidently not much to his taste. Edward replied sadly, 'I know there is nothing kingly about me but I have tried to mix with the people and make them think I was one of them.'[43] This was surely an attempt to make Baldwin acknowledge the value of a less formal, more democratic monarchy. But Edward could still perform ritual gyrations impressively, even heroically. During one summer parade, for example, a madman threw what looked like a bomb, but turned out to be an unloaded pistol, in front of the King's horse. Edward did not flinch. At the State Opening of Parliament on 3 November 1936 the King also behaved impeccably, though he was almost overcome by the smell of mothballs in the peers' robes. But he disappointed spectators by minimizing the ceremonial, arriving in a closed

Winterhalter's portrait of Queen Victoria, Prince Albert and their family, 1846.

Prince Edward received a naval education.

George V: a sailor-king 'happiest aboard his yacht'.

Lady Elizabeth Bowes-Lyon on her engagement to Prince Bertie.

Lessons at Windsor for Princesses Elizabeth and Margaret, 1941.

King Edward VIII by Walter Sickert.

Royal 'Conversation Piece' by James Gunn, 1950.

Queen Elizabeth II with Prince Charles and Princess Anne, 1952.

The growing royal family, 1965.

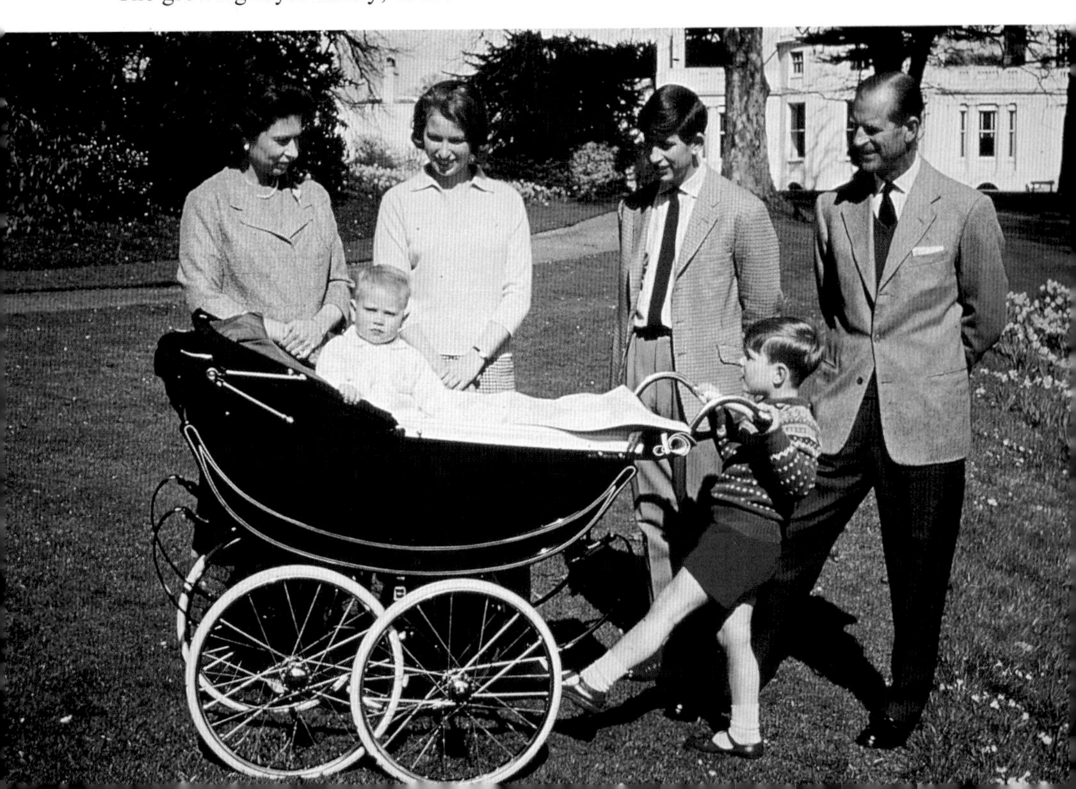

Majesty on the move: Coronation, 1953.

The balcony tableau: Coronation, 1953.

Princess Margaret by Cecil Beaton, 1958.

Daimler instead of showing himself in an open carriage, and wearing a cocked hat instead of a golden crown.

Where he seldom disappointed was in the human contacts he established with his people when he toured their workplaces and entered their homes. Later in the month he had two signal triumphs of this sort, 'kinging' (as he called it) brilliantly on the public stage while behind the scenes, concealed in a fashion almost inconceivable today, a personal drama was being played out which would bring Edward's reign to its premature end.

On 11 November the King visited the Home Fleet at Portland. He mingled with officers and ratings, refused to wear a waterproof during a wet inspection, led the singing of 'Tipperary' in a smoking concert and made an impromptu speech that brought the house down. King Edward found stooping to conquer easy and enjoyable. Yet he was conscious of the artificiality of his role and resentful of the time he had to spend away from the real world of Wallis. This is not to say that he was insincere in his concern for the welfare of working people, which he displayed in unforgettable fashion in South Wales a few days later. He was moved to tears by the rusting steelworks, the endless dole queues, the slums in the shadow of slag heaps, the shabby men (often war veterans), the prematurely aged women and malnourished children. The King was greeted with flags, cheers, hymns and banners saying 'We need your help.' He responded famously, 'Something must be done to meet the situation in South Wales and I will do all I can to assist you.'[44]

Edward mainly hated unemployment because it was a seed-bed for Bolshevism. He was a paternalist who regarded Welsh miners as creatures to be kept contented, said the writer Vincent Sheean, not men and brothers. Yet insofar as his impulse was altruistic, it was a mood of the moment. The King returned to London, bought some magnificent emeralds for Wallis, attended a glittering dinner with Chips Channon and told his hostess that he approved of splendour. Geoffrey Dawson was not far wrong in asserting that Edward had 'never shown the slightest interest' in social distress 'when away from his popular tours'.[45] Later, when the Duke of

Windsor was reminded that he had said something must be done, he apparently replied: 'Oh, what?'[46]

Ephemeral though the King's preoccupations with the underprivileged might have been, they were also disturbingly novel. Queen Victoria had pulled down the blinds of her railway coach when travelling through the Black Country. Edward VII, as his grandson later observed, would just 'sit in an open landau, receive an address, snip a ribbon and declare something open, retiring . . . to dine with his girl friends'.[47] George V carried out many industrial tours, but always maintained his distance and his dignity. He would surely have deemed it a vulgar stunt to borrow a trowel from an unemployed workman and learn how to mix plaster, as King Edward did in South Wales. He would certainly have considered it improper to emphasize that something must be done by banging his fist on a table in the presence of the Minister of Labour, as Edward also did. Other ministers took a dim view of this, too, fearing that the opposition would use the King's démarche to embarrass the government. Actually the Labour Party itself resented royal interference. Idealists like George Lansbury might wish to salute the 'Democratic King',[48] but most socialists thought sovereign sympathy no substitute for state aid. They wanted action, not distraction. Moreover, they agreed with the Tories that the King should steer clear of politics. At Westminster, therefore, Edward's behaviour was widely regarded as unconstitutional and there were rumours that he 'aimed at making himself a mild dictator'.[49] But did this provoke an Establishment conspiracy against the King? Did a cabal led by Baldwin, Lang, Dawson and Hardinge use the affair of Mrs Simpson for their own ends? Was Edward 'diddled out of the crown', as he later claimed, 'by sinister influences'?[50]

No doubt the Prime Minister, the Archbishop of Canterbury, the editor of the *Times* and the King's private secretary were at one in regarding Edward as lamentably ill-suited to his position. Baldwin told Reith that the King had 'the mind of a child' and was incapable of appreciating his responsibilities. But there is no evidence of a plot; indeed, they all appear to have felt that Edward might be redeemable if only he could detach himself from Mrs Simpson. Baldwin even hinted that a surreptitious liaison would be all right.

To postpone and so, he hoped, to prevent an actual marriage, Alec Hardinge wrote to his master on 13 November, brusquely warning that the press would soon break its silence, that the government might then resign and that Mrs Simpson should at once go abroad. Harold Macmillan described Hardinge as an anachronism from the 1900s whom Edward VII would even then have sacked as outmoded. Edward VIII thus had some cause to interpret his private secretary's missive as a hostile manoeuvre by the old gang. In that Dawson and Baldwin had approved the letter, he was correct. But he was wrong to think that they were trying to resolve the crisis by driving him from the throne.

The King's response was to shun Hardinge and ask Walter Monckton to act as his personal adviser. The loyal Monckton, who acknowledged that he bowed easily, bent over forwards to do so. But Edward, whose paranoid feelings grew with age, later accused him of getting 'a GCVO for selling me down the river'.[51] In fact the King sealed his own fate. He summoned the Prime Minister to Buckingham Palace on 16 November, the day before he set off for South Wales, and announced his intention of marrying Mrs Simpson. Edward said that if she was unacceptable to the British government and people, as Baldwin maintained, he would abdicate. The Premier was saddened by this decision, for he 'really loved "the little man"'. But, like many others at the time, Baldwin 'did not think him quite sane'.[52] The King seemed to be transfigured by his passion. His countenance, the Prime Minister said, 'wore at times such a look of beauty as might have lighted the face of a young knight who had caught a glimpse of the Holy Grail'.[53]

Queen Mary, to whom Edward confided his intention for the first time the same evening, was far less sympathetic. This was the worst experience of her life. She could hardly bear the humiliation of it all and vainly tried to persuade Edward to put public duty before private happiness. But he was deaf to her pleas and she became the most implacable enemy of 'the adventuress' who had ensnared her son. It was Queen Mary, more than anyone else, who ensured that Wallis was ostracised by the royal family. And it was Queen Mary who comforted Prince Bertie the next day as he sobbed at the prospect of having kingship, for which he felt entirely unfitted, thrust upon him.

For a few days towards the end of November it looked as though this cup might pass from him. Esmond Harmsworth, son of the press magnate Lord Rothermere, suggested to Wallis that King Edward could contract a morganatic marriage. This meant that he would not confer royal rank on his commoner bride. Mrs Simpson thought it a romantic as well as a pragmatic proposal and the King, somewhat less willingly, supported it. The Prime Minister and the Cabinet did not, whereupon Edward authorized Baldwin to consult the dominion governments. Prompted from Whitehall, they proved almost equally hostile. In reality the plan never had a chance of success. Morganatic marriage had been a German practice, but it was alien to British traditions and would have required an Act of Parliament. This, as many observed, would simply have given legal expression to the fact that the King's wife was unworthy to be Queen. Edward was bound to take the advice he had solicited, and on 2 December Baldwin delivered a virtual ultimatum: abdication or the renunciation of Mrs Simpson. Meanwhile an obscure bishop, appropriately named Blunt, had given an address stating that the coronation was no 'mere piece of national "pageantics"' but a holy sacrament, and commending the King to God's grace. The press opened the floodgates and, as far as most of the British people were concerned, the abdication crisis began. It proved literally to be a nine-day wonder. During that time, according to the *Annual Register*, the country went through 'a period of strain and agitation similar in many ways to that of the great banking crisis of 1931'.

The press, like the nation, was divided. Many popular newspapers, notably those of Rothermere and Beaverbrook, supported the King. Others, especially the *Times* and the *Daily Telegraph*, took the government's side. All treated the sovereign with respect. But he was shocked by their new candour. Edward 'foam[ed] at the mouth'[54] when the *Yorkshire Post* first broke the news, and accused the government of having inspired it. All the influence at his command was brought to bear on Fleet Street. The King 'instructed'[55] the Prime Minister to censor the *Times* and demanded that Beaverbrook should keep Mrs Simpson's name out of the *Daily Express*. In fact Beaverbrook, whom Edward had summoned back from America, may well have helped to drive Mrs Simpson out of the country in a desperate attempt to keep the King on the throne: Churchill later alleged that bricks were thrown through the windows of her palatial Cumberland Terrace residence at the press baron's behest. She was certainly 'loathed' for having 'stolen the beloved' King. There were rumours that people were plotting to assassinate her, and his equerry Sir Dudley Forwood remains 'surprised that she wasn't murdered'. To protect her from press and people the King sent Mrs Simpson abroad on 3 December. She was escorted by Lord Brownlow, a lord-in-waiting so dim that Evelyn Waugh once said it was 'a great intellectual strain to find words simple enough to converse' with him.[56] Brownlow was unable to shake off the pack of reporters who dogged their heels across France. The chase, which was filled with alarums and ended at a villa in Cannes, added an unwelcome element of farce to the last days of Edward VIII.

The King's champions made various efforts to play for time and to postpone what had been almost inevitable even before the nation became aware of the crisis. Mrs Simpson offered to withdraw from the scene. But it was an equivocal gesture and the government, like the King, concluded that it would make no difference. Edward himself proposed to calm anxieties by retreating abroad while remaining on the throne. But this was impractical. Winston Churchill, stirred by the romance of royalty in distress, excited by the rhetorical possibilities of defending the King and eager to scupper Baldwin, counselled delay at all costs. He whimsically advised Edward to immure himself inside Windsor Castle and station the royal doctors at the gates. Communists and Fascists, also keen to fish in troubled political waters, demonstrated on behalf of the monarch. Crowds formed in front of Buckingham Palace, singing the National Anthem and waving signs saying 'We

Want Edward' and 'God Save the King from Mr Baldwin'. However, the 'King's Party' was a little more than a miscellany of malcontents. Almost to the last Mrs Simpson was apparently confident that, led by Churchill, it could carry the country when Edward dissolved Parliament. Ribbentrop even thought it would mount a coup, and was nervous about going out to lunch on 11 December because he feared shooting in the streets. But the King's Party got no encouragement from the King; he had no stomach for constitutional novelties of that kind.

Doubtless he also recognized that public opinion was turning inexorably against him. More and more people expressed indignation that the Defender of the Faith should renegue on his duties and marry a foreign divorcée. Cinema audiences in South Wales watched newsreels of the King's visit in sullen silence. Socialists agreed with Liberals and Conservatives that 'the authority of Parliament must be upheld'.[57] On 7 December Baldwin told the Commons that 'the present state of suspense and uncertainty' could not be prolonged without grave risk to 'national and imperial interests'; and when Churchill pleaded for patience he was howled down. His royal quixotry cost him and the nation dear: it helped to keep the appeasers in power until the Second World War.

By now Beaverbrook had recognized that, as he memorably told Churchill, 'Our cock won't fight.' Encouraged by Mrs Simpson, their cock was too busy feathering his own nest. The King was determined that his exile should be comfortable and that nothing should jeopardize the financial settlement which Walter Monckton had been negotiating since 4 December. In order to maximize it Edward even lied about the size of his personal fortune, telling the Duke of York, Churchill and his other advisers that it amounted to about £90,000. The true figure was more like £1.1 million – some £30 million by present values. As even his official biographer admits, the distraught King 'behaved like a crooked fool'.[58] As payment for his life interest in Sandringham and Balmoral he secured promise of an annuity of £25,000 (roughly £800,000 in today's money), probably from the Civil List. It was not the first or the last time that royalty concealed its private wealth in order to prise open the public purse. But it was a dangerous expedient. When, as quickly and inevitably happened, Edward's deceit was exposed it created much bad blood. In fact his golden handshake inaugurated a royal feud which divided the House of Windsor for a generation.

Scarcely a hint of this was apparent when the King's three brothers assembled in the octagonal drawing room at Fort Belvedere on the morning of 10 December to sign the instrument of abdication. The following day Winston Churchill arrived to polish the text of Edward's farewell speech. Not realizing that he had been duped over the money and still overflowing with sympathy for Edward ('poor little lamb'), Churchill intoned Marvell's oft-quoted lines on the death of Charles I:

> He nothing common did or mean
> Upon that memorable scene.

That evening the Duke of Windsor, as the King-Emperor became, broadcast to his former subjects from Windsor Castle. He famously announced that he could not discharge his heavy duties 'without the help and support of the woman I love'. Less famously, he drew attention to the 'matchless blessing' of the 'happy home' enjoyed by his brother Bertie, who took the title of George VI, adopting his father's name to establish his legitimacy. It was an involuntary tribute to the merits of an old-fashioned royal family, and pointed up Edward's own failure to re-create the sovereign institution along contemporary lines – to fashion, as it were, an art deco monarchy in the sharp-edged, chromium-plated spirit of Mrs Simpson. But most people thought this a boon. 'Mrs Simpson was a godsend,' said Baldwin, though he did not go so far as Noël Coward, who suggested that statues of her should be erected all over England for the blessings she had bestowed on the country. The Prime Minister did believe, though, that if Edward had stayed on the throne he might have caused real problems as British policy hardened towards Nazi Germany.[59] He also concluded that kingship was strengthened by the change of kings. Tony Benn recalls listening to the abdication broadcast as a boy and being told by his father, himself a socialist MP, that British political leaders would 'always sacrifice the monarch to safeguard the monarchy'. As it happened, the monarch had sacrificed himself and the monarchy safeguarded itself by resurrecting the hallowed traditions of George V. It faced the future by looking to the past.

5

REBUILDING THE ROYAL HOUSE

George VI clung to the solid ground of convention because the abdication crisis struck him like an earthquake; he feared that the whole fabric of the monarchy might 'crumble under the shock and strain of it all'.[1] Others agreed and, although historians now say that the earthquake was just a 'hiccup',[2] he had real cause for concern. Inside the Palace, courtiers reckoned that the entire structure of throne and empire had been grievously undermined. Outside, there was an epidemic of what Labour MP Aneurin Bevan called 'boudoir hysteria'. When Baroness Rothschild heard that Edward had abdicated she exclaimed: 'What a bloody shit! Now we're going to get a republic!'[3] She over-reacted. But the prophecy of the 4th Marquess of Salisbury is less easy to dismiss: he said that the monarchy could not withstand this 'terrible blow' but that its full impact would only be felt after 'fifty years'.[4]

Undeniably the system of hereditary succession on which the dynasty depended had been found wanting. Edward had repudiated the crown, and rumours abounded that his brother Bertie was 'wholly unfitted'[5] to wear it. It has been said – and denied – that serious consideration was given to bypassing him and promoting one of his younger brothers. If so, the Dukes of Gloucester and Kent were each deemed unsuitable in their different ways. Nor was it acceptable to skip a generation and make the future Elizabeth II – then aged ten – Queen, with her grandmother Queen Mary as Regent. Whatever the truth, the fact that these proposals were even mentioned 'didn't do the monarchy any good';[6] they damaged its prestige and undermined its mystique. The manner of Edward VIII's going had, as Harold Laski said, let subjects see through the 'magic that screens the throne as they have not done since the time of George IV'.[7] Now, according to an American resident in London, royal personages were being spoken of as human beings, not as deities; 'the Hallelujahs have been soft-pedalled; the taboo is off'.

If the people 'wondered about the future of the monarchy',[8] their MPs discussed it. A handful of socialists on the far Left, though they praised Edward VIII for his 'warm-hearted interest in the welfare of the common man', belittled the sovereign institution itself. Their leader, James Maxton, described it as 'the outstanding symbol, the very head and front of a class society'.[9] The monarchy had had a great fall, he said, and all the King's horses and all the King's men couldn't put it together again. However, only five MPs supported (and 403 opposed) his motion for a more 'dignified', republican form of government. Yet one Tory, Sir Arnold Wilson, claimed that in a free vote a hundred MPs would have followed Maxton into the lobbies. Moreover, the Labour Party now adopted a more matter-of-fact tone towards the Crown. Its leader, Clement Attlee, argued that the monarchy should be less surrounded by privileged influences and less cut off from 'the masses of the people'.[10] From George VI's viewpoint this smacked too much of the approach of his brother. Haunted by portents of the collapse of the House of Windsor, the new King believed that it could only be saved if he imitated his father.

George VI was helped by the fact that he was a virtual replica of George V. They were both conventional men dedicated to stultifying routine – by no means a disadvantage for a constitutional monarch. Both were decent, decorous and dogged. Their interests were almost identical – shooting, clothes, medals. They wrote in the same laborious copperplate. They had the same memory for detail and the same eye for the minutiae of etiquette. They enjoyed the same lavatorial 'humour' and unkind chaff: on a train journey to Devon Lord Halifax told George VI that he had been born in that county, which prompted the King to point at each shack and barn *en route* and ask, 'Is that where you were born, Halifax?'[11] The two kings had the same respect for paternal authority, the same devotion to their wives, the same commitment to old fashions in everything. Both had volcanic tempers and shouted at their servants. Neither had been trained for kingship. Both wept at the prospect of it and sacrificed themselves to their royal duty.

However George VI, though a better husband and father, was more consumed by a sense of his own inadequacy. His stammer was such 'mental torture'[12] that he had avoided exposure to the public as much as possible. His health was delicate. Even by George V's standards, he lacked mental agility. He was, as R. A. Butler said, a 'dull dog'.[13] All his life Bertie had been eclipsed by the glib, golden-haired David; one of their tutors said it was 'rather like comparing an ugly duckling with a cock pheasant'.[14] As an adult Bertie had worshipped his brother, 'the blue-eyed boy of the whole world'.[15] When the 'intolerable honour', as his wife called it, descended upon Bertie, he had what amounted to a nervous breakdown. How could he possibly fill the 'ghastly void' left by the senior sibling?[16] How could he compare with a royal star? As David Cannadine says, 'It was as if people had expected Clark Gable and they'd ended up with George Formby.'

In the event this scarcely mattered, because when King George came to the throne a new star was born – his Queen. Brilliantly displaying those essential but barely compatible royal attributes – majesty and the common touch – she was, says John Grigg, 'beautiful, charming, sweet, affectionate, almost cuddly'. But she also exuded regal dignity on the public stage – taking a leaf out of Queen Mary's book, she invariably referred to 'the dear public'. In the belief that the new King should remain on his pedestal, both to differentiate him from his predecessor and to make a virtue out of his natural stiffness, the Queen insisted that she should do the unbending. Yet she still encouraged him to play the leading man, to smile and wave instead of hiding and hesitating, to master his phobias and nerve storms, to control his temper. The Queen did not always succeed, and Palace servants recall occasions when the King 'became so out-of-control that he actually struck his wife'.[17] Usually, though, she turned away his wrath; one rage she transformed into laughter by putting her hand on the King's pulse and saying, 'Tick-tock, tick-tock, it's going too fast'.[18]

Before the abdication Elizabeth and her husband had been regarded as dreary country cousins, not even smart enough to rate invitations from leading society hostesses such as Emerald Cunard. After it they became the focus of loyalty, not to mention snobbery, and the Queen's glamour was deliberately enhanced. The King himself showed couturier Norman Hartnell romantic royal portraits by Winterhalter and suggested that he should 'capture this picturesque grace' in the dresses he was to design.[19] Accordingly he revived frothy Victorian crinolines which made the most of Elizabeth's fresh complexion and warm smile, and thus helped to create royal images which synthesized 'public grandeur and private probity'.[20] The society photographer Cecil Beaton completed Elizabeth's transformation into a fairy queen with pictures so elaborately doctored and retouched that they amounted to 'cosmetic surgery' on celluloid.[21] Beaton made the Queen slimmer and sexier; but she emerged, too, as more wholesome than the brittle, glittering Duchess of Windsor, whom he also photographed. He cleverly conjured up domestic allusions as well as imperial echoes, portraying her in the role of tweedy mother as well as tiara'd matriarch.

Meanwhile the communications media were bent on the same task. Newspapermen responded eagerly to Baldwin's appeal to 'rally behind the new King', repair 'whatever damage the country has suffered' and 'maintain the integrity of the monarchy'.[22] But it was an uphill task, as Chips Channon noted, for Edward had been 'the most popular man in the world'[23]. He was, German ambassador wrote, 'every girl's, as well as every sportman's and every soldier's, ideal'.[24] At first the public, reluctant to transfer its loyalty, showed a marked coolness. Fleet Street manfully stressed the King's record of selfless social work, his unpretentious lifestyle, his plucky struggle against his speech impediment, his happy family and his similarity to George V. Many instances were given of the new King's reversion to the old order: his punctilious attendance at church; his rehabilitation of the royal stables at Windsor, which his brother had closed down; his re-employment of dismissed servants at Sandringham and Balmoral; the recalling of his father's old secretary Lord Wigram, who had been put out to grass as Keeper of the Royal Archives; the exclusion of the international fast set from the court circle; and the restoration to favour of the hereditary nobility.

Film-makers promoted the new regime with equal fervour. Even more than journalists, cameramen focussed on George VI's radiant Queen – if her personality could be summed up in a single epithet, said the *Times*, it would be 'radiant'.[25] In the cinemas coverage of royalty increased: 89 out of 101 Movietone newsreels included royal items in 1937, compared to 43 the previous year. Two feature films about Queen Victoria, previously the subject of total censorship, proved popular. They were *Victoria the Great* and *Sixty Glorious Years*; to ensure that they said exactly what the Establishment wanted, Sir Robert Vansittart, Permanent Under-Secretary at the Foreign Office, secretly took a hand in writing the scripts. From the first, wireless also played its part. Though finding King George awkward and uninspired, and dourly noting the presence of a hundred jewelled cigarette cases in his bedroom, Reith was the original Gold Microphone Pursuivant. As one of his conversations with the King reveals, both men took it for granted that the BBC was a propaganda agency designed to defeat 'left-wing influences'.[26]

Left-wingers such as Kingsley Martin, editor of the *New Statesman*, were 'nauseated by the sycophancy and ballyhoo of royal propaganda',[27] which reached its climax during the coronation month of May 1937. The date of the ceremony had been left unchanged because the preparations were already in train, but the fact that the sovereign himself had changed gave new importance to the crowning. It would exorcise the trauma of the abdication, display the resilience of monarchy and parade the confidence of empire. It would, in short, show the world that Britain was mighty yet. All this explains the enormous effort and expenditure – £524,000, two and a half times more than the cost of George V's coronation.

London was transformed by coloured hangings, Union Jacks, floral decorations, gilded crowns, illuminations, acres of red, white and blue bunting, millions of gilt lions and unicorns. Armies of workmen turned forests of timber and 570 miles of steel tubing into stands along the route. The travel firm of Thomas Cook paid the Duke of Wellington £10,000 to give their clients a privileged view of the procession from Apsley House on Hyde Park Corner. Stores competed to display their patriotism: Selfridge's, for instance, exhibited a huge sculpture entitled *The Empire's Homage to the Throne*. The *Times* welcomed the sublime day by asserting that the democratic monarchy was so involved in all aspects of the community that 'The Crown is the necessary centre, not of political life only, but of all life.'[28]

This hardly seemed to be hyperbole as the brilliant cavalcade wended its way to Westminster Abbey. Two miles long, it was a *tableau vivant* of past glories, a shining reminder under grey skies that a quarter of the globe was still painted red on the map, a picture of medieval romance in the midst of the devil's decade. Instead of mechanized might here was militarism in masquerade, 'frogged tunics, aigrettes, bearskins, leopard pelts, kilts, striped turbans, scarlet coats, plaid pantaloons, gilt cuirasses and waving plumes – all the pageantry of impracticality wherein England's genius for poetry and empire equally thrive'.[29]

The Abbey, with tiers of seats almost up to the roof, resembled a magnificent theatre. It was ablaze with stars and garters, crimson robes and scarlet uniforms, blue silk breeches and white court dresses, sparkling diamonds and glowing rubies, ermine capes and gold copes. The King looked gaunt, nervous and pale, despite the theatrical make-up which he wore on public occasions. But he made a dignified entry in his mantle of imperial purple with its immense velvet train borne by nine pages in scarlet and gold. Centre-stage, he solemnly underwent the mystic rites: the swearing of oaths; the anointing with holy oil; the investment with sword, spurs, orb, ring and sceptre; the crowning, when a shaft of sunshine lit up his golden tunic; the acclamation; the enthronement; and the acts of homage, which were followed by the crowning of Queen Elizabeth. No one was more inspired by the pomp and circumstance than the King and Queen themselves. As drums rolled and trumpets blared, they emerged from the Abbey in a state of spiritual exaltation, even euphoria. 'After you've been crowned you're never the same again,'[30] exclaimed the Queen later.

In its first major survey Mass Observation, an early form of public opinion poll, discovered that most of the King's subjects were also deeply moved by the coronation. Crowds watched the procession with shining eyes and paid devout attention to the service as it was transmitted over loudspeakers. Listeners to the wireless were 'thrilled', often to the point of tears, by the 'voice pictures' of the BBC – some worried about whether it was proper to eat during the ceremony. In the evening, outside Buckingham Palace, enthusiasm for the new sovereign reached a climax with cries of 'We want the King!' George, responding *sotto voce*, 'The King wants his dinner', duly led his family on to the floodlit balcony, where they were greeted with tumultuous cheering from the vast crowds.

Yet a surprising number of people were resistant to what Ritchie Calder, a radical journalist, called 'the greatest spectacle of its kind the world has yet staged'.[31] Weary Liberals such as Lloyd George, who regarded the King as 'a nitwit' though he admired the effervescent Queen, dismissed the coronation as 'all mumbo-jumbo with the Priest Zadock'.[32] Informed socialists such as Lord Ponsonby complained that inviting three or four working men to the exclusively aristocratic ceremony was 'just a patronising sop'.[33] Citizens in the street quizzed by Mass Observers criticized 'the patriotic jingo of flag-wagging' and the 'artificially bumped-up' ceremonial. One man said that, although it would be a pity to rob the populace of 'this colourful make-believe', it was 'too dangerous a weapon to be in the hands of the people at present in power in this country'.[34]

Protests about the 'luscious coronation propaganda' indicate that it was effective. Members of the Establishment, at any rate, clearly believed that the road of excess led to the palace of wisdom. The Archbishop of Canterbury announced that the country was now nearer the kingdom of heaven. He and the Duke of Norfolk viewed film taken in the Abbey by forty newsreel cameramen (all wearing full evening dress) in order to cut out 'anything which may be considered unsuitable for the public at large to see'.[35] Lang had in mind regal tics, stutters or agonizing silences like those which had punctuated Prince Bertie's closing speech at the British Empire Exhibition in 1925. The Archbishop had already excluded television from the ceremony precisely because it would have been live and so there would have been no chance of censoring it. But all he excised now was a close-up shot of the normally indomitable Queen Mary wiping away some tears. His efforts ensured that the coronation was presented exactly as the royal family wanted. The moving pictures made a powerful impression on the 20 million Britons who attended the cinema each week: the Empire was in safe hands, and the father of the royal family had been hallowed as the paterfamilias of his people. George VI would be able to serve out the 'life sentence' imposed by his office in the manner of George V. For, as the *Times* affirmed, successful kingship relied 'not upon intellectual brilliance or superlative talent of any kind, but upon the moral qualities of steadiness, staying-power and self-sacrifice'.[36]

This may not have been very complimentary to the new King, but it was chiefly intended as a disguised attack on his predecessor. The Duke of Windsor, who denied reports that he listened to the ceremony on the wireless in exile near Tours in France while knitting a blue sweater for Wallis, was the spectre at the coronation feast. He was, as the *Morning Post* acknowledged, 'the absent one who will throw a long shadow across many hearts today'. It was impossible to forget him, impossible to avoid the thought that he would have transformed the crowning ceremony from a jittery ordeal into a jaunty triumph. In private people still argued about the man born to be king: some 'really liked' him 'whatever his shortcomings';[37] others declared bitterly that he had let them down. An American reported to President Roosevelt that despite 'the enormous press build-up' given to Edward's conscientious understudies, he was still more popular than they were, to judge from the number of their respective toasts in London pubs.[38] To counter this, the BBC and the respectable papers tried to pull down the blinds on Edward VIII as effectively as they had on Mrs Simpson before the abdication crisis.

Nevertheless there were some final comments on Edward's unsuitability for kingship. Lord Beaverbrook went so far as to say that Geoffrey Dawson directed a 'reign of terror' against Edward in the *Times*; but its mildness can be measured in the valedictory editorial expressing incredulity at Edward's sacrifice of high responsibilities to personal preferences and placing the blame on his unfortunate choice of intimates, an 'exotic' coterie remote from the people. Archbishop Lang was somewhat more forthright – though, following the ancient convention that the king can do no wrong, he too directed his fire mainly at 'evil counsellors'. In a broadcast on 13 December the Primate expressed disappointment that Edward had abandoned his sacred trust and sought 'happiness in a manner inconsistent with the Christian principles of marriage, and within a social circle whose standard and way of life are alien to all the best instincts and traditions of his people'.

The new King and the two Queens who dominated him, his mother and his wife, secretly approved of the Primate's address. But the press could not attack the king over the water too harshly 'without the double risk of impairing the dignity of the Crown' and provoking a reaction from the large number of people who still held him 'in great affection'.[39] The real aim was to make Edward 'the world's prize forgotten man'.[40] So records of his abdication broadcast, which had provoked a sympathetic reaction in his favour, were censored: although available in America they could not be bought in England, where royal discs were popular and there were twice as many gramophones as radios. The leading newspapers, following the *Times*, went out of their way to avoid mentioning the Duke of Windsor. The BBC consigned him to an historical *oubliette*, refusing even to transmit his eloquent appeal for peace from Verdun in 1939. The five newsreel companies ignored him entirely for almost a year after the abdication, and barred film of his wedding from every screen in Britain. The Royal Academy omitted him from the special coronation exhibition featuring portraits of every monarch from George III to George VI. And there was an informal ban on discussing the abdication in Pall Mall clubs.

The new court also demonstrated its disapproval of those who had pandered to the *ancien régime*. Brownlow discovered from the newspapers that he had been replaced as lord-in-waiting. Lady Cunard was ostracised. Like many others, pilloried by Osbert Sitwell in his poem 'Rat Week', she now claimed hardly to have known Mrs Simpson and tried to distance herself from the monarch whom she had once addressed as 'Majesty Divine'.[41]

A thinner diet of flattery was one of many changes to which the Duke of Windsor now had to accustom himself. He seems to have had little idea what exile would be like or even where he would go after abdication. In the event he stayed at Baron de Rothschild's house near Vienna, Schloss Enzesfeld. Unable to join Mrs Simpson in France until the divorce was finalized, he spent lonely months connected to her only by a bad telephone line. Even his personal servants had refused to follow him. 'He suffered a lot' by not having a proper staff or an important programme of events, says Sir Dudley Forwood. For company the Duke relied mainly on his old friend, the brash, ebullient Fruity Metcalfe. Metcalfe's great merit was that he treated Edward 'as a perfectly ordinary human being' – although, his widow adds paradoxically, he was always 'very deferential'. He accompanied the Duke on his energetic skiing and shopping expeditions, and stayed up into the small hours playing cards with his master or listening to him perform on the bagpipes. He imparted some of his own *joie de vivre* to a man who expressed no regrets about what he had done but whose moods swung from febrile cheerfulness to nervous depression at Mrs Simpson's slightest reproach. But Metcalfe failed to prevent the Duke reading some of the hate mail and press censure which poured across from England. Edward had been brought up to believe that there were three types of human being – men, women and royalty. Now he was discovering that there was a fourth – the once and former king.

Edward envisaged that after the abdication he would revert to something like his status as Prince of Wales, failing to appreciate that he would have a far more exiguous and equivocal role as ex-King than as Prince. The Duke proposed to spend a year or two on the continent while Bertie settled into his new office; then he would return to Fort Belvedere and enjoy the privileges of his rank while undertaking the agreeable light duties of an honorary younger brother. The Duke also assumed that he would have a permanent hot line to the King, who had always hero-worshipped him. But George VI was reduced to a gibbering wreck by his brother's insistent telephone calls, which the Germans unprofitably tapped. First the new King rationed his brother's calls, then instructed him not to ring at all unless for some urgent reason. Other humiliations followed.

The Duke was excluded from the Civil List. The Labour Party would not permit him to receive a state pension without some parliamentary enquiry into the royal finances, which King George was determined to avoid. So, indignant that Edward had lied about his assets, the King offered to pay him a smaller pension out of his own pocket. The Duke protested vehemently that his brother was reneging on their agreement when he had given up everything. Edward, obliged to cater for Wallis's extravagant tastes, became increasingly manic about money. The quarrel about cash went on with growing rancour until 1938. Then, to anticipate, the Duke was granted some £21,000 a year. Half came from the selling of his life interest in Sandringham and Balmoral. King George paid the other half himself on condition that his brother did not visit England without official permission. It seems, incidentally, that while negotiating Edward's annuity King George managed to persuade the Treasury that the monarch's private income should be freed from tax.[42] This concession was so generous that it enabled the royal fortune to grow immeasurably, and it was so secret that the sovereign's tax-free status soon appeared to be an immemorial tradition. But wealth on this scale, amassed in this manner, inevitably distanced sovereign from heavily taxed subjects. Like King Midas, Queen Elizabeth II was to pay a heavy price for this golden touch. The Duke of

Windsor, meanwhile, was beginning to pay the price for his great renunciation – pariahdom.

Shortly before Mrs Simpson's divorce decree became absolute, in May 1937, the King told the Duke that none of the family would attend his wedding. He broke the news with some embarrassment, for he himself had suggested that his brother should get married not on the Riviera, with its playboy associations, but at the Château de Candé near Tours, which was owned by an industrialist named Charles Bedaux. Nevertheless, for the royal family to condone a match which the country and the Established Church had opposed, said the King, would be harmful to the monarchy. The Palace put pressure on friends and courtiers such as Lord Brownlow to refuse invitations to the wedding. So what seems to have been planned as a kind of alternative coronation became an undignified, hole-in-the-corner ceremony. Only Walter Monckton and a handful of hangers-on appeared. Lacking his brothers as 'supporters', the Duke asked Fruity Metcalfe to be his best man. Denied a royal chaplain or any respectable Anglican clergyman, he had to rely on the services of a renegade English parson whose bishop, Hensley Henson, believed Mrs Simpson's third essay in matrimony to be 'doubly bigamous'. Still, the Rev. J. A. Jardine proved adequate and the ceremony took place on 3 June 1937.

The unkindest cut of all was the King's refusal to bestow on Wallis the coveted title of Royal Highness. The convention was that a wife took her husband's rank. Since Wallis had not been deemed fit to do so when Edward was King – had not even been deemed fit to be a morganatic queen – he had abdicated. Now Wallis was deemed unfit even to share his rank as a royal duke, and became instead a morganatic duchess. She resented the slight, but seemed to think that being created HRH was just a matter of 'extra chic'.[43] The Duke, however, 'burst into tears' and told his spouse that she would always be HRH to him.[44] He regarded the withholding of this title as a mortal insult which signified his family's decisive rejection of Wallis: they had branded her as an outcast. The Duke was outraged by what he later called a 'cold-blooded act' which raised a 'kind of Berlin wall' between him and home. He engaged in a lifelong campaign to rescind the decree, causing acute social embarrassment by expecting people to curtsey to Wallis. In consequence relations with his family, despite occasional attempts at reconciliation, were poisoned for good.

When the Duke warned, after the wedding, that all these humiliations would lead to their 'complete estrangement', the King replied spiritedly: 'How do you think I like taking on a rocking throne, and trying to make it steady again? It has not been a pleasant job, and it is not finished yet.'[45] The task was made infinitely harder by the unusual circumstance that his predecessor was not only alive but, as the King artlessly remarked, 'very much so'. Bertie loved David, but worried that he might steal the limelight with some sort of come-back; he feared that the Windsors would find further ways to damage the House of Windsor. As the British ambassador to Washington recorded, '. . . the King does not yet feel safe on his throne, and up to a point he is like the medieval monarch who has a hated rival claimant living in exile'.[46] The Duke also bore certain resemblances to Princess Diana in the early 1990s: he was a rogue royalty whose glamour could divide loyalties. Nothing makes life more difficult for sovereigns than a regal loose cannon aboard the ship of state.

As mutual suspicion burgeoned into mutual paranoia, the King was sustained, perhaps even directed, by family and courtiers. Queen Mary, who had lost two stone during the abdication crisis, could not have been more staunch. She had promised her husband never to receive Mrs Simpson and urged the new King to sustain the boycott even if it meant keeping his brother at arm's length. Queen Elizabeth was equally implacable, but professed sorrow rather than anger; there are hints that some relations doubted her sincerity, and the Princess Royal sneered at her sister-in-law's 'cheap public smile'. According to Chips Channon the court hated Wallis 'to the point of hysteria'. Certainly Wigram, Hardinge and Lascelles (who reckoned that Edward had received every gift from the gods except a soul) stiffened King George's resistance. Channon, who was extremely well informed, further asserted that the King and Queen were the 'puppets of a Palace clique'.[47]

The conservative courtiers, who formed a 'closed ring'[48] reinforced by aristocracy and government, wanted to turn the clock back to King George V's reign. They had detested Edward VIII's aberrancy, but now they distrusted George VI's capacity. Accordingly they tried to make him a *roi fainéant*. Before the coronation his stressful Christmas broadcast was cancelled; so was the Indian durbar. This should have taken place, along the lines of George V's, during the winter of 1937; but his private secretaries felt that it would be too much of a strain for George VI. They may have been right, for he agonized over official occasions: the King prepared himself for the State Opening of Parliament by sitting at his desk in the imperial crown, and before Trooping the Colour he wore the Brigade of Guards bearskin while gardening. Now courtiers made it clear that his duty was to take advice, shun the Windsors, preserve his dignity, bring his wife and children into the picture, and follow in his father's footsteps. Although the King did sometimes try to assert himself, rumours of his feebleness gained wide currency. In the German embassy Reinhard Spitzy concluded that King George was 'stupid . . . weak and ineffectual', whereas his 'clever' wife was the 'power behind the throne'.

Meanwhile, troubles great and small marred the Duke of Windsor's marital bliss. He and the Duchess travelled to Venice for their honeymoon, setting off in a long convoy of cars transporting equerries, valets, maids, detectives and 266 pieces of luggage. He was not amused when, during the long delay while all their impedimenta was transferred to a train, English passengers leaned out of windows and booed him (though romantic French ones cheered). Plainly the public mood in Britain had turned against the Windsors, and in private even Churchill disparaged their 'court of dagoes on the Loire'. During the honeymoon there were tensions: Wallis blamed Edward for having been jockeyed off the throne, and he blamed himself for having failed to make her royal. Later the Duchess of Kent refused to visit them and the snub received much publicity. Sometimes, though, it was the smallest pinpricks which wounded most. Shortly after the honeymoon Barbara Cartland witnessed the Duke dining at

Maxim's in Paris: he wanted some butter but was unable to attract the waiters' attention.

It was in a mood of angry disillusionment, therefore, that the Duke attracted the world's attention. He let the pro-Nazi Charles Bedaux arrange a visit to Germany in the autumn of 1937. The Duke's professed purpose was to study housing and labour conditions, itself a reminder of his Welsh tour and thus anathema in Buckingham Palace. But although he did have sympathy with German working people, admired the Nazi achievement in conquering unemployment and hoped to make pacific overtures to Hitler (who had sent good wishes on his wedding), the Duke's main motives were surely personal. Perhaps, like a retired matinée idol, he longed to return to the spotlight. Certainly he wanted a state visit on which his wife would be properly acclaimed. As Sir Dudley Forwood says: 'The fact that Hitler put his train at our disposal and we were very much treated as guests of honour pleased HRH because he was able, for his beloved, to share in a kind of state occasion.'

Everyone was anxious to impress. The visitors arrived in their usual immaculate fashion, and the Germans ensured that they saw only show-places. Everywhere the Windsors were greeted with enthusiasm, much of it undoubtedly spontaneous. At one mining town 'the people shouted with joy, children had the day off school, flowers were scattered in the streets'. The Duke responded by going down the pit, evincing an interest in technical innovations, and displaying an obvious concern for the poor. As one witness says, he revealed himself as 'a former king who could be touched'.[49] The Duke was overwhelmed by his reception, particularly at a dinner given by his Brownshirted cousin Charles of Saxe-Coburg. Here the Duchess of Windsor was acknowledged as royalty by royalty: her place card bore the German equivalent of HRH. Edward himself tried too hard to please. Reinhard Spitzy, who acted as his ADC, recalls that the Duke constantly clicked his heels, not realizing that such imperial customs had no place in the populist Third Reich. Worse still, the Duke several times gave the Nazi salute, even responding to Hitler himself in kind.[50] Apparently Edward was uneasy about the practice, perhaps reflecting on the scandal which Ribbentrop had caused by saluting George VI in the Hitler manner. At one point the Duke congratulated himself on the 'cunning' way in which he had disguised the salute as a wave. But he also justified having saluted unambiguously by saying that it was just 'good manners'.[51] Even so, the English newsreel companies remained loyal enough to delete the gesture.[52]

There were other awkward incidents. His hosts explained that a concentration camp which they passed was a place 'where we keep cold meat'.[53] When he insisted on making an unscheduled visit to the royal palace of Württemberg, the Duke found himself in a Colonial Exposition where maps displayed Germany's imperial demands, including portions of the British Empire. Staying with Goering at Karinhall, the Duke watched the General dropping wooden bombs from a toy aircraft on his nephew's model trains. The meeting with Hitler was cordial. But the Duke, proud of his fluent German and irritated that the Führer insisted on using an interpreter, occasionally interpolated: 'False translation.' Hitler assumed that his guest shared Nazi aspirations, and the Duke said nothing to disabuse him. They mostly talked about the need for Anglo-German friendship. The Führer was impressed by the Duke and achieved some rapport with the Duchess, dilating on his architectural enthusiasms and boasting that Nazi 'buildings will make more magnificent ruins than the Greeks''.[54] Afterwards he said that Wallis 'would have made a good Queen'.[55]

The Windsors' triumphal progress restored their self-esteem. Meeting them in Paris shortly afterwards the American ambassador, William Bullitt, told Roosevelt that the Duke was calmer and more confident. The Duchess was more '"gracious"', talking in what she thought was an English accent (actually 'a rather nasal cockney') and now bereft of 'that spontaneous wit and twinkle which used to make her very attractive'.[56] Anyway, the Windsors were now confirmed in their pro-German prejudices, strengthened as they were by the Duke's ties of blood. Like many at the time, he regarded Hitler as a bastion against Bolshevism. He stubbornly refused to recognize the evils of the Third Reich, despite having had better opportunities than most to appraise them; and just as obstinately refused to believe that the Nazis would make propaganda out of his tour – in fact they did so ruthlessly. The regime strengthened its hold on the working classes by advertising itself, apparently with ducal support, as their friend. In short, the entire episode was worse than a crime; it was a blunder.

In England the court seethed silently. The press could not avoid reporting the news but it largely forbore to comment, continuing the policy of official disregard. Many of Edward's left-wing adherents, remembering that Hitler had smashed the German trade unions and recognizing that the Duke was (to paraphrase Harold Laski) about as much of a socialist as John D. Rockefeller, lost faith in him. The Labour politician Herbert Morrison, an ardent devotee of royalty, advised him to keep out of the public eye. But this was a slap on the wrist compared to the reaction in the United States, where a tour was planned. Americans warned that the Windsors came as Nazi propagandists and allies of that enemy of labour Charles Bedaux. A cartoon in the *Detroit News* showed the Duke asking a shabby, cloth-capped labourer, 'On your salary, how do you buy your wife a wardrobe for the winter season?'

As a result he cancelled his American tour and, his plans to return home continuing to meet official opposition, he remained in France. His grievances festered, particularly when the arbiters of status disagreed about the Duchess: *Debrett* gave her high rank, *Burke* gave her low rank, and the *Almanach de Gotha* ignored her altogether. The Windsors invented offensive nicknames for his English relations. They called Queen Elizabeth the 'fat Scotch cook' ('Cookie' for short) because she reminded them of 'a cook giving notice'.[57] She was also known as 'the dowdy Duchess' and 'the Monster of Glamis'. Edward described his brother Bertie as a 'cad' and Henry of Gloucester as 'the Unknown Soldier'. Late in 1937 the Duke gave an interview, which was suppressed, in which he said that he would be willing to serve as president of some future English republic. In the meantime the Windsors established a quasi-regal court in Paris and on the Riviera. Here they adhered to the old German convention: the smaller the principality, the more minute its attention to etiquette. But luxurious though their existence was, many visitors found it a pathetic parody of life at Buckingham Palace.

There King George VI, despite feeling haunted by his eldest brother and plagued by his handicaps, was gradually finding his way. He had sacrificed his agreeable life as a country gentleman and accepted the stern discipline of his office. He had submitted to being fenced in by formality, modern replacement for the divinity that once hedged a king. He kept up a tradition which consisted largely of keeping up appearances. But at a time of mounting European tension, concluded an American journalist, King George had 'given the British nation a new sense of solidarity in which the monarchy plays a semi-mystical part'.[58] In this he was energetically assisted by Neville Chamberlain, who took over as Prime Minister on Baldwin's retirement a fortnight after the coronation. The new Premier stayed at Balmoral with the royal family, where he enjoyed fishing in the Dee, though he seldom caught anything. He did, however, hook the King. Although he was still 'stiff and speechless'[59] with other ministers, George found it easy to talk to Chamberlain. The King became an ardent admirer of the Premier and an eager supporter of his policy of appeasing Germany. So, indeed, did Queen Mary, who was now apt to say that Britain had 'backed the wrong horse' in the First World War.

This was a surprisingly common sentiment at the time: Lord Mount Temple, for instance, publicly expressed the hope that in the event of another war the partners would change. However, democratic France was Britain's most important ally against the menace of totalitarianism. It was therefore appropriate that, in July 1938, King George should make his first major state visit to Paris. Carefully planned as an attempt to revive the spirit of the Entente Cordiale, it was an outstanding popular success. But more than this was required to overcome the deep mistrust between the ancient rivals. Within a few months the French Premier, Edouard Daladier (himself a bull with rubber horns), damned the conciliatory British government root and branch. He described the King as a 'moron' and the Queen as 'an excessively ambitious woman who would be ready to sacrifice every other country in the world in order that she might remain Queen Elizabeth of England'.[60]

The earnest, well-meaning King wanted to do more than take part in ceremonial functions. Of course, he was not hyper-active like his eldest brother. Indeed, when staying at Windsor Kenneth Clark was 'shocked' by how little the King and Queen 'did with their day; she never rose before 11'.[61] The King devoted little energy to cultural pursuits, though he adored dancing and played tennis with skill and ill temper. His neglect of the arts and sciences, Lord Crawford complained, amounted to a boycott – though, unlike his father, the King did not shake his stick at the paintings of Cézanne. But George VI did yearn to intervene personally in the great political issues facing the nation – none more vital than the matter of war and peace. He was given little opportunity. The Foreign Office quashed his proposal to appeal personally to Hitler as 'one ex-Serviceman to another'. Ministers also rejected the King's suggestions that he should communicate with Mussolini and send 'a friendly message direct to the Emperor of Japan'.[62]

Behind the scenes the King was more successful in getting his own way. In July 1938, for example, Lord Runciman refused the thankless task of leading a mission to find out what concessions Czechoslovakia might be prepared to make in order to pacify Hitler. Then King George asked him to go and, a royal wish then being virtually a command, Runciman 'couldn't very well refuse'.[63] Later the King encouraged an intrigue against the Jewish War Minister, Leslie Hore-Belisha, who was struggling to modernize an army still in love with the horse and the lance. Eventually Chamberlain removed him from this office. More important, King George allowed himself to become identified in public with the policy of appeasement. When Chamberlain made his first dramatic flight to Germany, he told his sisters that the King was 'as excited as a boy'. When the Prime Minister returned from Munich, the King sent him 'heartfelt congratulations on the success of your visit'[64] and appeared with him on the balcony of Buckingham Palace before a wildly cheering crowd. That the King should share the general sense of relief was understandable; that he should encourage the almost universal applause was unwise. In so doing the King endorsed a policy which was subject to a vote in the House of Commons, and supported a politician who had actually brought back the antithesis of 'peace with honour'. This was 'the biggest constitutional blunder that has been made by any sovereign this century'.[65]

By contrast, the royal tour of Canada and the United States in the summer of 1939 was one of the greatest triumphs of George VI's reign. He was first invited by the Canadian Prime Minister Mackenzie King, who wished to promote Québecois loyalty and to persuade an English court 'still living in the reign of the Stuarts' that the dominion was more than just a colonial outpost. Roosevelt had his own agenda. He wanted to strengthen links with European democracies, in the hope of deterring Hitler, without offending American isolationists. He therefore determined on an informal visit in which the keynotes should be 'simplicity and naturalness'.[66] Staff at Buckingham Palace were not accustomed to this, and elaborate details of royal requirements were transmitted to the White House. Nevertheless, on what was the first visit of a reigning British sovereign to the New World, the King and Queen proved extraordinarily relaxed and received a rapturous welcome. Ironically the Duke of Windsor, who had long been idolized in America, contributed to the enthusiasm. Evidently trying to steal their thunder with his peace broadcast from Verdun, he laid himself open to the charge of spite as well as appeasement.

Roosevelt kept clear of the family feud but behaved like a benign uncle. He welcomed the King and Queen to his house at Hyde Park, fed them on beer and hot dogs, and insisted that they enjoy rest and recreation. The President exercised power without pomp, a lesson to visitors who enjoyed pomp without power. Unfortunately he also gave the impression that American help would be forthcoming if Germany attacked England, an impression that the King injudiciously passed on to a journalist. But if King George made no diplomatic breakthrough, he achieved a spectacular public relations coup. Americans voted Queen Elizabeth 'Woman of the Year'. As she said afterwards, 'that tour made us . . . I mean us, the King and myself'.[67]

It made them in the sense of conferring vital ingredients of prestige and self-confidence which they had previously lacked. Liking and respecting the royal couple (though heaving a sigh of relief when they left), Roosevelt had virtually given them a presidential endorsement. In his blithe-spirited way he had also shown them how to combine dignity with informality. This democratic skill came naturally to the Queen, who seemed to achieve a personal rapport with everyone – perhaps through the brillance of her eyes. Harold Nicolson, who made this observation, concluded: 'she is in truth one of the most amazing Queens since Cleopatra'. The King had to try harder. But he discovered in America that the 'high-hat business', which his father had considered essential, must now be modified by 'the common touch'. This was for him 'a new idea of kingship'.[68] It was also a synthesis of the sovereign styles of George V and Edward VIII. It enabled George VI to overcome the trauma of the abdication, to eclipse the Windsors, and to enhance the position of the monarchy in the years of trial ahead. This is not to say that the King was transformed overnight. Like other members of England's elite, he tended to see war as a tiresome intrusion into a privileged existence – one in which field sports loomed large. At the end of August 1939, King George lamented the interruption to shooting in a marvellous year for grouse: it was 'utterly damnable that that villain Hitler had upset everything'.[69]

6

BROTHERS AT WAR

There was a marked contrast between the fortunes of the royal brothers at war. King George VI remained in England with his wife and daughters and shared the privations of his subjects. He faced the Blitz and endured the bombing of Buckingham Palace. He was a staunch supporter of Winston Churchill, who declared that the King and Queen were now 'more beloved by all classes and conditions than any of the princes of the past'.[1] This was the King's finest hour. As an old courtier says, 'His making was, of course, the war.'[2] The Duke of Windsor, on the other hand, had 'pro-Nazi'[3] leanings, wanted to do a peace deal with Hitler and threatened to become a quisling king. When Germany invaded France he fled to Spain and Portugal. After various bizarre episodes the Duke was made Governor of the Bahamas, where he and the Duchess spent the war demonstrating that they were the 'arch-beachcombers of the world'.[4] By 1945 the British public regarded the Duke with complete indifference, as 'a sort of dead sensation'.[5] This, at any rate, is the standard version of what the estranged brothers did in the second global conflict to menace the House of Windsor. But, like most standard versions, it is truth alloyed with myth.

Of King George's grit and tenacity there is no doubt. But it is often forgotten that he put these virtues entirely at the service of Neville Chamberlain during the first months of the struggle. Neither the shipwreck of appeasement nor Britain's feebleness during the 'Phoney War' undermined the King's faith in his Prime Minister; he remained 'a hundred per cent pro-Chamberlain'[6] even in May 1940, when it became plain that the Premier had lost the confidence of the Commons. And George preferred Lord Halifax as his successor, not least because his rival for the post, Winston Churchill, had supported Edward during the abdication crisis. Halifax had seen Hitler as another Gandhi and had proved about as capable of standing up to the Führer as Little Lord Fauntleroy would have been capable (to paraphrase Duff Cooper) of standing up to Al Capone. Even now the 'Holy Fox', as Churchill nicknamed him, wanted to make overtures to Nazi Germany. Probably this further endeared the spindle-shanked aristocrat to the King, who was himself initially 'a little défaitiste'.[7] He stood somewhere between his staunch wife and his compromising mother. Queen Mary was such 'an enthusiastic member of the compromise peace party' that a 'very angry' Churchill 'tried to stop people seeing her'.[8] She retaliated by attempting to prevent Chamberlain's secretary, Jock Colville, from transferring his services to Churchill.

In the event, of course, Churchill swept into office and swept all before him. The new Premier turned up late to audiences or cancelled them altogether. He did not keep the King fully informed and insisted on the appointment of adventurers such as Lord Beaverbrook, who did not find favour with the monarch. Churchill usurped the King's position as confidential correspondent of Roosevelt, who once simply failed to answer a royal letter. King George's instinct was to put his trust in princes and not politicians – even princes like Paul of Yugoslavia, whom Churchill aptly nicknamed 'Palsy'. The Prime Minister made inspiring speeches and he, not the sovereign, became the embodiment of Britain's fighting spirit. However, although tensions remained between the Palace and 10 Downing Street, Churchill proved personally as well as politically irresistible. At their informal Tuesday luncheons, where they would serve each other from a buffet sideboard, King and Premier held long private conversations. As a royalist, a Conservative and a patriot, Churchill naturally appealed to King George. He also charmed the King: at Christmas 1940 he sent his sovereign a siren suit.

Like Churchill, George VI habitually wore uniform during the war. But having a warrior premier, he had little scope to be a warrior king. Accordingly he developed a new role for himself – king of morale, binding up the nation's wounds. He and the Queen suffered with their subjects and comforted them in the midst of destruction and death. They visited bombed houses and were proud when Buckingham Palace itself was hit – though the King was severely shaken by the experience and privately suspected that the attack was part of a German plot to kill him and put his elder brother on the throne. Actually the bombing of the Palace gave the Ministry of Information a great propaganda opportunity: it sent forty journalists to cover the event, and their reports played variations on the theme of the 'King with his people in the front line'. The story made headlines all over the free world, provoked indignation in the United States and 'immediately dissipated bad feeling' in the rubble-strewn slums of London. As Queen Elizabeth famously remarked, 'Now we can look the East End in the face.'

That comment reveals the difficulty which the monarchy confronted during wartime. Previously it had been the focus of national celebrations – now, however, the King and Queen were associated not with a reign that was happy and glorious but with a rain of terror from the skies. Instead of appearing in a gold coach surrounded by cheering crowds, the royal couple were pictured against a backcloth of ruins and misery. Indeed, they were 'always shown the people who had the worst tragedies happen to them'.[9] And their subjects typically remarked that 'Kings and Queens don't make much difference when it comes to wars.'[10] According to the Ministry of Information, the press and the wireless, they were greeted with massive demonstrations of loyalty in bombed areas. But the truth, as revealed by the (admittedly unsophisticated) Mass Observation surveys, was that their reception was muted.

Some victims of the Luftwaffe considered it good of the King and Queen 'to think of us'. Others criticized royal tours of the blitzed districts: there 'wasn't time' for this sort of 'fuss' when clearing up had to be done.[11] It was all very well for the King to speak of the 'honourable scars' of Buckingham Palace when he had other homes to go to, as well as warm fires and good food. Even the Duke of Kent's death in 1942 in a flying accident while on active service did not provoke much sorrow among those who had formerly admired his film-star looks. 'There's hundreds of others dying the same way every day,' said one interviewee, 'and nobody shares the grief of their wives and families, and at least the state will look after the Duchess and her children handsomely whereas these poor devils have to bring up their children as best they can.'[12] But the Duke's death probably did more for the royal family's popularity than any other event between 1939 and 1945: what mattered in a people's war was equality of sacrifice.

King George thus made every effort to show that the royal family was sharing wartime privations to the full. The shattered windows of Buckingham Palace were not replaced with glass. Royal ration books were the order of the day. Lighting and heating were restricted at Crown residences. A line was drawn round baths to indicate that only five inches of water could be used. The King publicized his Pig Club, and the Windsor greys were photographed working for their keep. The Queen stripped Windsor of surplus furniture and had it distributed to bomb victims. The Princesses knitted gloves and collected tinfoil. George VI's entire reign could be summed up, according to A. J. P. Taylor, by meals of spam served on gold plates.

This was a potent image of a democratic monarch; but to some extent it was a false image. There is plenty of evidence that the royal diet was supplemented from royal farms, estates and other sources. At a Buckingham Palace luncheon Joseph Kennedy, the American ambassador, was offered the choice of hare or pheasant. Lord Reith was served a dinner of soup, ham mousse and chicken, strawberry ice and strawberries and cream. Margarine was widely used in the household but only butter, the pats monogrammed with crowns, appeared on the monarch's table. Enormous supplies of tinned food had been accumulated at Buckingham Palace and Windsor but these were 'reasonable precautions', as the Comptroller of Supply ingenuously recorded, and there was 'no question of hoarding'.[13] In the national interest Churchill exempted himself from rationing, and it is clear that food coupons played equally little part in the life of the royal family.

Similarly, since the Queen had to make a good impression, her adherence to 'austerity dressing' was purely nominal. Like other members of her family, she received 1,277 clothing coupons a year in excess of the ordinary ration, which fell from 66 to 48 as the war progressed. The Queen tried to avoid ostentation and forbade extravagant embroidery, but Norman Hartnell was allowed certain indulgences. For example, he painted by hand 'garlands of wax-like lilac and glossy green leaves on a gown of white satin, with which Her Majesty wore ornaments of diamonds and rubies'.[14] Dressing the part during the war was a delicate art, and the Queen evidently mastered it in order to comfort the afflicted. Thanks to the King's influence in high places the royal family was also able to avoid wartime trials that afflicted the comfortable. When Lord Halifax became British ambassador in Washington, King George wrote asking him to despatch regular supplies of Bronco soft lavatory paper which 'is unprocurable here'.[15] They were presumably sent in the diplomatic bag.

Much was made of the King's determination to go down fighting if need be – he and his wife practised shooting in the grounds of Buckingham Palace. Still more was made of the Queen's refusal to desert him or to evacuate the Princesses to Canada. However, the capitulation of King Leopold of the Belgians damaged the standing of monarchy in general and warned of the fate which would overtake a crowned head in the hands of a dictator. King George sympathised with the much-vilified Leopold and rejected proposals to strike him off the roll of Knights of the Garter, but also felt that Leopold 'should have left the country and established his government elsewhere'.[16] Clandestine contingency plans made for King George to do so included the provision of 'safe houses' *en route* to the port of Liverpool.[17] Queen Mary, who spent the war at Badminton in Gloucestershire with sixty-three servants, was terrified of being kidnapped by Nazi parachutists. Determined 'to take one with me', she secreted a small pearl-handled revolver in her parasol.[18] In readiness to escape the invasion she also kept four suitcases packed, one crammed with jewels.

Meanwhile King George, Queen Elizabeth and their children spent their days at Buckingham Palace, avoiding the night-time raids by travelling down to Windsor Castle each evening in an armoured car. At least, this was the intention; but the Queen filled the armoured vehicle with so many personal possessions that the family often had to resort to the Daimler. Even so, the King told the Canadian Prime Minister that he found the bombing a considerable 'strain' and that they all 'slept in a shelter each night'.[19] The royal security measures were kept secret even from their own subjects, who might not realize that the preservation of a national symbol involved the special treatment of a privileged family. That the symbol was still immensely potent is illustrated by Enoch Powell, who agreed on a suicide pact with a brother officer: they would shoot themselves with their service revolvers if the King surrendered.

Everyone took heart from the fact that, as a popular song had it, 'The King is still in London'. But George VI himself was increasingly frustrated by his emblematic role. His efforts to exert influence on important policies were thwarted – though he did persuade Churchill not to accompany the D-Day invasion in 1944 by threatening to come himself. George even found it hard to impose his will on small matters such as uniforms and medals – though these were large matters to him. The King's one major tour of the war, to French North Africa in 1943, was spoilt by 'desert tummy'. He did, it is true, establish a good rapport with Dwight D. Eisenhower, though the General was irreverent behind his back, joking about whether to address the monarch in a cable as 'Dear Kingie, Dear Georgie, or Dear Rex'.[20] The King also made a favourable impression on the troops, who greeted him with 'tumultuous' acclaim. But he found it impossible to empathise with them in the electric fashion of, say, General Montgomery or Admiral Mountbatten.

One of King George's problems was that Alec Hardinge, his private secretary, hampered his efforts to be democratic.

According to Harold Macmillan, Hardinge was 'idle, supercilious, without a spark of imagination or vitality'.[21] Queen Elizabeth was largely responsible for Hardinge's replacement, a month after their return from Africa, by Alan Lascelles, who proved almost equally conservative but rather more flexible. One of Hardinge's supporters, Oliver Harvey, commented: 'The King is fundamentally a weak character and certainly a stupid one. The Queen is a strong one out of a rather reactionary stable.'[22] In fact Hardinge's dismissal resulted in the introduction of fresh blood into the royal household. Instead of drawing his courtiers exclusively from aristocratic regiments, the King appointed a handful of officers from the fighting services. One new recruit was Group Captain Peter Townsend, who had flown Hurricanes in the Battle of Britain. He too was nervy and had a speech impediment – he once announced Sir Oliver Harvey as 'Sir Oliver Hardy, Your Majesty.' The King took to Townsend at once and he helped to make court life less stiff and formal, at least behind the scenes. It was Townsend who accompanied Princesses Elizabeth and Margaret into the rejoicing crowds around Buckingham Palace on 8 May 1945, Victory in Europe Day. Their existence had been so cloistered that the adventure would have been 'unthinkable' only a few years before,[23] but now they went incognito and unrecognized into the exultant throng – a rare venture into anonymity – and joined in the loud cheers for their parents. They must, however, have noticed that the day belonged to the Prime Minister. As one witness reported, when Churchill appeared the public mood turned from enthusiasm to ecstasy and 'there was a deep, full-throated, almost reverential roar'.[24]

Nevertheless, the electors did not choose Churchill to carry out the social reforms which they saw as their just reward for wartime sacrifices. So the royal family were left alone to bask in the glow of victory. Memories of a heroic monarchy at one with the people in their hour of need grew fonder as they grew fainter. Indeed, this chapter in what Churchill called 'our island story' took on the status of a legend. By contrast the Duke of Windsor had faded into the background, by the time he resigned from the governorship of the Bahamas in March 1945. 'Queer to think he was once King of England,' remarked one contemporary, 'and now nothing, and nobody cares.' Some did care, though, against all the odds. In fact recollections of the Duke as a socially concerned King were still strong enough to cause unease at Buckingham Palace. 'He made mistakes, but he had a good 'eart,' went one verdict. Other judgements were hostile, reflecting on the Duke's playboy propensities, his idleness, his selfishness. One man called the Duke of Windsor a 'scoundrel'.[25] Worse epithets have since been flung at him, and the rumour has grown that during the first year of the war the pro-German Duke might actually have been a traitor.

The suspicion of perfidy was strengthened by the British government's attempt to suppress captured German documents relating to the Duke and by conspiracy theories about the art historian and spy Anthony Blunt. After the war he was allegedly despatched to Germany to retrieve 'the Windsor file', which implicated the Duke in treachery against his homeland. Later, when Blunt's own betrayal of his country was exposed, he supposedly bought his immunity from prosecution with silence about the royal matter. Such charges, during the 1980s, made uncomfortable reading for the present royal family, who did not want the Duke resurrected as a quisling king. Doubtless this was one reason why Philip Ziegler was given access to the Royal Archives to write the Duke's official biography; he has done his best to explode unsubstantiated accusations and to rehabilitate the Duke.

Perhaps his conclusions are rather too favourable. True, the Duke of Windsor was by no means alone in advocating a negotiated peace in 1940. Not only did his mother agree with him, but Lord Beaverbrook suggested that he should campaign for it in Britain – Edward was only deterred by the prospect of having to pay UK income tax. But the Duke went further than other guilty men and constantly played into German hands. When appointed during the 'Phoney War' to a liaison job in France, with the rank of major-general, his garbled gossip about Allied war plans reached the ears of the German envoy in The Hague. Having fled across the Pyrenees after Hitler's invasion of France, the Duke negotiated with the enemy, through a Spanish intermediary, about retrieving possessions he had left behind. Intelligence reports reaching Buckingham Palace revealed the Duke's contacts and the implication seemed plain: the Duchess wanted to become Queen at any price. Ribbentrop, too, thought that the Windsors might be used in such a capacity and wove a fantastic plot to kidnap them. Nothing came of this, but *en route* to take up his post as Governor of the Bahamas, in August 1940, the Duke caused outrage by saying, 'Of course, if I'd been King there'd have been no war.'[26] Subsequently the Duke vexed Churchill by his defeatist statements and his unsavoury associations with such characters as Axel Wenner-Gren, 'a violently pro-Nazi Swede'.[27] More than two decades later, long after the full horrors of Nazism had been revealed, the Duke told Lord Kinross: 'I never thought Hitler was such a bad chap.'[28]

All this is impossible to excuse. Yet Ziegler is probably right to maintain that the Duke's conduct, though 'heinous', did not amount to treason. Edward may well have dreamed of returning to the throne. But the suggestion that he would have accepted it as 'a gift from a victorious German government completely ignores the enormous patriotism which was one of his driving forces'.[29] Foolish, naive, petulant, egotistical and rash the Duke undoubtedly was; but there is, as yet, no solid evidence that he consciously acted against the interests of Britain. Indeed, his behaviour is to be explained in personal, rather than in political, terms – it was essentially a by-product of his overpowering infatuation with Wallis. His prosecution of the family feud stemmed from the fact that they had slighted her. His disgraceful haggling about the terms on which he would take up his post in the Bahamas, at a time when England was in mortal peril, was an attempt to maintain her dignity. His attempt to visit the United States before even embarking on his job was a sop to Wallis; and he would not offend her Southern susceptibilities by receiving blacks. He severed relations with his brother and vilified Queen Elizabeth, whom he blamed for the official instructions which forbade curtseying to the Duchess. To Lord Halifax in 1941 the Duke poured out 'a story of grievances – bitter, bitter family grievances and other things never to be forgotten or forgiven.

And then a thousand petty things not worth recording but all the stories of an injured soul.' Some of his complaints were justified, Halifax considered. His secretary, Charles Peake, agreed: 'It is a pity that the Royal Family cannot behave with common decency to him. Distance, frigidity one expects, and is no more than he deserved. But civility (which costs nothing) might certainly be given and if given would deprive him of one well merited grievance.'[30]

There were even members of the royal family who endorsed this view. Lord Harewood, for example, accepted that the Duke had been condemned for putting private life before public duty; but he also felt that the King and Queen were denying Christian virtues such as forgiveness and family affection. However the dominant Queens, Mary and Elizabeth, supported by Puritan courtiers like Alan Lascelles, grimly insisted that the monarchy's image could only remain samite white if the Windsors were sentenced to perpetual boycott and banishment. Churchill did allow them occasional visits to the USA, but the lavish state in which they travelled offended an America now embroiled in the war. So for the most part the Duke fretted away at what the Duchess called 'a double-zero job' in a 'lousy' Caribbean 'dump'.

The Duke resigned as soon as he decently could, shortly before the end of the war, and returned to Europe. He achieved a formal reconciliation with King George and hoped to obtain some kind of ambassadorial role in the United States – one which would give him an official position, with peripatetic duties that were not too onerous and tax-free status. The last particularly preoccupied Wallis, whose obsession with money had helped to turn Edward into a royal Scrooge. When his diplomatic aspirations were dashed – the Duke was too much of an anomaly to fit in anywhere – he plumped for France, a republic peculiarly indulgent towards an ex-king.

Wallis set out to create a Parisian court which would outshine that of London, a Grand Trianon to rival Buckingham Palace. Her domestic arrangements were, indeed, of such sybaritic splendour that even the jaded cosmopolitan plutocrats who made up their social circle were amazed. 'Every detail was perfect,' says one guest,[31] and everything was the best – gilt antique furniture and crystal chandeliers, jewelled *bibelots* and tiger-skin sofas, Meissen figurines and Aubusson carpets. Outstanding chefs produced 'the finest food in the world',[32] and host and hostess were models of elegance and good manners – the Duke always stood at the door until departing guests were out of sight. But the atmosphere enveloping the Windsors was tragic.

At best there was frenetic gaiety over canasta and jigsaw puzzles, cocktails and gossip, sword dances and songs from popular musicals such as *Oklahoma*, with the Duke tinkling on the piano. Dressing-up was the most popular after-dinner recreation – once Wallis made the Duke don a tutu and a blonde wig and told him to dance *Swan Lake*. At worst there were tearful scenes, diatribes against Communists and Jews, a litany of discontent during which, as Kenneth de Courcy says, Wallis 'steamed [the Duke] up to extreme aggravation with his family'. Above all there was a corroding sense of futility. Often the Duke had nothing to do but walk the dogs. The Duchess tried to impose some purpose on their idle existence in the familiar manner of the rich, moving from place to place in the hope of getting somewhere. She organized her husband's journeys with military precision. Every hotel bedroom would contain his prized Persian rugs, favourite photographs, monogrammed sheets. In the dining rooms he had special food and was waited on by his own liveried servants. Yet there was a pervading sense of pointlessness about the Duke's round. He might vary golfing, gardening and entertaining with going on holiday but, as Lady Pamela Hicks (Lord Mountbatten's daughter) says, what did that mean? 'Life was one big holiday, but a boring holiday.'

Life in Britain meanwhile, during the austerity years after the war, was taking its toll on the Duke's brother Bertie. The King, liking a socialist government no better than his parents did, was shocked by the voters' ungrateful rejection of Churchill; passing a polling station in 1945 Queen Mary asked the Tory candidate, 'How are we doing?'[33] Now, for the first time, the monarchy was faced by a Labour Party, led by Clement Attlee, with a majority in the House of Commons. That the King had never warmed to Attlee was not surprising:

they were poles apart politically. At the beginning of the war the King had criticized him in one royal audience, from which Attlee apparently emerged looking chastened, for his failure to support Chamberlain. But personally, too, the stammering King and the taciturn Premier were incompatible. George complained that at their meetings Attlee 'never talked at all', and he referred to him privately as 'Clem the Clam'.[34]

But in practice Attlee proved almost as indulgent towards his sovereign as Ramsay MacDonald had been. The Prime Minister agreed to take the Order of the Garter out of politics and place its gift in the hands of the King, who redesigned the ancient ceremony of investiture along modern lines. At King George's behest Attlee appointed Ernest Bevin Foreign Secretary instead of Hugh Dalton, who was the 'anarchist son' of Canon Dalton, George V's tutor – evidently the royal family never forgave him for being a class traitor. The hostility was mutual: Dalton considered George VI to be about as inanimate as an animate monarch could be, and he noted waspishly that the proposals in his first budget which most interested the King were those concerned with raising surtax.[35] Attlee, though, defended expenditure on royalty even when the rest of the country was tightening its belt. He secured a vote in the Commons for money to refurbish Clarence House and to support the new establishment of Princess Elizabeth. It was quite a mistake to imagine that the royal family lived luxurious and easy lives, the Prime Minister maintained; its members were approachable people, working hard and living simply. About a third of the public were unconvinced, especially when the King, Queen and Princesses went on a tour of South Africa during the desperately hard winter of early 1947. In such circumstances George found it difficult to be a 'People's King', to strike that delicate balance between 'close identification' with, and 'mystical aloofness' from, his subjects.[36] By contrast, Attlee found it so easy to be a royalist Premier that in 1951 he even timed the general election with an eye to the Crown's convenience.

Other Labour ministers were less partial. Sir Stafford Cripps dismissed royal pageantry as 'all bunk and bunting'.[37] Hugh Gaitskell found the King and Queen awkward and unnatural: both were 'extremely conservative' and assumed that socialism meant the end of the world as they knew it. When King George met the Labour minister Lord Stansgate, Tony Benn's father, he asked plaintively: 'What bits of my empire have you given away today?'[38] Chips Channon, an astute observer of high life, concluded that the King had not concealed 'very skilfully his dislike of the Socialists for all the ones who had been in waiting are vitriolic about him. But no one hated him – he was too neutral; hence he was a successful and even popular sovereign.'[39]

As all this suggests, the King could never be reconciled to his new ministers or to their policies. He did everything possible to slow down the introduction of state control of industry. He had grave doubts about the welfare state and could not understand why people needed free teeth. He disliked trade union power and feared the advent of egalitarian republicanism. Most of all he deplored the collapse of empire and the loss of the jewel in Britain's imperial crown. The King had always taken a hard line on India, advocating the imprisonment of nationalists like Gandhi. But now he apparently favoured the appointment of his flamboyant cousin Admiral Lord Mountbatten as last Viceroy. Mountbatten, who felt that he might damage his own and his family's reputation by failure, expressed reluctance to assume the task. But the King urged him to do so, saying that if he succeeded it would redound to the credit of the royal family. Also, he knew that Mountbatten would do his best to 'see fair play for the [Indian] Princes'.[40]

However, when India did become independent the King – no longer an Emperor – 'minded frightfully' about changing his signature from GRI to GR.[41] Yet he did adapt quite easily to his new position as Head of the British Commonwealth. This was another invention, a wholly factitious office, but it gave a new and 'important dimension' to the Crown.[42] As the Empire contracted physically the monarchy expanded morally, much as the Papacy had done after the loss of its secular power in 1870. The monarch became head of a voluntary, multi-racial organization of some fifty countries, many of them republics. Perhaps the Commonwealth was shadow rather than substance. Maybe it was eventually doomed to extinction. But in the short term it filled the vacuum left by the Empire. It also enhanced the sovereign's prestige, giving him a world importance comparable to that of an international spiritual leader.

Accommodating the monarchy to changes that were more or less unpalatable imposed almost unbearable strains on the monarch himself. 'How I hate being King!' he once exclaimed. 'Sometimes at ceremonies I want to stand up and scream and scream.'[43] His rages, or 'gnashes', grew worse. Sitting next to him at dinner could be 'absolutely terrifying': he would suddenly get 'extremely annoyed about some quite trivial thing and there would be a violent explosion'.[44] Crowds and open spaces particularly unnerved the King, and the South African tour provided both. As he drove through an excited black throng an African burst through the cordon and gripped the hood of the King's open car. Standing by to repel boarders, the Queen bashed his hands with her parasol and he was eventually overpowered by police – his intention had been to give Princess Elizabeth ten shillings for her birthday. The incident so rattled the King that he started shouting orders at the chauffeur. Fearing an accident, Peter Townsend, in the front seat, turned round and told the King to shut up. Like the Queen, Townsend had learned the knack of suppressing the King's tantrums. According to Alastair Forbes, the equerry once 'had to hit him with his swagger stick to stop him going over the top'.

In personal terms, succeeding to the Crown as he did proved a catastrophe for King George. It took him away from the only life in which he felt happy – country life and family life. 'He loved nature, he loved walking, he loved sport,' says Peter Townsend. Like his father and mother respectively, he enjoyed shooting and 'wooding' – cutting back undergrowth. He adored his wife and children, relishing domestic entertainment. The King's sense of humour did not rise much above apple-pie beds and the radio comedy *ITMA*, though he did solicit smoking-room stories from Tommy Trinder. He danced with enthusiasm, favouring the hokey-cokey and the boogie-woogie, and sometimes leading the conga through the half-lit corridors of Buckingham Palace. After one post-war dinner at Windsor a group of dignitaries including Anthony Eden, Sir Stafford Cripps and General 'Pug' Ismay allowed themselves to be equipped with shovels and brass pokers from the fireplace, mustered into a squad and marched past the King and Queen in slow time down the length of the drawing room. But guests tended to exhaust the monarch, who had few intimate friends. As the 1940s progressed he suffered physical illness – arteriosclerosis brought on by cigarette smoking – as well as psychological stress. The King preferred to follow his outdoor pursuits alone or in small parties; and he liked gatherings of his immediate family – 'us four', as he called them – at home. 'We are the royal family,' the King wrote in his diary, 'and we must stick together.'[45]

They had always been a tightly knit unit despite the inevitable separations caused by royal duties. Princess Elizabeth, born in 1926, and Princess Margaret Rose, who appeared four years later, had led 'extraordinarily sheltered' lives.[46] They seldom met anyone outside the charmed circle, and their education was quintessentially royal. Queen Mary insisted that their governess should teach them 'all about the royal families of Europe, and the dates of all the kings and queens, when they were quite small, because she thought this was the most interesting thing of all'.[47] But despite the ministrations of the headmaster of Eton and the substitution of American history for German lessons in 1940, neither she nor her sister received an academic education – now apparently a source of regret to her. Their mother though it was more important to 'spend as long as possible in the open air, to enjoy to the full the pleasures of the country, to be able to dance and draw and appreciate music, to acquire good manners and perfect deportment, and to cultivate all the distinctively feminine graces'.[48]

This was the debutante training of the day, and the two Princesses had some contact with girls of that background. They attended dancing classes, staged amateur theatricals and enrolled in the Guides – the First Buckingham Palace Company; Elizabeth won 'many more badges than anyone else . . . because of her hard work and dedication to what she was doing'.[49] During the war Princess Elizabeth also joined the women's regular army, the Auxiliary Territorial Service

(ATS). This was a great propaganda coup. One East Ender remembers pictures of 'the present Queen as a young girl in an ATS uniform and a pair of dirty old dungarees underneath a car, getting it cleaned and straight, [which] had to be seen to be believed. But it became [plain] that she was one of us and that's how they were built up.'[50] Courtiers maintain that 'joining the ATS was a tremendous help to her because she did see how other people lived'.[51] Queen Elizabeth II, who set much store by her military experience, agrees: 'One had no idea how one compared with other people.'[52] But the comparisons were not quite what they seemed. Before the Princess arrived at Camberley the previous batch of trainees had had their own course cut short so that they could polish and whitewash everything in sight. And other 'new recruits' whom the Princess met were actually instructors in disguise.[53]

How did such careful nurture affect the nature of the two Princesses? According to those who know them, the standard answer is the correct one. Elizabeth was dutiful, conscientious, reserved, with a 'passion for tidiness'[54] and good order that bordered on the neurotic. Notwithstanding her favourite quotation – 'moderation in all things' – she had her father's fierce temper. Despite her precocious gravity, she had her mother's sense of humour. Like her mother, too, Princess Elizabeth had a steely will. Lord Airlie possesses a photograph of her as a curly-haired girl behind the wheel of a scarlet toy car that was his prized possession as a boy: the picture's significance lies in the fact that he had been determined to prevent her from riding in it but that she had got her own way. Lord Mountbatten was similarly thwarted when he taught her to ride: despite his most earnest pleas she refused to use a side-saddle except on state occasions. By contrast, Princess Margaret was wilful in the manner of her uncle, the Duke of Windsor. 'Warm and demonstrative', she was her father's 'plaything'.[55] She was 'fun-loving' and 'espiègle', says Veronica Maclean, 'more brilliant' than her sister – but less reliable. Margaret had a talent for music and mimicry; in fact she possessed 'great natural gifts' for amusing and entertaining which might have made her a 'huge success' on the stage. At the same time she could be difficult and temperamental, as sulky out of the limelight as she was bouncy in it. The ailing King, who did not want Margaret to grow up (he kept both his daughters in short skirts for as long as possible), was partly to blame. 'He spoilt her rotten,' says a member of the household at that time. 'He knew she wasn't going to be head girl.'[56]

Elizabeth, to her parents' distress, decided from early adolescence whom she wanted as her head boy. He was, of course, Prince Philip, son of Prince Andrew of Greece and Princess Alice of Battenberg. Philip had been born in Corfu in 1921 and, after his parents' separation in 1930, spent a frugal, peripatetic childhood. Often he stayed in the palaces of other European descendants of Queen Victoria. Sometimes he wore hand-me-down clothes provided by his uncle, Lord Mountbatten, who eventually more or less adopted him. Philip went to school at the spartan academy of Gordonstoun, which was first located at his sister's castle in Germany and then moved to Scotland when its Jewish founder, Kurt Hahn, faced persecution from Hitler. Afterwards Philip became a cadet at Dartmouth and served with distinction in the Royal Navy during the war. His Viking good looks and air of derring-do captivated Princess Elizabeth. Mountbatten, whose dynastic and other ambitions King George somewhat resented, 'did all he could to encourage' the relationship.[57] But Philip was at first thought unsuitable, despite sharing many of King George's tastes and views. Having been a 'naughty' and 'headstrong' youth,[58] Philip now seemed a rough, licentious sailor. Moreover he had a host of disreputable German relations, some of whom had been involved with the Nazis.

Once again, in the aftermath of another war, the House of Windsor was threatened with Teutonic contamination. Privately, royal family solidarity was manifested in curious ways. For example, Princess Alice of Athlone made sterling efforts after the war to help her imprisoned Brownshirt uncle, Duke Charles of Saxe-Coburg-Gotha: she and her husband 'humiliated ourselves' by lunching with the US Governor of Coburg, 'a Jewish-French American whom we did not think a suitable representative of his great country nor the sort of person one would select to instruct the Germans in democracy!'[59] King George VI solved his public German problem by the familiar expedients of delay, alias and ostracism. His daughter's betrothal was postponed until she was twenty-one and had completed the South African tour *en famille*. Philip, whose family name was Schleswig-Holstein-Sonderburg-Glücksburg, adopted his uncle's name of Mountbatten and became a naturalized Englishman. And his sisters, all of whom had married German princelings, were not invited to the wedding; nor were other relations who might tarnish the bright new royal image. Also excluded, to his surprise and chagrin, was the Duke of Windsor. He had once more caused the King intense anguish, this time by agreeing to publish the story of his early life. Being barred from his niece's wedding finally convinced the Duke that he was a perpetual outcast, and the brothers' relationship deteriorated accordingly.

The wedding, which took place at Westminster Abbey on 21 November 1947, was an uneasy compromise between grandeur and austerity. Fearing adverse publicity, the Palace scaled down its initial request for extra clothing coupons. Nevertheless there was criticism of Princess Elizabeth's elaborate trousseau from brides who could not be married in an ivory satin dress designed by Norman Hartnell, embroidered with flowers and embellished with diamonds, pearls and crystals. The wedding itself provided a brilliant splash of pageantry at a time when post-war shortages were at their most acute. An American journal wrote: 'The glamour of it all, in the midst of Britain's drab existence nowadays, has jerked millions out of their one-candlepower lives and tossed them into dreamland.'[60]

As the couple went off to the Mountbattens' stately home, Broadlands, for their honeymoon there seemed to be no reason why the royal family should not live happily ever after. Although Princess Elizabeth had reduced his domestic quartet to a trio, the King was reconciled to his new son-in-law, whom he had just created Prince Philip, Duke of Edinburgh. Now George looked forward to the satisfactions of grandparenthood. Assisted by the Queen, he himself had weathered the storms of abdication and war. As post-war economic recovery eased social tensions, he hoped to consolidate the position of his popular but ceremonial monarchy. And, although Margaret was something of a worry, he had complete faith in his elder daughter: she had dedicated herself to the service of the Commonwealth in a ringingly sincere twenty-first birthday broadcast from South Africa, and would carry on his work impeccably when the time came. But, surely, she had years to spend on motherhood as well as on her royal apprenticeship.

However, in the next few years the King's health deteriorated rapidly. He had two major operations, – the second one, in 1951, for the removal of a cancerous lung. George resisted becoming an invalid. So that he could continue with his outdoor pursuits he had special equipment designed, including a battery-powered, electrically heated waistcoat and fur gloves. Wearing them on the last day of his life, he went out shooting hares at Sandringham – his own happy hunting ground. That night, on 6 February 1952, the King died in his sleep.

7

THE IMAGE OF A QUEEN

Princess Elizabeth had pledged her destiny to country and Commonwealth under African skies. When she next saw them, in 1952, they must have seemed the clearest she had known for many months. The worries of the past year had closed in on her and her young family. As the King's health had worsened she and her husband had been pressed into more engagements. Throughout 1951 the shadow on the King's lung had darkened the political scene long before his nervous doctors finally ordered the excision of the cancer. After the surgery the King seemed to rally, but he could not undertake arduous journeys, so his daughter and her husband replaced him on the long trip to East Africa, Australia and New Zealand planned for 1952.

The royal couple arrived in Kenya on the first leg of their journey, and spent the night of 5–6 February at Treetops, built into a massive fig tree as an observation platform for big game. The Princess woke early on 6 February, to continue her photography. Far away in Sandringham her father would not wake at all.

A footman found George VI dead in bed that morning, and in London the private secretaries scattered to tell their elders. Edward Ford hastened to Queen Mary, and Lady Cynthia Colville told the stoical old dowager that the third of her sons was dead. Lady Cynthia's own son, John Colville, found Churchill, now Prime Minister once more, still in bed and in tears. Colville ventured that he would get on well with the new monarch. 'All he could say was that he did not know her and that she was a child.'[1] Child or no, she was now Queen, and the news reached her late. Alan Lascelles had devised a series of fatuous code words for royal eventualities. 'Hyde Park Corner' was the code for the death of George VI.[2] A telegram bearing these words was sent to Kenya but never arrived; it was a radio report which alerted the private secretary, Martin Charteris. He telephoned the Duke's own secretary, Mike Parker, at Sagana Lodge, to which the royal couple had now returned. Parker desperately tried to pick up the BBC on his radio for confirmation. 'When I heard bells ringing I waited and waited with my fingers right through the floor until I heard the distant voice of John Snagge. So I woke the Duke and told him, and it was his job to tell the Queen that her father was dead. Probably the worst moment of his life.'[3]

This couple, whose lives were now changed utterly, behaved in very different ways. When Charteris arrived he found the new Queen composed, 'seated at her desk, very upright, high colour, no sign of tears', ready to dictate telegrams to the Commonwealth countries she was to have visited. The Duke was shattered. His wife's career was beginning; his had ended. Charteris recollects: 'After all, she was going to be Queen. That was her destiny. But for him it was a change he didn't particularly want. . . . He was rather holding himself back. He had the *Times* up in front of his face, like a shield'.

As Elizabeth II drove away from Sagana the press photographers lined the route with their cameras hanging limply, in passive respect. So the first powerful icon of the new reign was the young Queen, in black, descending alone from her aircraft to meet the aged Churchill, his ministers and her uncle Gloucester. She had hesitated to don mourning until the last moment and, seeing the black limousines on the tarmac, had exclaimed to Pamela Hicks, 'Oh God, they've sent the hearses.'[4] The royal matriarchy closed ranks around her: the grandmother; the mother, widowed at fifty-one; and the sister – George VI was buried with the honours and affection due to the war leader he would have liked to be. His older brother came over for the funeral, looking jaunty, some thought. The Duchess was not invited to the ceremony, and the Duke himself, after a bleak meeting with the unforgiving Queen Mother, was not even invited to the funeral dinner at the Palace.

Churchill persuaded the Queen Mother to stay in public life, with her own lavish establishment. According to Colville he even dangled the Governor-Generalship of Australia before her.[5] The widow grieved sincerely, but it was not difficult to induce her to soldier on. On 17 February she issued a statement that she wished 'to continue the work we sought to do together' and moved into Clarence House; she is there still. The Queen and her now thoroughly unsettled consort changed places with her and moved into Buckingham Palace. Philip put the case for keeping it as offices only, but got a testy reply from Churchill: the monarch must live over the shop. And the shop assistants were unchanged. The Palace staff, from Lascelles downwards, were kept on.

There was soon a further snub to Philip. His uncle, Mountbatten, had unwisely boasted that the Mountbattens were now on the throne. One of the guests at his table was the head of the Hanoverian family in the male line, Prince Ernest Augustus. The Hanoverians might have lost their Cumberland dukedom in 1917 but they knew they had a friend at court in Queen Mary, great-granddaughter of George III and upholder of what she called 'the old royal family'. Queen Mary sent for John Colville to protest at this takeover by the upstart Battenbergs. 'She begged me to inform the Prime Minister at once that when King George V had chosen the name of Windsor for the royal house he intended it to be in perpetuity. . . . I went back to Downing Street and told Winston Churchill, who was indignant.'[6]

A strongly, but ably, worded memorandum from Philip himself failed to sway the Cabinet, and on 9 April a royal proclamation declared that the Queen's descendants would continue to bear the Windsor name. 'I'm just a bloody amoeba,' Philip raged, and bided his time. In fact he sprang from the most fecund line of royal amoebas in all Europe – not the Mountbattens from whom he took his surname of convenience, but the Danish Glücksburgs, his father's family. They had provided Danish kings in unbroken male line for a dozen generations and went back to Gorm the Old a thousand years before. But his own life had always been spent in transit, as a desirable alien in British service. Now the promising naval career which his contacts and abilities would have guaranteed had vanished. He had lost Clarence House, which he had had renovated at vast expense, to the mother-in-law whose influence was all-pervasive. Worst of all, wizened courtiers like Lascelles shut him out from decisions. Crusted old operators, which was how Philip saw them, had a myriad ways of keeping this upstart in his place. He was not the male equivalent of a Queen Consort, sharing the throne. He resented this bitterly and did not conceal his resentment. Old courtiers speak of the high level of passion which he injected into arguments with them.[7] He was, indeed, so violent that they were reluctant to raise contentious matters with him unless they were of great moment. But this simply reinforced Philip's sense of his own unimportance. 'If you have a king and queen,' he told Basil Boothroyd, 'there are certain things people automatically go to the queen about. But if the queen is also the Queen they go to her about everything.'[8]

As consort but not the Consort, Philip sometimes tried to assert himself in public, trampling on ancient British sensitivities in the process. On 26 February 1952 he watched a stormy debate in the Commons from the Peers' Gallery. His presence and behaviour were noted by many MPs, and a stern missive went to Churchill from a Tory backbencher whom he had not previously encountered. As recently released papers in the Public Record Office reveal, J. Enoch Powell told the Prime Minister that 'H.R.H. should not again avail himself of our debates'. The only previous attendance by a consort had been when Prince Albert watched the Corn Laws debate in 1846, to audible protests from Bentinck and Disraeli. Churchill's private secretary, John Colville, enquired of the Chief Whip what the reaction had been. Had the Prince been impassive? Patrick Buchan-Hepburn, the Chief Whip, replied that most Members had not been put out by his visit, but had noted that 'he did not exactly maintain a "poker face" during the Debate, which was, of course, in the first degree party-political.'[9] The Prince, like Albert before him, never set foot in the Commons again.

There was much that Philip could have done to clear away outdated rituals at court, and a few courtiers were sympathetic. The supple Charteris remembers the young Philip with affection, despite his initial sulkiness. The attempted name change had been a bad beginning. It was 'partly due to a suspicion that Admiral Mountbatten might be too keen on interesting the Queen in his own ideas'.[10] But with the Queen Mother so much in evidence, the necessary antibodies to Mountbatten were always available. Only over time was Philip able to gain something of the status that his uncle craved for him, being created a Prince of the United Kingdom in 1957. He never ceased to lobby for the Mountbatten name to be taken up by the royal House. His persuasive powers, and even more those of Mountbatten himself, eventually won the day. By 1960, as R. A. Butler wrote, Queen Elizabeth had 'absolutely set her heart' on the change. She persuaded the government to 'advise' her to make the change, so that ministers would have to accept constitutional responsibility for it. Some were reluctant to do so, including Butler himself, who resented being saddled with this awkward piece of royal business while the Premier, Macmillan, was abroad. But the Queen's wish prevailed and she expressed her 'special gratitude' to the Prime Minister.[11] Just before the birth of their third child, in February 1960, the Queen declared her 'will and pleasure'. She announced that those of her descendants who were neither Royal Highnesses nor Princes and Princesses would carry the surname Mountbatten-Windsor. In fact her younger children pre-empted the change. Princess Anne (in Mountbatten's lifetime) and Prince Andrew signed their marriage registers as Mountbatten-Windsor. The *Daily Mirror*, conjuring with the Queen's German connections, asserted that this 'controversial compromise' would 'NOT be applauded by the British public'.[12] But the amoeba was preserved for posterity.

While her husband chafed the Queen flourished. There was much press hyperbole about a new Elizabethan age. Britain felt free at last of wartime austerity. The two senior statesmen of the Commonwealth, Churchill and Menzies, doted on her. The former who had first been elected in the reign of her great-great-grandmother, no longer thought her a child. She was to remember their sessions as fun, and he brought out her own wit. When he saw her horse beat his into fifth place at Lingfield races he telegraphed his congratulations. She replied by return. 'Most grateful. . . . Sorry you were not in closer attendance.'[13] Menzies was equally charmed. On her post-coronation tour of Australia his adulation verged on the mawkish. At Canberra, quoting the obscure Elizabethan poet Barnabe Googe, he proclaimed:

> I did but see her passing by
> But I will love her till I die.

Elizabeth II's youthful freshness touched most hearts. She had the additional advantage of a government which was generally uncontroversial. The veteran Churchill had no appetite for domestic confrontation. Many of his ministers had personal links with the Queen and her courtiers. James Stuart, Secretary of State for Scotland, had been the first man her mother loved. Stuart, Macmillan and Lord Salisbury were all closely related to the Duchess of Devonshire, who was Mistress of the Robes, while the courtiers Charteris and Colville were linked by marriage or descent to former Conservative chief whips. (Peter Townsend later recalled his shame that his cousin Hugh Gaitskell was a socialist: 'there was not a single socialist – at least above stairs – at Buckingham Palace'.)[14] The natural governing elite, now clustered around its sovereign, provided a congenial base without tempering her formal neutrality. The one incident which could have severely embarrassed her – Churchill's stroke in 1953, when the country was without either a Prime Minister or a Foreign Secretary (because Eden was ill) for some months – was resolved by this tight ruling circle without the press realizing what was afoot. If Churchill had died, the Queen would have found herself calling on a caretaker Prime Minister who was the grandson of Queen Victoria's last Premier – the 5th Marquis of Salisbury. Salisbury would have kept the seat warm for his friend Eden, who was assumed then, and when he eventually took over, to be the natural successor.

In the same secluded manner the royal financial arrangements were sympathetically handled when the Civil List for the new reign was considered in 1952. George VI, as Phillip Hall's painstaking researches have shown,[15] had achieved complete immunity from taxation, since he had won the right to claim back taxes deducted at source. This was described as 'natural' by the Chancellor, R. A. Butler, in the 1952 debate. The royal family received generous annuities, with a built-in allowance for inflation to be used in a discrete fund to make allowances for later inflation. The state also agreed to pick up the bill for staff engaged on maintenance of the royal palaces.

The Queen's grandmother performed a last service by dying without fuss with just enough time for a period of mourning before the coronation. Queen Mary's death was genuinely lamented at that comparatively new part of the royal tradition, the Lying in State. One ghost remained by the bier. The Duke of Windsor, prudently leaving his Duchess to her own devices, came to his mother's funeral. He wrote to his wife, 'What a smug stinking lot my relations are, and you've never seen such a dubious worn-out bunch of old hags as most of them have become.'[16] He was not invited to the lunch afterwards, whereas such seedy figures as Prince Paul of Yugoslavia were – an extraordinary snub.[17] Any illusions that his favourite niece would rehabilitate him were swiftly shattered. Martin Charteris was present at Elizabeth II's encounters with her uncle: 'I think she highly disapproved of the Duchess and in a way she also disapproved of the Duke, because I don't think she's the sort of woman who believes in abdication. It's letting down the side.'[18]

It was conveyed to the Duke that he would not be welcome at the coronation. In one sense everyone else was welcome, thanks to the relatively new medium of television as well as radio. But in another it remained a tribal ritual of the old aristocracy. Every peer was invited, but only a handful of backbench MPs. The master of ceremonies was the 16th Duke of Norfolk, Hereditary Earl Marshal of England. As a young man this Woosterish figure had presided at George V's jubilee and George VI's coronation. When a nervous peer enquired if he would be excluded from the Abbey because he had been divorced, Marmaduke Norfolk snorted: 'Good God man, this isn't Ascot!' By a further paradox Norfolk was a Catholic, organizing a ceremony which, by definition, excluded Papists from its sacrament. Financial assistance came from the elegant Minister of Works, David Eccles, determined not to stint the show, who rashly referred to the Queen as his leading lady.

She was not that, but she was, as never before or since, the star. This was a sacrament of service, to both Church and State. She would be the central figure throughout, either robed and majestic, or in a simple shift as at the anointing. The ancient ritual, reinvented for the twentieth century, could be renewed afresh if the Queen could be seen by her peoples. Advised by her husband and Mountbatten, she had won over the august figures who wanted to exclude television. Churchill was convinced, and when Archbishop Fisher protested against filming the sacramental part of the service, which lasted 13½ minutes, the Premier retorted: 'Just time for an old man like me to retire.'[19] Thus did the young Queen enhance the magic of monarchy.

A whole generation defines its youth by that day: they were warmed up by news of the conquest of Everest; they were enthused by the early morning radio; they drove or bicycled through the grey drizzle to the home of a friend or neighbour who owned a television set. The master of television commentary, Richard Dimbleby, reflected the pageantry, the dignity and the happiness of an occasion which three hundred million people throughout the world watched with curiosity and some admiration. Richard Crossman, journalist and left-wing MP, took himself off to the country but could not resist being a consenting viewer in private.

> I had expected to read a book but in fact I sat looking at the whole service in the Abbey. . . . Comparing notes with those M.P.s who chose to go into the Abbey or to sit outside on the stands by the House of Commons one finds that everyone is certain they had the best of it. . . . My own feeling was that the ceremony was completely out of gear with modern democracy but this is apparently shared by a minimal number of people. . . .[20]

Another television viewer, watching in Paris, was the only

other human alive who could know just how well his niece had done. 'A woman can go through the motions far more gracefully than a man,' the ex-King wrote to a friend.[21]

For the British the young Queen provided a day of supreme reassurance. Yet the carriages (called clarences) containing the Commonwealth Prime Ministers had shortly before been sold off to the film tycoon Alexander Korda and had to be bought back in time for the ceremony. And one of them was drawn by the last two horses that could be rounded up in London and these were 'doubtfully trained to resist the shouts of the mob'.[22] Still, the Queen in her lighted and glittering State Coach; the cries of 'Vivat Regina'; the solemnity of the anointing; the rotund Queen of Tonga waving gaily in the rain; the ancient Churchill in his Garter robes: these images stayed with the nation. They also stayed with Elizabeth II. (North of the border, by contrast, the royal image-makers miscalculated: the Queen caused lasting offence by receiving the Honours of Scotland in 1953 wearing a simple blue dress amidst dignitaries kitted out in splendid robes.) Whatever mishaps the future held, after the coronation she could feel set apart for life. As Robert Graves irreverently remarked after meeting her, 'the holy oil has certainly taken for that girl'. It had taken for the country too. Three years later two sociologists, Edward Shils and Michael Young, wrote of the magic moment when the 'frail creature who has been brought into contact with the Divine' is transformed as priest/king 'from a mere person into a vessel of the virtues which must flow through him into his society'.[23]

As the royal family left the Abbey on 2 June few would have thought that the hapless conduit for these virtues would be not the Queen but her younger sister. Princess Margaret was seen to brush a hair from the uniform of the man at her side, Group Captain Peter Townsend. The press began to play with the rumours about them, with a generous dose of humbug. 'Newspapers in Europe and America are openly asserting that the Princess is in love with a divorced man and wishes to marry him,' sniffed *The People*. 'The story is of course utterly untrue. It is quite unthinkable that a royal princess, third in line of succession to the throne, should even contemplate a marriage with a man who has been through the divorce courts.'[24]

Suddenly the full solemnity of the priest/king's vows fell upon a young woman who had never been required to make them. The public thought it knew Princess Margaret well. This was the prankster portrayed by the Princesses' former governess Marion Crawford – 'Crawfie'. 'More than once I have seen an equerry put his hand in his pocket and find it, to his amazement, full of lime balls. I am sure the last person he suspected was the demure-looking little girl at the end of the table.'[25]

History does not record whether Group Captain Peter Townsend DSO, DFC, ever found lime balls in his pocket. He had been seconded to the Palace as an equerry in 1944. At that time Princess Margaret was fourteen, Townsend twenty-nine. She soon had a crush on him, not lessened by the slow-motion break-up of his marriage. A Deputy Master of the Royal Household, which was what Townsend became, can easily lose touch with his own household. Margaret had grown to maturity with a fast set in attendance – dashing lads destined to be dull dukes or lifelong playboys. Townsend has recorded an extraordinary picture which leaves no doubt that Margaret had devastating sex appeal, like her uncle Edward VIII before her. 'She was a girl of unusual, intense beauty, confined as it was to her short, slender figure, and centred about large purple-blue eyes, generous, sensitive lips and a complexion as smooth as a peach. She was capable, in her face and her whole being, of an astonishing power of expression. It could change in an instant from saintly, almost melancholic composure to hilarious, uncontrollable joy.'[26] A gifted mimic and singer, she could be egocentric and demanding; but Townsend also found 'a rare softness and sincerity'.

When George VI died, his younger daughter was shattered. She leaned on Townsend, the older man and confidant, whom she had known since her childhood and who was identified with such intimate memories of the late King. They grew closer. Townsend might have asked to be posted away, but he did not. One day at the beginning of the coronation year the two decided that they loved each other. This information was conveyed to the close royal circle, where it was received with perturbation more than outright hostility. But Townsend's fellow courtiers were horrified. Often their families had served the crown for generations and they were jealous that Townsend, from a much humbler background, had been on such good terms with King George VI. The prospect of the equerry's marrying Princess Margaret and lording it over them was appalling. Carpeting Townsend for impertinence amounting to lèse-majesté, the old private secretary Lascelles spluttered: 'You must be mad or bad.'

Townsend's divorce meant that he could not remarry within the Church of England – the very Church which was about to anoint Margaret's sister as its Supreme Governor. Under the Royal Marriages Act of 1772 the Queen's consent was needed until Margaret attained her twenty-fifth birthday. Lascelles remembered the abdication, and the last time love had got the better of duty. Through John Colville he approached the Prime Minister. The Queen could not give her consent if the Prime Minister advised against it, but the advice should be dressed up as delay. The disingenuous message conveyed to Margaret was to wait for her twenty-fifth birthday, two years away. Meanwhile Lascelles and the Queen's press secretary – yet another Colville – advised that Townsend be got out of the country. Once the press had the story in detail after the coronation, the need was urgent. He was shunted away as air attaché in Brussels whilst Margaret was on a visit to Southern Rhodesia.

Townsend was not liked by Princess Margaret's circle and recalled by one of them today as being 'self-centred and insensitive'. One recent royal biographer catches this mood. 'He was a talker, mostly about himself, in a tormented, self-deprecating way which appealed to some women but not to most men. Prince Philip, for one, was not particularly drawn to his sort.'[27] The Princess, meanwhile, carried out a brilliantly successful tour of the West Indies. 'People forget what star quality she had,' her lady in waiting Elizabeth Cavendish remembers; 'She was like the Princess of Wales today.'[28] One resident noted sourly in his diary that the Princess was under orders not to dance with coloured folk. Noel Coward wrote, 'I should think that any presentable young Jamaican would be a great deal more interesting to dance with than the shambling Billy Wallace . . .'[29] Shambling Billy, the wealthy grandson of the architect Lutyens, led all the rest in the contest for her hand. He was one of her main consolations among the 'Margaret set' as 1954 rolled by. It says something for Princess Margaret's tolerance that in an implicitly authorized biography she nodded through Coward's description of an amateur revue which she and Wallace organized. 'The whole evening,' the Master wrote in his diary, 'was one of the most fascinating exhibitions of incompetence, conceit and sheer bloody impertinence that I have ever seen in my life.'[30]

But the charms of Billy Wallace were resistible and for more than two years Margaret waited for the Group Captain to return. When he did, in October 1955, there was a new Prime Minister. Anthony Eden, like Townsend, was a glamorous, highly-strung divorced man. Townsend's cousin, Hugh Gaitskell, was the favourite to take over from Attlee as Leader of the Opposition. Under the pressure from them, the courtiers and the churchmen, however, were well prepared. The government informed the Queen that since the marriage would not be recognized by the Church of England, it would threaten the throne. A Bill of Renunciation would be drawn up, under which Margaret would have to give up her title, right of succession and Civil List income; that would be the price of a civil ceremony and a new life as Mrs Peter Townsend. The country seemed to speak of little else. The debate was along class lines: the *Times* argued for faith and duty, while the popular papers argued (and polled their readers) in favour of love.

It was an uneven contest. The Princess had (and has) deep religious convictions and fierce loyalty to her sister. ('My sister is God's representative in this realm,' she recently told the writer A. N. Wilson.) Elizabeth Cavendish was close to her during the decision. 'One's got to remember that divorce then was not acceptable, and in the end she put the Crown before her own sense of happiness.' On 23 October the Princess learned from her sister over dinner how rigid the government's position was. The next day the *Times* thundered that the position of the Queen, through whom her subjects 'see their better selves ideally reflected',[31] would be damaged by a marriage which these same subjects would see as no marriage at all. With this salvo ringing in their ears, Townsend and Margaret met at Clarence House 'mute and numbed at the centre of this maelstrom', as he remembered it. Together they scribbled out the statement which most thought at first must have been drafted for them. 'Mindful of the Church's teaching that Christian marriage is indissoluble, and conscious of my duty to the Commonwealth', she had decided against a civil marriage. Townsend did not accompany her to see Archbishop Fisher, who in his own inimitable way thanked the powers he thought responsible. 'What a wonderful person the Holy Spirit is!' he exclaimed. Townsend took his wistful charm off into exile. Thirty-eight years later, in his eightieth year, the Group Captain returned to take tea at Clarence House with the Princess and her mother among their bygones.

With hindsight the Princess was badly betrayed by the guardians of the world to which, in the last analysis, she clung. Later her own marriage and those of her two married nephews and niece were to collapse in turn. It was left for Townsend, a touch smugly, to reflect in later life that his own civil marriage to a Belgian girl had survived, whereas 'the Princess's marriage, consecrated by the Church, is itself now no marriage at all'. She did not sustain the image of the Windsors as moral exemplars. She provided the classic case of an individual of some talent endlessly fluttering in the gilded birdcage of monarchy. If, since then, she had wanted to answer the attacks on her lack-lustre performance of royal duties she could have argued that she had paid her dues to the respectability of the Windsors in 1955. It had not rubbed off on her. 'My sister was made out to be the goody goody one,' she later told Andrew Duncan. 'That was boring, so the Press tried to make out that I was wicked as hell.'[32] But as she became less central to the monarchy it came to matter less whether she was respectable or not.

For her brother-in-law, Windsor respectability was to be a lifetime burden. This restless over-achiever was condemned to the perpetual under-achievement of walking three steps behind the Queen, making up for her shyness with his own brand of brutal bonhomie. John Grigg, the Windsors' most candid friend, concedes that Philip's contribution during these early years has always been undervalued.

> In their public appearances together he carried the show during the first fifteen years of the reign, rather as Queen Elizabeth had done for George VI. But compared to Queen Victoria's consort he was at a great disadvantage. Albert was in effect her private secretary – he ran the whole of her public affairs; he ran her office. He was her principal adviser in all purposes. That was far from the case in 1952. There was a very substantial bureaucracy in place – private secretaries, assistant secretaries, and what have you. Philip was right outside that; he was regarded with some suspicion by those people and resented their attitude to him.[33]

The young Queen might have chosen to weave him in. Apart from making him Regent in the event of her death, she did not do so.

As a result Philip became over-intrusive in those areas where he could make an impact, without being kept in check by the court mafia. He encouraged his wife to follow her father's and grandfather's tradition of the Christmas broadcast, first on radio, then on television, and when she proved desperately wooden with prepared texts he tried to make helpful amendments. Because of his own facility with the microphone he was not always a patient critic. One internal memorandum some years later referred to the fact that the stilted text handed over to the BBC producers had the look of something designed to be written, not spoken. They had particularly noted the phrase 'My husband and I' instead of 'we', only to be told that this had been a late addition by the Duke.[34] Sometimes the long-suffering producers had to resort to petty deceptions to get him out of the way.

Philip survived by making space for himself, and by taking a series of initiatives aimed at personal achievement. He roamed the palaces attempting to pull the flunkeys out of their periwigged torpor. He went after new technology with a zest that made him a premature yuppie. The National Playing Fields Association, the Duke of Edinburgh's Awards Scheme, the Central Council for Physical Recreation, Voluntary Service Overseas – all benefited from his energy and bore with fortitude his clumsier interventions. He stuck with a task once he

George V's Silver Jubilee celebrations in London's East End

Edward Prince of Wales and Mrs Simpson at the races, 1935

King Edward VIII leaving an aircraft of the King's Flight, which he inaugurated in 1936

King Edward VIII and Mrs Simpson during the *Nahlin* cruise, 1936

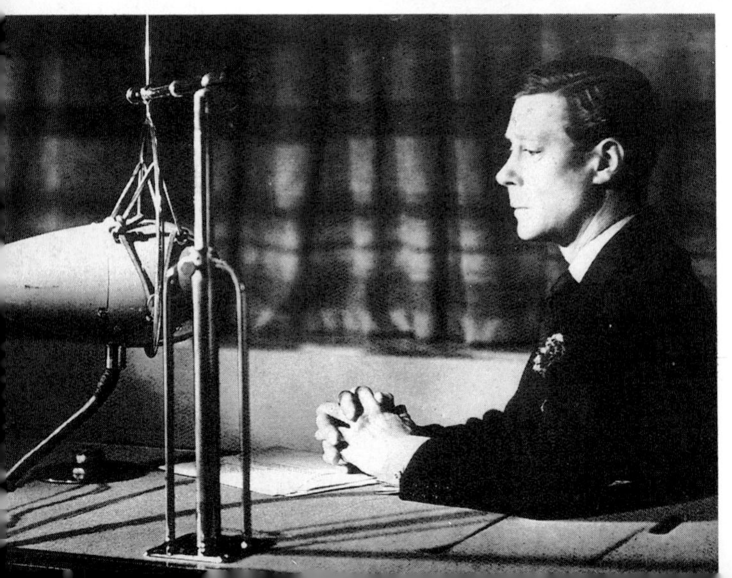

The Duke of Windsor broadcasting his abdication speech, December 1936

King George VI and Queen Elizabeth on the balcony of Buckingham Palace after their coronation, May 1937

The Duke and Duchess of Windsor on their wedding day, May 1937

The Duke and Duchess of Windsor meet Hitler, 1937

The Duke of Windsor gives the Nazi salute on this official visit to Germany in 1937. His equerry, Dudley Forwood (with moustache) is on the right

King George VI and Queen Elizabeth inspect bomb damage at Buckingham Palace, 1940

Princess Elizabeth, watched by her mother, at an ATS training centre, 1945

King George promoted self-sufficiency by founding a "Pig Club" during the war

Three queens in mourning at the funeral of King George VI, 1952: Queen Elizabeth II, Queen Mary and Queen Elizabeth the Queen Mother

A marriage that never was: Princess Margaret and her father's equerry, Group Captain Peter Townsend, during the royal tour of South Africa, 1947

A marriage that might have been: Prince Charles and Camilla Parker-Bowles, 1975

The Queen at "The Times" office with Rupert Murdoch: the man who has done more than anyone to change popular attitudes towards the monarchy had imposed it on himself, and something of the relentless activism he had learned at Gordonstoun stayed with his creations even when he had moved on. In the process he sometimes left bruised feelings too. Richard Crossman encountered the young Duke for the first time at the laying of the foundation stone for the new Coventry Cathedral. 'The Duke is a great deal rougher than I expected, with a slightly wild look in his eye. Although the Prime Minister [Eden] was in the room he spent the time talking to Maurice [Edelman] and me about Crush and Bulge [Khrushchev and Bulganin, the Russian leaders then visiting Britain]. "They've arranged that we should give them tea," he said. "I think it's bloody silly."' Crossman concluded, 'When he called it bloody silly he was criticising no one except the Prime Minister. We may have trouble with this young man'.[35] This was Gordonstoun Man in action: earnest, impatient, physical.

He was bent, too, on making his eldest son in his own image. Whilst Princess Anne was in many ways the son he never had, the full force of his expectations fell on the sensitive, good-natured heir. To have a mother who is a national institution is a disadvantage. To have a father, often away (he was away for six of Charles's first eight birthdays), who wants to replicate his own tough childhood can be a disaster. One who knew Prince Philip well in the fifties says: 'The most stupid thing in the whole royal family was not making Philip a Consort and giving him something to do. So he made the family his thing, and "ruled" it very badly. In this present family it is Philip who dominates and has caused the problems; no love, no affection, no understanding, but education according to rules and plans and standards.'

Philip wanted, says another authority, 'a real man's man. He wanted a blunt, outspoken sportsman, rough-and-tumble sort of guy.' What he got was a shy, diffident boy with slightly knock knees, slightly flat feet and a slight twitch in his mouth. Whenever he had a toy which his sister Anne wanted, she got it. Charles relied on his nanny, Nurse Lightbody, 'much more than the average little boy would do'.[36] He would hold back and ask her permission to do things: 'Should I go, Nanny?' And sometimes, because he was prone to colds, she would forbid him to swim. But Philip tended to overrule her on the grounds that coddling the child was bad for him. He obviously disappointed his father, who 'cut the ground from under Prince Charles at every opportunity. He never praised him; he never encouraged him.' Their relationship uncannily resembled that of George V and his eldest son; and Queen Elizabeth II, whose husband 'wears the trousers in the house', did not interfere any more than Queen Mary had done.[37] So Charles grew up believing that he was not much good, which had a profound effect on his personality. Philip's own view was different, of course. He considered that he was an enlightened parent, offering freedom of choice at every stage. Looking back, he said: 'I was careful not to make a rigid plan – I haven't for any of them – until some sort of forseeable situation arose.'[38] Within this liberty Charles went on from his first day school, Hill House, to his father's prep school, Cheam, and then to the grimmer world of Gordonstoun.

When Charles began with his first governess/tutor, both his parents were abroad. When he was chauffeured for the first time to Hill House in 1957 his father had been absent for four months. To be fair to Philip, he behaved just as any conventional naval officer of his generation would have done: away for long periods at sea, sons off at some distant public school. Prince Philip's flagship, after his marriage, was the royal yacht *Britannia*, as it remains to this day. It was his toy, an adequate compensation for a former naval personage, and his travels in it were supplemented by his use of the Royal Flight, whose planes he often piloted.

All this array of transport was at the Duke's disposal when he departed on 15 October 1956 for a five-month tour of the Commonwealth, built around an invitation to open the Olympic Games in Melbourne. The Duke's wanderlust was never slaked. As he scrambled around the Falklands and Ascension Island there was press speculation that his marriage was even more on the rocks than he was. Old stories about the bachelor set he had frequented with his Mountbatten cousin David Milford Haven and the royal photographer Baron Nahum were recycled. He had continued to meet these friends for lunches every week at the so-called Thursday Club, which met at Wheeler's Restaurant in Old Compton Street. There they went in for drinking, telling bawdy stories, singing raucous songs and playing practical jokes. Philip's louche associates puzzled, perhaps perturbed, the Queen, who made enquiries about his 'funny friends'.[39] Doubtless she realised that her husband needed a safety valve, though she may not have appreciated his climbing over the walls of Buckingham Place (as happened on at least one occasion) and arriving home smelling of port.

Enough was known about the Thursday Club and the lifestyle of some of its members to set off press gossip about Philip's private life. The Duke has always had a brusque way with such speculation. 'Have you ever stopped to think that for the last forty years I have never moved anywhere without a policeman accompanying me? So how the hell could I get away with anything like that?' he asked the journalist Fiammetta Rocco in 1992.[40] To which the ribald answer in 1956 was always that you got away with it by getting away from it on a long cruise in southern waters.

Nothing would have transpired from this cruise, however, had it not been for the marital problems of his private secretary and former boon companion Mike Parker. Before the royal party returned Parker's wife Eileen went to see the Buckingham Palace Press secretary, Commander Richard Colville. She intended to sue her husband for adultery. Colville asked her to delay any statement until after the royal return, but her solicitors leaked it to the *Sunday Pictorial* while the *Britannia* was approaching Gibraltar. Parker knew what to expect; 'I had seen what happened to Peter Townsend, and the tail of his comet going about, and I saw what the press had done to him. I didn't want that, and I didn't want it to get anywhere near the Queen or Prince Philip.'[41] He resigned in Gibraltar and flew on to London, whilst the Queen went in the opposite direction to greet her spouse. At London Airport Parker met Colville, an apparently friendly face in a mass of inquisitive press men. 'You're on your own now, Mike,' he said.

Shaken by the excited speculations of the foreign press, the Queen's private secretary, Sir Michael Adeane, put out a statement: 'It is quite untrue that there is any rift between the Queen and the Duke of Edinburgh.' This did not have the intended effect. What did dampen the gossip, though it flared up again with every lengthy solo visit made by the Duke to distant parts, was the couple's obvious if unostentatious affection for each other and the birth of two further sons in the sixties. The Duke remained unapologetic about his circumnavigation. At the Mansion House in the month of his return he argued that he had 'strengthened, I hope, the close links which exist between the Crown and the people of the Commonwealth'.

The Commonwealth countries, now including republics in Asia, were happy to see the Queen as the sovereign of some but the Head of them all. Few then echoed the worries of Enoch Powell about the legislation which gave the Queen her style and titles in 1952: 'I said this was a contradiction . . . how, if the Commonwealth is composed of self-governing nations, can it offer unitary advice to the Crown? And how can the Crown, which governs this country on advice[42], be head of a Commonwealth which it cannot govern on advice?' In the early fifties this conundrum was conveniently set aside. The Asian states settled equably for a fiction, and the Anglo-Saxons tried to turn the fiction into fact.

The avuncular Menzies set the tone. In his autobiography he described how a new Governor General was chosen for Australia in 1952. Menzies, the Queen and Lord Salisbury all wrote down three names as their choices for the post. Why Lord Salisbury? Because 'Bobbety Salisbury . . . knows everyone of consequence and has great judgement.'[43] By happy chance all three concurred on the nomination of Sir William Slim. Despite their differences the first generation of Commonwealth leaders, the men who walked behind Churchill in the coronation procession, saw the organization as more than a convenience. Then came the Suez crisis, a potential test to destruction. The Commonwealth, like Britain, was riven. For the first time the Queen found herself embroiled in passionate controversy, in both her roles.

When the new Egyptian leader, Gamel Abdel Nasser, nationalized the Suez Canal in 1956 the British and French governments prepared for military intervention. Lord Mountbatten, who had returned to the Navy, was now First Sea Lord, charged with the responsibility for preparing a seaborne invasion. Initially he had argued for a short sharp expedition to seize Port Said and negotiate from a position of strength. His misgivings grew as the various stratagems to force Nasser to back down failed. He wrote to the hawkish General Templer: 'If we were fighting a visible enemy who was trying to dominate the Middle East by force of arms I should back you to the limit . . . but there is no such enemy. . . . The Middle East is about ideas, emotions, loyalties. You and I belong to a people which will not have ideas which we don't believe in thrust down our throats by bayonets or other force. Why should we assume that this process will work with other people?'

Mountbatten, the ex-Viceroy of India, knew the force of this argument in the Commonwealth. 'I fear that respect for the U.K. has vanished utterly from Asia and Africa,'[44] wrote Nehru to him. In August 1956 the First Sea Lord drafted but did not send a letter of resignation to the Prime Minister; later he presented it theatrically to the First Lord of the Admiralty Lord Hailsham, who briskly 'wrote him an order to stay at his post'.[45] Two months later, when the Anglo-French invasion fleet was on the high seas, the Leader of the Opposition broadcast his scathing critique of this action, reminding the nation of the bitter hostility of the vast majority of the Members of the United Nations. Unknown to him, Mountbatten had written to Eden along the same lines two days earlier, breaking all tradition for a serving military commander. Eden pressed ahead, and the Suez operation stumbled to its lamentable finale. Mountbatten's hostility was never publicly revealed, nor to this day do we know what his contacts were with the Palace both before and after his nephew Philip sailed away.

Twenty years later, Mountbatten told the writer Robert Lacey that the Queen had been opposed to Suez but powerless to prevent it. A letter to Mountbatten in her own handwriting confirms his story but has been kept out of the public domain. Certainly the view that the Commonwealth would be irrevocably, and perhaps fatally, split would have weighed heavily with the young monarch. The response of the Commonwealth leaders to the Anglo-French invasion had (Menzies apart) been a harsh one. What passed between her and her British Prime Minister at their meetings is not known. Sir Edward

Heath, then Chief Whip, says now that if royal doubts were conveyed to Eden 'he never passed them on to his Cabinet colleagues'.[46] Mountbatten has been treated with some scorn by Eden's official biographer because he did not disseminate his doubts earlier beyond his immediate chiefs. This 'seriously misled the Prime Minister and the Egypt Committee, virtually amounting to a dereliction of duty'.[47] With, his record and his royal links he could have had a major impact on the military preparations. The royal links, however, chafed both ways. Public opposition by Mountbatten might have involved the Palace in bitter political controversy.

Demoralized by American hostility, Russian bluster and a massive run on sterling, Eden now found himself deserted by his Chancellor, Harold Macmillan. Also a majority of his own Cabinet favoured a ceasefire. The Suez expedition was a humiliation, both for those who had opposed the expedition and for those who lamented the consequent triumph of Nasser. Eden's health, too, was ruined. He saw the Queen at Sandringham on 8 January and told her that he wanted to resign at once. It seems to have been agreed there and then with the Queen's private secretary Sir Michael Adeane, that a senior party figure should tender advice on her exercise of the royal prerogative in seeking the most suitable replacement. Lord Salisbury was chosen to take soundings on the two obvious candidates, R. A. Butler and Macmillan. Events then unfolded with breathtaking speed.

Eden said farewell to his Cabinet colleagues on 9 January 1957. That same day Salisbury and the Lord Chancellor, Lord Kilmuir, saw Cabinet ministers individually. Each was asked the much-quoted question: 'Which is it to be, Wab or Hawold?' That was all. The Chief Whip, and the chairmen of the party and of the 1922 Committee, were asked their views; ministers outside the Cabinet were not. Backbenchers were not polled. The Conservative Party in the country (which opinion polls showed to be for Butler) was not consulted.

By the following morning Lord Salisbury was on his way to the Palace. The overwhelming choice, he told the Queen, was Harold Macmillan. She took one second opinion – that of the aged Churchill himself, who concurred with the party grandees. The press had tipped Butler, but he now began a long career as the nearly man of Tory politics.

Salisbury acted as he did to avoid embarrassment for the Queen. It was thought that she should have an unambiguous report, leaving her with a clear choice. Eden had followed the precedent of Bonar Law in making no recommendation himself, although he would have expressed a negative view of Macmillan if asked. What is surprising about the 1957 exercise is that, despite its outcome being so clearly at variance with what was expected, few queried the result. The new administration was in great peril, and the Conservative Party's natural tendency to cling together in adversity was reinforced by the speed and skill with which Macmillan established himself. Nevertheless the Queen could have taken wider soundings. Salisbury and Churchill, after all, were by then at the very end of their political lives.

Suez, as one resigning minister put it, was 'no end of a lesson'. When the young Queen welcomed her husband back in February 1957 she too had taken it to heart. A certain national innocence had been wiped out with the fiasco. The complacent enthusiasms of the new Elizabethan Age seemed ragged. The British were in a questioning mood. And for the first time those questions would extend to the monarchy itself.

8

A MATURING MONARCHY

At first sight the early years of the Queen's maturity, from Suez to the investiture of her son as Prince of Wales, were a time of fulfilment. She seemed to refine the Windsor family model associated with her parents. She completed her family. She saw her sister make what seemed a modern and intriguing marriage. She presided over colonial independence abroad and political change in Britain with apparent good humour, and was unscathed by the new satire vogue which politicians found so unnerving. Yet in early middle age Elizabeth II and her husband seemed a touch boring. Unfortunately the prescribed treatment of new image-making was to cause more problems than it solved.

For the first five years of her reign the Queen enjoyed good publicity. Her family life had continued seamless and unbroken in the pattern established by her parents, and resistant to gossip about the Duke's absences. She was as wholesome as she was dutiful, with the patina of the coronation still upon her – the image of the 1955 Annigoni portrait. Her cousins began to find spouses and produce children. The Townsend affair was eclipsed when her sister Margaret made a love match with a photographer, Anthony Armstrong-Jones. They had been introduced by Lady Elizabeth Cavendish in her Chelsea house: 'I hadn't any doubt that they would get on. Their minds worked in the same way. Their humour was the same. They had a great deal going for them.'[1] Armstrong-Jones kept his relationship secret; and he took revenge on his friend Kingsley Amis, who had unwittingly blustered that Princess Margaret 'has no mind at all',[2] by dropping him far from home whilst Armstrong-Jones sped off for a late-night rendezvous with her. His bohemian background and plentiful step-parents raised eyebrows, as did his lack of blue blood. But the family liked him, and still do.

Only those who knew him best realized that there was a downside to his common interests with the Princess. As her biographer puts it, 'They were too much alike in temperament and too different in background for the marriage to be a happy one – once their love became commonplace, as it was bound to do.'[3] But all this lay in the future. Their engagement was announced just after the birth of Prince Andrew, and the first televised royal wedding became another Dimbleby spectacular. For a while it seemed that Margaret and Tony, now Lord Snowdon, would become alternative royals – unstuffy, witty and a touch raffish, running a court for the chattering classes as the Queen withdrew into family life. The arrival of her third child (followed by Prince Edward in 1964, and a son and daughter for Margaret) marked a period of royal fecundity, and the expanding royals were drenched with adulation. In October 1956 Malcolm Muggeridge had voiced misgivings in the *New Statesman*[4] that the Queen and her family had become not so much a symbol of religious values as a substitute for them. Three years later the leftish Sunday paper *Reynolds News* assessed one of its own readership surveys and concluded that 'reverence for royalty has become the national religion'.[5]

This made headway difficult for the critics who did surface, as disillusion with the political establishment grew in the wake of Suez and the uprising in Hungary. Few asked what the monarchy was for; that was still self-evident. But more asked what it was not for. Muggeridge's article, 'The Royal Soap Opera', introduced a linkage which has been a commonplace ever since; he pointed out that 'there are those who find the ostentation of life at Windsor and Buckingham Palace not to their taste'. Because he was generally polite about the monarch, all this could be taken in good part. But criticism in the *National and English Review* in August 1957, although a much more obscure magazine, could not. This was because its author, Lord Altrincham, was a young Tory radical peer. His father, Edward Grigg, had toured with the Prince of Wales and had later been ennobled. From boyhood Altrincham had seen the great occasions of royalty from the sidelines. He was, and remains, a fervent monarchist. He knew courtiers, and mixed with them. He did not like what he had seen. Now he was owner/editor of a monthly review, and he devoted a whole issue to the monarchy.[6]

Writing as a candid friend, he attacked the Queen's advisers and the way in which she came across in public. The entourage was 'a tight little enclave of English ladies and gentlemen' who were 'almost without exception of the "tweedy" sort'. The people who were seen around her, he said, did 'not reflect her new role as the sovereign of a democratic country and of a multi-racial Commonwealth'. He noted that 'courtiers are nearly always citizens of one Commonwealth country – the United Kingdom'. One phrase, however, achieved instant notoriety. The tweedy set, he suggested, had trapped the Queen within their own limited world: 'The personality conveyed by the utterances which are put into her mouth is that of a priggish schoolgirl, captain of the hockey team, a prefect and a candidate for confirmation.'

Altrincham, who renounced his peerage in 1963 to become plain John Grigg, did not intend the Queen to be his target. 'I thought that the words put in her mouth were grotesquely unsuited to her as a young inexperienced woman. She was made to talk in a very condescending and hieratic way.'[7] Nevertheless the young peer was lambasted as a traitor to his class. The Duke of Argyll wanted him hanged, drawn and quartered. Altrincham was attacked in a London street by an elderly buffoon who thumped him on the jaw in view of the television cameras; the judge who tried the subsequent case declared that '95 per cent of the nation are disgusted and offended at what was written by Lord Altrincham'. In contrast

Bill Connor (Cassandra) of the *Daily Mirror* telephoned to say, 'I thought you'd like to know that our readers are now supporting you in a ratio of thirteen to four'.[8]

Muggeridge's article was picked up and republished in the United States, under the provocative title 'Does England Really Need a Queen?', to coincide with a royal visit. Heavily misquoted, the piece cost him his contract at the BBC and much personal abuse. The playwright John Osborne took up the soap opera theme in *Encounter*, declaring that 'My objection to the royal symbol is that it is dead; it is a gold filling in a mouth full of decay. When the mobs rush forward in the Mall, they are taking part in the last circus of a civilisation which has lost faith in itself and sold itself for a splendid triviality.'

These forays could be brushed aside; Altrincham could not. Sir Edward Ford, then an equerry, recollects that tweediness was no occasion for guilt. 'We laughed it off. We didn't mind being called tweedy. If you've got to go to Sandringham in the depths of winter you've damn well got to wear tweeds to survive.' On the point of their common background, 'of course there is some value in having people of a like mind and similar friends and contacts, particularly when they are interchangeable . . . we were chosen on the old boy network'.[9] Lord Charteris, then assistant private secretary, remembers that 'I don't think [the Queen] liked it and I don't see why she should. The courtiers disliked it very much . . . but I did see that there was something of great importance in what John Grigg said . . . we were a bit stuffy, you know.'[10]

Change was slow. Charteris was one of the modernizers: 'The dear old court is a long-established institution, and we are the descendants of our predecessors.' While the Duke of Edinburgh was firmly in the modernizing camp the Queen, for all her youth, was a natural conservative. 'The Queen has got absolutely impeccable negative judgement . . . she can always see what's wrong,' says Charteris. 'She's very sound but she's not a tremendous positive in this way. She is not a person who is passionately stamping the ground to change everything.'

The first fragment of the old order to be chipped away was the annual presentation of debutantes at court. The royal tours and speeches were streamlined. Ceremonies previously confined to London, like the Royal Maundy service, were moved around the country. The Queen began to meet a wider cross-section of her subjects, at garden parties, at informal lunches, on formal visits. Sir Edward Ford recollects the opposition from officialdom when it was suggested that the Queen might chat to the ball boys and girls at Wimbledon. '"Oh," they said, "very difficult", so we had to make a guard of honour so that she could chat to some of them and the umpires on the way through.' The televised Christmas broadcast replaced radio for good in 1957. BBC producer Anthony Craxton plucked up courage to tell the Queen that her voice was too high-pitched and that she should not try to emphasize every word. Only age changed the pitch of a voice which was cruelly easy to caricature, and she would never be a broadcasting natural like her grandfather George V. In an effort to help, the Prime Minister, Macmillan, frequently returned to the theme of how the broadcasts could be scripted to be spoken rather than read.

Where the courtiers saw little reason to budge was on the failure of the royal entourage to absorb representatives from the Commonwealth. The key group, who knew and trusted each other, saw no reason to move aside – though sometimes they had to give ground. In 1960 Bill Heseltine, a young Australian, arrived for a year's secondment from the office of Sir Robert Menzies. Before major tours a little local talent was taken on – and here alone non-white faces could be seen. Before the Queen's visit to Nigeria in 1956 Major Ironsi of the Nigerian Army was seconded to Buckingham Palace for three months as an extra equerry. The only member of the Queen's staff who later became a head of state, he was assassinated in office. John Grigg believes that to this day the Queen's household has not taken his criticisms seriously. 'I think she hasn't got the imagination that Queen Victoria had [who] had an Indian as part of her personal entourage. . . . It's incredible that she should maintain an official family around her which so inadequately represents . . . this country, let alone the Commonwealth.'[11]

No one, however, has doubted the Queen's application on her Commonwealth tours. The Nigerian visit had gone well.

Five years later she paid a further visit to West Africa which was to demonstrate both her personal toughness and the way in which the balance and make-up of the organization were changing. Her attitude towards emergent black and brown nations would help to determine whether the Commonwealth could change from being a family club of the old white dominions, and do so at a time when one of them was outraging the world. South Africa, where she had originally pledged herself to the Commonwealth, was now a pariah. Dr Verwoerd's apartheid regime was told that if it wished to become a republic it must leave. The South Africans stalked out anyway in 1960. The senior Commonwealth statesman, Nehru, both appalled and impressed by the stubborn bigotry of the South Africans, invited the Queen to tour India in 1961, and for the first time she had the experience of touring Commonwealth republics (Cyprus, India and Pakistan) which had been part of her father's Empire.

Macmillan had a wider strategic design. He had told the South African Parliament that a wind of change was blowing through Africa; he did not want it to fill the sails of international Communism. If Africa was at stake, he would use the Queen. Ghana had been the first West African country to achieve independence. It had done so as a republic, under the volatile Kwame Nkrumah, but his regime had swiftly become a one-party state and there were explosions and mass arrests in the capital the month before her visit. The Queen's safety could not be guaranteed. Noisy MPs pressed Macmillan to advise her to drop the visit. Winston Churchill wrote to the same effect, in his last detailed letter to his successor: 'Nkrumah might leave the Commonwealth. I am not sure this would be a great loss.'[12] But knowing how open Nkrumah then was to Russian influences, Macmillan wanted the visit to go ahead. He sent Churchill's tough former son-in-law Duncan Sandys to Accra with instructions to 'try it on the dog'. Nkrumah was obliged to ride with Sandys along the planned processional route. No bombs were thrown. The Redeemer, as Nkrumah was known, 'lived to tell the tale'.

The Queen knew the Prime Minister's mind, and that if she faltered the next ceremonial procession could well see

Nikita Khrushchev at Nkrumah's side. She was adamant that she would go. Thus the sovereign spared the Prime Minister from giving advice which she knew he was trying to avoid, but which, if given, she would have had to accept. 'What a splendid girl she is,' Macmillan exulted to his press secretary, whose diary continued: 'The House of Commons, she thought, should not show lack of moral fibre in this way. She took very seriously her Commonwealth responsibilities, and rightly so, said the P.M., for the responsibilities of the U.K. monarchy had so shrunken that if you left it at that you might as well have a film star.'[13]

The tour went off faultlessly, and Macmillan wrote to the new American President, Jack Kennedy, to urge him to push through the financing of Nkrumah's Volta Dam: 'I have risked my Queen; you must risk your money.'[14] In its mixture of courage and application the tour of Ghana brought out the best in Elizabeth II. Some time later Sir Edward Ford took the politician-turned-diplomat Geoffrey De Freitas to kiss hands on appointment as High Commissioner in Ghana. 'I said, "She will talk to you for ten minutes and then she will make it quite clear that the audience is finished and then you leave." Well, he came out forty-five minutes later and said, "I've spent three weeks going around the Foreign and Commonwealth Offices to find out about Ghana and I've learned more in the last forty-five minutes than in all those three weeks."'[15] De Freitas was not averse to flattery, but the honeyed words coated a nugget of truth. The Queen is a meticulous absorber of briefings and has a retentive memory. The Commonwealth Office was merged with the Foreign Office in 1968, but in one sense the Queen remains the incumbent in post. Throughout the sixties she would have been obliged to align herself with decolonization. That was ministerial advice, under both Conservative and Labour governments. But she went further, in building relationships with leaders like Kenneth Kaunda in the emergent states; they were to gratify some of her prime ministers, but enrage others. By following Macmillan's advice about the dissolution of the Central African Federation, ignoring 'loyal' white Rhodesians and later ostracizing the breakaway Smith minority government, she made sure that the monarchy did not suffer guilt by association with the white racist regimes of southern Africa.

For all his political skills, Harold Macmillan was running out of time. A vast purge of his Cabinet in 1962 had masked the sacking of his Chancellor, Selwyn Lloyd. One of those to go was Lord Kilmuir, who had conducted with Salisbury the soundings which led to the Queen's initially sending for Macmillan as Prime Minister. Kilmuir had famously proclaimed that loyalty was the Conservatives' secret weapon; now he discovered that it was not. One disaster after another rocked the government. First it was diplomacy, then spies, then sex. At the beginning of the year De Gaulle had vetoed Britain's application to join the Common Market, destroying at a stroke the centrepiece of Macmillan's strategy, in which the Queen had been deployed to ease Commonwealth fears of desertion. At the same time Harold 'Kim' Philby, long suspected of being a Soviet agent, disappeared from his residence in Beirut. 'There is something odd about this,' the British ambassador to the Lebanon wrote to the Foreign Office, but 'it is not the first time that journalists have slipped away quietly on special assignments.'[16] In March it was officially admitted that he was a Soviet agent, the 'third man' who had tipped off the diplomats Burgess and Maclean twelve years before, enabling them to flee to Moscow. The net was also closing around the 'fourth man', the art historian and Surveyor of the Queen's Pictures, Sir Anthony Blunt. He was much interviewed by MI5, but for the moment remained mute.

The press had an appetite for more. In another spy scandal the previous year they had over-reacted when a minor Admiralty clerk, John Vassall, was found guilty of espionage. They alleged, wrongly, a link to an equally obscure minister, Tam Galbraith. Galbraith resigned, and Macmillan resolved not to be panicked by the press again. Two journalists were jailed for refusing to reveal the sources for some of the wilder stories. Their colleagues were not averse to revenge.

Macmillan was slow to react to the clouds of sexual scandal that swirled around the Minister for War, John Profumo. It was alleged that he had had a relationship with a 'woman of easy virtue', as Lord Hailsham memorably called her. Christine

Keeler was also involved with the Russian naval attaché, Evgeny Ivanov. Warnings delivered to Downing Street by Sir William Carr, chairman of the *News of the World*,[17] were disbelieved until the story was aired in the House of Commons. Profumo denied the allegations indignantly; his colleagues believed him. Then, when it became clear that the press had letters written by him to Keeler, and that the intermediary in the affair, a fashionable osteopath named Dr Stephen Ward, was blabbing the truth, he confessed.

There followed a hunt for scapegoats. The man who had been everyone's darling, Stephen Ward, was arrested on 8 June and charged with being, in effect, Keeler's pimp. By this time the rumour mill was grinding fast. On 12 and 13 June the Cabinet discussed the affair in a near panic. Macmillan noted that 'deplorable speculation about individuals prominent in public affairs is now rife'.[18] Ward had a talent for making skilful and flattering portrait sketches on demand. Many people had sat for him, including the Duke of Edinburgh and seven other royals, Macmillan himself, and the recently deceased Labour leader, Hugh Gaitskell. Ward had flitted on the fringe of many worlds. The press made desperate attempts to link his clique to another mighty scandal of the time, the divorce of the Duke of Argyll. Equally wild rumours alleged that another Cabinet minister enjoyed being chained to a radiator at society dinner parties, dressed only in a masonic apron.

The public began to believe that people in high places – politicians, aristocrats, even high court judges – were engaged in a vast cover-up. The Duke of Edinburgh did not escape unscathed from his acquaintance with Ward, which dated back to Thursday Club days: Ward had been a friend and protégé of the royal photographer Baron. Two days after the Macmillan government finally set up an enquiry under Lord Denning to investigate 'rumours affecting the honour and integrity of public life', the *Daily Mirror* published a story which said that 'the foulest rumour being circulated about the Profumo Scandal has involved a member of the Royal Family. The name being mentioned is Prince Philip.' The rumour, it said, was 'utterly unfounded'.[19] One of Philip's latest biographers, a former employee of *Mirror* chairman Cecil

King, talks knowledgeably about photographs from Ward's private collection, allegedly featuring the Prince and his friend Baron, which found their way to the safes of Odhams Press and were then impounded by the police for their investigations into Ward's activities.[20] Since no copies have ever been published, speculation is otiose. A few days later Ward committed suicide and never heard the guilty verdict against him. His sketches of the royals, then on display in a West End gallery, were secured for cash by an anonymous buyer and were never seen again.

The government was dealt a heavy blow by the Profumo Affair, which seemed to incriminate the entire Establishment. One of the principal Labour muck-rakers, Richard Crossman, wrote gleefully in his diary, 'I can't think of a more humiliating and discrediting story . . . the lying, the collusion and the fact that Royalty and the Establishment back Profumo.'[21] Lord Denning's enquiry in fact substantially cleared the government. But it was not so reported by a hostile press, and Macmillan's authority was substantially weakened by the number of his backbenchers who believed, with his bitter critic Nigel Birch, that it could never be 'glad confident morning again'.

Macmillan had already told the Queen that he might not wish to go on. On 5 September, before the publication of the Denning Report, he wrote again to her about 'the political situation, the leadership of the Party, and the life of the present Parliament. I have not yet reached a decision in my own mind as to how things ought to be handled[22]. . . .' As the muttering on the benches behind him continued, he made up his mind. On 20 September he recorded in his diary what passed at his weekly audience with the Queen. He told her that he would not have an election in 1963, nor would he lead the party into one in 1964; the change would come about in January. The Queen seems to have seen trouble coming. 'She feels the great importance of maintaining the prerogative intact. After all, if she asked someone to form a government and he failed, what harm was done?'[23]

This question became a practical one a month later. Macmillan had half resolved to rescind his decision and carry on when, on the eve of the Conservative conference in Blackpool, he was struck down with the agonizing effects of an inflamed prostate. Told by the first doctor he saw that this was caused by a tumour, he feared the worst. Macmillan instructed R.A. Butler, the deputy whom he believed to be too pusillanimous to succeed him, to hold the fort. Lords Home and Dilhorne (Foreign Secretary and Lord Chancellor) had said in Butler's presence that if there had to be a sudden change they would be available to take soundings, since they were not candidates for the succession. But once Macmillan had been whisked into hospital they visited him, after which Home went to Blackpool to inform the conference of what Macmillan had already told the Queen by couriered letter to Balmoral – that it was his intention to resign. This turned the conference into an American-style convention: politics on the hoof, not in the back room.

Recent legislation brought in to allow Anthony Wedgwood Benn to renounce his peerage and seek re-election to the Commons now enabled any peer to follow suit. Macmillan's favourite for the succession, Lord Hailsham, noisily disclaimed his own peerage and reverted to being Quintin Hogg. But as he rushed from one Blackpool event to another, wide-eyed with excitement and with his baby in tow, Hailsham ruined his chances. Some years later Macmillan reflected: 'Hogg was far the best – the only one of genius. But he destroyed himself at that unlucky Blackpool, with his baby and his tin of infant food.'[24] A more reluctant peer now moved into the spotlight – Lord Home. From his sick-bed in London Macmillan received a stream of party functionaries and switched his support to the newcomer. The hapless Butler was preparing his speech for the Saturday rally when Home told him that he would be having a medical to see if he was fit for the job. 'He told me just before my speech,'[25] Butler plaintively remembered.

The party soundings taken by Lord Dilhorne and a coterie later castigated by Iain Macleod as the 'Magic Circle' of Old Etonians purported to show the largest group of MPs and an overall majority of the Cabinet in favour of Home. Chief Whip Redmayne had asked questions favourable to Home of the former, while Dilhorne's computations (an overall Cabinet majority for Home) showed Macleod to be for Home – at best an error, at worst a falsification. Butler's widow has subsequently written of eight ministers who pledged him their support; Dilhorne calculated only three.[26] On the night of 17 October Macmillan prepared a lengthy memorandum for the Queen, 'should she ask my advice'.

The news that Home was to be the recommendation leaked out overnight, and a number of dissenting ministers protested. Macmillan was unmoved, noting in his diary: 'If we give in to this intrigue there would be chaos. Butler would fail to form a government; even if given another chance (for the Queen might then send for Wilson) no one else would succeed.'[27] This was unlikely. A party with less than a year before an election would have rallied behind the Queen's choice out of self-preservation as well as loyalty. Macmillan meant to ensure that the Queen made the choice he advised. The timetable was now crucial. His letter of resignation arrived at the Palace at 9.30 on 18 October. He was no longer Prime Minister from the moment the Queen accepted it, but two hours later she came to the hospital, tearful and shaken, to consult him.

> She said, very kindly, 'What are you going to do?' And I said, 'Well, I'm afraid I can't go on.' And she was very upset . . . then [she] said, 'Have you any advice to give me?' And I said, 'Ma'am, do you wish me to give advice?' And she said, 'Yes, I do.' So then I said, 'Well, since you ask for it, Ma'am, I have with the help of Mr Bligh prepared it all, and here it is.' And I just handed her over my manuscript. Then I read it to her, I think.[28]

The Queen handed the bulky manuscript to Adeane 'looking like the Frog Footman', Macmillan remembered. He told her that 'I thought speed was important and hoped she would send for Lord Home immediately – as soon as she got back to the Palace.'[29] The Queen and Adeane departed and did just that. But the dissident ministers still had a strategy: if they could persuade Home that enough of them would not serve under him they might prevent his accepting the Queen's offer. While the Queen was with Macmillan the three leading contenders – Butler, Hailsham and Maudling – met with Iain Macleod, Chairman of the Party, in Butler's office at the Treasury. They all agreed to serve under Butler. But by then Home was on his way to the Palace. Butler's biographer asks 'why, if [Macmillan] felt so certain of the constitutional correctness of the advice he was proffering, it needed to be implemented with quite such precipitate haste; equally properly, a query arises as to the uncritical alacrity with which the Palace fell in with both the nature and the timing of Macmillan's scheme'.[30]

Did Macmillan leave the Queen with no other choice? Hailsham, as Lord President of the Council, had sought leave to make his own representations to his monarch. Adeane turned him down. Hailsham today says simply: 'I think she was placed in a position where she either had to accept the advice of the outgoing Prime Minister from his sick-bed, or reject it and make a choice of her own. I'm quite sure that of those two disagreeable alternatives she chose the right one.'[31] Enoch Powell, fiercest of the rebels, condemns Macmillan outright. 'Harold Macmillan violated the constitution in my view, for, having stated that he intended to resign, he acted as if he had not stated that he intended to resign, and continued to offer advice. He said, "Ma'am, I am going to find out who I would recommend to you to succeed me if you were to ask me after I had resigned." That's . . . a contortion not uncharacteristic of the gentleman who offered it.'[32]

In his influential *Spectator* article the following January Iain Macleod excoriated the 'Magic Circle' but said nothing of the other circle – the one around the monarch, whose members would by breeding and inclination have seen Home as a most congenial choice. Home was a peer, and for the first month of any premiership he would be in limbo, seeking election to the Commons. Nothing like this had happened before. Yet the Queen apparently sought no other advice. Home, returning from his audience charged with forming a government, had the sovereign's touch as surely as if he had already kissed hands. Butler crumbled. 'You see, I had up against me such a terrific gent,' he said fifteen years later.[33]

The terrific gent had a year of office, to which he devoted only two skeletal chapters of his memoirs. In them Home described how he introduced a system, with arcane rules, for electing the next leader. Although 'the Magic Circle had almost everything to be said for it', Sir Alec Douglas-Home (as he then briefly was) conceded that at least in an election 'everything was seen to be open and above board'.[34] If the Tories changed their leader within a Parliament, they, like Labour, would offer a single name for the monarch. Only where the two-party system broke down in 'hung' Parliaments would the element of royal choice remain.

One incident during Douglas-Home's administration, hushed up at the time, deserves recording. After the government had been forced to acknowledge the treason of Kim Philby, its security interrogator William Skardon redoubled his attempts to crack the defences of Sir Anthony Blunt. The confrontation has become legendary, and formed the basis for Alan Bennett's play *A Question of Attribution*. Offered immunity from prosecution, 'the suspect thought long and hard, then got up, stared out of the window, poured himself a drink, and after a few minutes confessed'.[35] But there were problems. The qualities which made Blunt a good spy also made him a good courtier: absolute discretion, the ability to blend into any background, the skill of flattery and the ability to perform difficult missions.

Blunt had done King George VI a signal favour when he accompanied the royal archivist Sir Owen Morshead to Wolfsgarten in 1945, to retrieve from the castle of the Dukes of Hesse documents compromising to the Duke of Windsor. A visit years later to the late Kaiser's residence in Holland was said to have the same motivation.[36] But the Duke's official biographer, Philip Ziegler, says that none of the papers related to him. The material was brought back to London and vanished. Its exact nature cannot therefore be verified, though documents were handed back to the Hesse family in 1951. The Wolfsgarten expedition remained highly sensitive. When Peter Wright was preparing for one of the later interrogations of Blunt he was summoned to see Sir Michael Adeane. 'The Queen,' said Adeane, 'is quite content for him to be dealt with in any way which gets at the truth.' But there was one exception. 'You may find Blunt referring to an assignment he undertook on behalf of the Palace – a visit to Germany at the end of the war. Please do not pursue this matter. Strictly speaking it is not relevant to considerations of national security.'[37]

This seems somewhat excessive if all that was found at Wolfsgarten was some old letters of Queen Victoria's. We do know that other material on the Duke was sensitive enough to lead to exchanges between the British and US governments later on, when it became clear that documents in American hands might be published. It is unlikely that Blunt's mission gave him any power over the royal family, though it may have amused him to pass its secrets on to the Russians. By 1964 he would have to rely on cool nerve and hope for regal gratitude. Blunt, a particular favourite of Queen Mary, had after all insinuated himself deep into royal circles – it has been alleged that he was the mystery man who bought up the Ward sketches when they were exhibited in 1963.[38]

Such was the man who was offered immunity from prosecution in 1964. His interrogators ended his silence by pledging their own. At the Palace Sir Michael Adeane was told of the offer, and of what was now known about Blunt. He has never spoken about what, if anything, he told the Queen. The advice on which he acted came from the Home Secretary, Henry Brooke. Why was Blunt kept on, first in 1964 and then, incredibly, as a special adviser after his formal retirement in 1972? Lord Charteris recollects that

> Anthony Blunt was kept on as a member of the household after he had confessed because that was the advice given to the Queen by the Home Secretary . . . it was thought better that Anthony Blunt should just go on, because he was talking to the security services, and that's what happened. And of course very few people in the household knew that he was a traitor. I think it was a mistake to keep him on as Surveyor Emeritus; better if he'd just disappeared. But as someone so rightly said to me the other day, why wasn't he made a GCVO? And the answer was that we knew enough then to make sure he wasn't.[39]

His obituarist in the *Dictionary of National Biography*, Michael Kitson, remarked that 'both Blunt's own actions and the treatment of him not only by the public but also by officials were permeated at every turn by the class divisions in British society'.[40] Where his social inferiors would have rotted in jail for a lifetime, Blunt was 'punished' by the withholding of the

Grand Cross of the Victorian Order to add to his knighthood. Or so it seemed, until much later a very different kind of Prime Minister came along.

Harold Wilson, however, was not that different. Indeed, the two Harolds' similarities were more remarkable than their differences, not least in their attitude to the monarch. They were sentimental and sententious, and where they could use her for their own purposes they did. After his narrow victory in the 1964 election Wilson took his family to the Palace to meet the Queen; it was her first experience of a Labour government. The intellectuals within it, Richard Crossman and Anthony Crosland, fretted at what the former called 'the thinness of it all' when involved in royal ceremonial. Of his induction to the Privy Council he wrote, 'I don't suppose anything more dull, pretentious or plain silly has ever been invented.'[41]

Coming to terms with Labour ministers was easy. Charteris helped hugely with his bonhomie, and the royals fell in with this spirit. The Queen Mother had always kept her right-wing views to herself. Prince Philip could take his frustrations abroad, pursuing his new enthusiasm – the World Wildlife Fund. The Queen and her sister made an effort to find common ground with these new ministers, so unlike the 14th Earl of Home. Princess Margaret mimicked the haughty, cheroot-smoking Crosland, and Barbara Castle quickly found herself seduced by the royal charm. 'I was admiring the Queen's dress, with a blue sash across it, and Princess Margaret plucked at it and said, "Darling it's showing your bosom too much." The Queen, referring to Charles's O Levels, said to her sister, "You and I would never have got into university."' When Mrs Castle left for a vote on the abolition of the death penalty, Margaret said, 'You mustn't miss that. I care very much about that.'[42] They had a convert in one easy session.

In the absence of written records it is hard to make even an interim report on Elizabeth II and her husband as they moved confidently through the early years of her second decade on the throne. We know what we know only because her ministers at that time were compulsive diarists and gossips, and not struck dumb in their memories of royalty like their political opponents. Crossman tells us, for example, that busy ministers were asked to travel to Balmoral because the Queen spent the early autumn there, whereas she would never come down for a Privy Council at *their* convenience in London. We know that through her officials she intervened or tried to intervene to stop proposals which affected her position, or even her image. Richard Crossman was staggered to find that when a maverick backbencher, Emrys Hughes, tried to introduce an Abolition of Titles Bill as a publicity stunt she pressed Harold Wilson to stop it being debated. Wilson gave way, only to be brusquely pulled back by Crossman and Roy Jenkins, who insisted that the Bill should be debated. Tony Benn, the Postmaster General, ran into a more successful Palace veto when he showed the Queen his proposed designs for new stamps.

> I was there for an hour. I took a lot of stamps with me that didn't have the Queen's head on them . . . and I said, 'I understand you've banned any such stamps.' She said, 'Oh no, not at all. Not at all.' 'Well,' I said, 'I didn't think for a moment that that could be the case.' She said, 'I've never seen them', so I opened my box and I put on the floor all these beautiful stamps that I'd designed. 'Oh,' she said, 'this is very interesting. They're lovely stamps.' Then I packed them up, and by the time I got from Buckingham Palace in the car to my office – about twelve minutes – the Palace had rung the Prime Minister's office and the Prime Minister had rung my office to say there was no question of these stamps ever being used.[43]

The Government had a tiny majority, and the Palace knew how to muzzle this cheeky minister. Later, Benn had another wheeze. He would have all the rulers of Great Britain, including the regicide Cromwell, in a series embossed as required with the effigy of the Queen. This was vetoed, not for the reason he expected 'but because Edward VIII was on it. Edward VIII was a greater threat to the monarchy than Oliver Cromwell'.

The Duke of Windsor had remained coldly ostracised by his family for the first twelve years of the Queen's reign. He was not invited to the wedding of her popular cousin Princess Alexandra of Kent in 1963. The Queen might have relented, but her mother did not. One courtier told Douglas Keay that the Queen's refrain was always, 'It's Mummy that matters. We mustn't do anything that hurts Mummy's feelings.'[44]

By the mid-sixties, however, some formal stigmas were fading. Divorce reached the royal circle when the Earl of Harewood, oldest grandson of George V and the first of the Windsors to have a distinguished independent career, had a child out of wedlock with the violinist Patricia Tuckwell, and was divorced by his wife. He wished to marry Miss Tuckwell, and under the archaic Royal Marriages Act needed the Queen's consent. She sought the advice of the Labour government, and the Cabinet duly obliged by telling her there was no objection. Harewood spent a period of internal exile from the royal family, pushed out of some of his figurehead jobs and, more painfully, from the directorship of the Edinburgh Festival. He regards the whole episode with justified distaste. 'The Royal Marriages Act is the most totally outdated piece of legislation . . . still on the books. . . . Divorce has very much been a taboo, of course. It's against the beliefs of the Church of England and the Queen is Defender of the Faith. Not I suspect a logical position any more, but that's only what I think.'[45] Harewood's divorce, remarriage and long career in the arts were to have longer-term consequences for the Queen's nearer kin. In the seventies and afterwards they could see that divorce was not a complete destroyer of status: life could and did go on.

All this was small consolation to the aged Duke of Windsor. He was eventually allowed to bring his Duchess back to one ceremony, tinged with bitter irony. In 1967 a memorial plaque to Queen Mary was to be unveiled outside her London residence, and all her living descendants were invited. So was the woman whom she had always refused to receive. Before the television cameras the Windsors took their place on the rostrum, nervous and fidgeting. The Duke greeted the Earl of Harewood with sympathy; he knew what his nephew had endured. The Queen and her husband were pleasant and unflappable. The cameras waited for the first fingertip touch between Wallis and the Queen Mother in thirty years. Would the Duchess curtsey – she who had been so curtseyed against? The press reported that she did not. But the cameras show a graceful movement between a bow and a bob. The Duchess was not submissive, but she inclined. For the rest of the Duke's life small contacts were resumed, ending with a visit to his deathbed by the Queen and Prince Charles. The British ambassador in Paris, Sir Christopher Soames, instructed the Duke's doctor that he could die before, or die after, but he must not die during the visit. The Duchess brought his body for burial at Frogmore near Windsor, and stayed for the first time at Buckingham Palace. There she was snapped at a window looking like some lost sheltering sparrow, unsure whether a haven has turned into a trap. She lived on until she was ninety, perennially pestered by Mountbatten to hand back her jewels to the British royals, and her wealth to charities over which they would preside. But Mountbatten's 'excessive zeal' was counter-productive, and the fortune went to the Pasteur Institute.

The nurture of the next Prince of Wales was a major preoccupation for his parents in the late fifties and early sixties. Charles had heard himself created Prince of Wales in 1958, scarcely comprehending it. After prep school his opinion was not sought on his next place of education. Lord Charteris, who would have favoured Eton, the courtiers' school *par excellence*, thinks Gordonstoun was chosen for its ability 'to bring them up to know what it's like not to be royal'. But above all it was where Prince Philip had cut a dash; 'for the son, if the father's been a tremendous success there, that gives him some problems in trying to live up to his father's reputation'.[46] And Gordonstoun was tough, even brutal. 'Where at Cheam he had found diffidence at Gordonstoun he came up against adolescent malice.'[47] The Prince survived, but he has never betrayed any yearning for his sons to repeat the experience. Even the proclaimed advantage of remoteness – that it would keep the press from harrying him – proved to be an illusion. His first gulped cherry brandy in a Stornoway hotel vied with the Profumo affair in the headlines. His exercise book was stolen and touted round the world. Only when he went to the Australian outback school Timbertop, an offshoot of Geelong

Grammar School, did Charles discover a peer group who could steer a course between the extremes of servility and hostility. His six months there were, he said, 'the most wonderful period of my life'.

Before Charles left Gordonstoun the Queen held a dinner party to discuss the next stage of his development. Its membership was similar in style to the group once gathered by Queen Victoria to discuss the future of her feckless eldest son. Harold Wilson and the Archbishop of Canterbury joined senior courtiers and the inevitable Mountbatten to offer their advice. Charles himself opted for Trinity College, Cambridge, where he would be under the eye of the new Master, Rab Butler. The old statesman let the heir know that he 'was holding three-quarters of an hour available for advice every evening', but found the prince happier to keep appointments with the young Chilean who was helping to write his memoirs, Lucia Santa Cruz.[48] He made friends more easily now. One of them was a Welsh socialist from Cardiff, Hywel Jones, who gave him a valuable insight into the Principality he had shortly to conquer. The royal family were about to have one of their periodic relaunches: Charles would have the starring role, at his investiture at Caernarvon.

The public life of the Windsors was now being handled with a lighter and more skilful touch. When Commander Richard Colville retired as press secretary in 1968 he was succeeded by the young Australian Bill Heseltine, a man who did not think that the techniques of public relations were inventions of the Devil. Prince Charles's own equerry, David Checketts, had a personal connection with the PR executive Nigel Neilson, who told any courtier who would listen that the Prince of Wales was 'a first-class product, being criminally undersold'.[49] Throughout 1968 Neilson seeded the press with favourable publicity about the Prince, and the Prince obliged with a diffident candour unlike the starchy attitudes of his elders. But they too were now persuaded to relax and enjoy a good portrayal.

Lord Mountbatten was preparing for Thames Television a vast film autobiography comprising twelve episodes of personalized and partisan history. It was a huge success. His son-in-law, the film producer Lord Brabourne, suggested to the Palace that a candid film portrait of the entire family should be made. 'The Palace staff – the senior ones – weren't very enthusiastic. The crucial person in this was Bill Heseltine. It was his enthusiasm and understanding that made it possible.'[50] The veteran BBC producer Dick Cawston was brought in for a series of consultations with Prince Philip. The aim now was not merely to launch Charles, but to present the human face of his family as well. 'The thing that had never come across about the Queen was her own personality and her tremendous sense of humour.' This was on display in the finished *Royal Family*, which was passed without cuts. The Queen listened patiently to the blundering and verbose American ambassador, told of an incoming ambassador who really did look like a gorilla when he came through the door, and made small talk with Wilson and Richard Nixon. The American President skilfully manipulated the royal family while on screen, cuing them instead of waiting for his own cues. The family organized a lochside barbecue. Prince Charles twanged a cello string which snapped in the face of an alarmed Prince Edward.

That programme was seen by 23 million viewers on its first screening. The royal icon seemed to come off the stamps and coins and into the home – these were just ordinary people. Ordinary people, however, would not have been able to retain power and copyright over *Royal Family*. It has not been seen for many years, but its work was done after one screening. In public opinion polls, there was an instant rise in the numbers who believed that the Queen was 'in touch with what is going on'. Daylight had shone on the magic and mystique of monarchy, and Bagehot's warrings seemed groundless.

As the embattled government struggled through 1968, under attack from Welsh and Scottish Nationalists, it looked to the coming investiture as a spectacle which could both woo the Welsh and enhance the British sense of wellbeing. This coincided with the strategy of the media-friendly royal advisers. Like his great-uncle in 1911, the Prince of Wales was to be put through a ceremony of reinvented ritual, flanked by Cardiff's finest (Home Secretary Callaghan and Welsh

Secretary George Thomas) and stage-managed by his uncle the Earl of Snowdon. First, however, the young man was sent to the University College of Wales at Aberystwyth to learn a little Welsh and rather more about the nation. The Welsh Language Society declared its opposition. Demonstrations and small-scale bombings by nationalist ultras calling themselves the Free Wales Army caused two fatalities. The Prince kept his nerve, and his advisers launched a media blitz for him in the weeks before the great day. Here his candour disarmed his critics. He told Jack De Manio on the BBC: 'As long as I don't get covered in too much egg and tomato I'll be all right. I don't blame people demonstrating like that. They've never seen me before. They don't know what I'm like. I've hardly been to Wales and you can't expect people to be over-zealous about having a so-called English Prince come among them.'

When he did come among them it was in a ceremony tailored for television. Lord Snowdon presided as Constable of Caernarvon, in a uniform of his own design which earned him the sobriquet 'Buttons'. Plywood chairs, a transparent perspex canopy, a gold and platinum crown (rumoured to have a ping-pong ball as its orb for lightness) – these were the trappings of a film set, to be used once and then discarded. The Prince managed the Welsh, and got in a small joke about his favourite *Goon Show* character, Harry Secombe. He took an oath, his hands between the Queen's, to be her 'liegeman of life and limb and earthly worship, and faith and truth I will bear unto you to live and die against all manner of folk'. The Welsh were won over. The Prince's Cambridge friend Hywel Jones was there. 'I suppose my view at the time was that it was going over the top, that it wasn't really required. . . . But I enjoyed going to it, and it was great fun. It was like a Habitat version of Lord Snowdon's dream of how the world would be in Caernarvon.'[51]

Following the Prince's interviews, and the television transmission of *Royal Family* a week before, the relaunch of the Windsors was complete. It had the dream ingredients of public relations, glamour and nostalgia, novelty and dignity, with a new star in an old tale. Its real triumph, one perceptive critic wrote, 'was in the way it realised its aim without apparently cheapening the monarchy'.[52] Republicans could only fret at the 'astonishing tinsel and glad rags of Caernarvon'. It was mock-Welsh, but it did not mock Wales. Warm sentiment had triumphed over intellectual disdain. Royal commentator Tom Nairn puzzled over 'just how such a sensible and mature population can so infallibly lose its marbles over fake-feudal buffoonery'.[53] It seemed to be game, set and match to the Windsors' new star, no longer knowingly undersold.

9

THE CRITICS GATHER

From her fortieth birthday to her Silver Jubilee as monarch the Queen and her advisers deliberated on how the royal appeal could be maintained. Following *Royal Family*, how much more daylight should be let in on the magic and the mystery? Prince Philip thought carefully about how the monarchy should be presented, and understood the medium of television. Throughout a decade of irreverent change and the satire boom his was the most sympathetic ear in the Palace when proposals were made to reveal more of the human face of royalty. But his restless energies had their downside; he had never had the gift of tact. At Balmoral Cabinet ministers found that he would take over their conversations with the Queen, bang on inexorably, and then say 'It's time for them to go.' But he could also be acute and sympathetic, encouraging them to persist with people who had impressed him. Thus he turned suddenly to Barbara Castle in the middle of a gilded Windsor soirée, saying: 'I'm very sorry Peter Parker never became chairman of the Railways Board. He worked with me, you know, on the Outward Bound thing, and I thought he was absolutely first class.'[1] Like Parker, most of the unwitting recipients of this royal recommendation got where he wanted them to go in the end.

Philip had drawn his own firm conclusions from the royal

tours of the sixties. In 1965 a visit to Germany had sealed new friendships and reminded him of old ties. The Windsors could now formally visit Wolfsgarten, and meet Philip's German kin. He came back to hold forth at length about the urgent need for Germany to be reunited, which provoked a veiled attack from the *Daily Mirror* and a warning letter from its chairman to the Prime Minister.[2] In contrast his patience with the Commonwealth was easily stretched. In Canada, where French Canadian separatists were agitating against the monarchy, he told an Ottawa audience, 'Look, we don't come here for our health. We can think of better ways of enjoying ourselves. . . . The answer to this question of the monarchy is very simple – if the people don't want it they should change it. But let us end it on amicable terms and not have a row.' His private views had been made very clear to Tony Benn a year earlier: 'The first thing to do is to get rid of the Commonwealth angle. They [the Canadians] don't want us and they will have to have a republic or something.'[3]

The Duke believed that at home people would still 'wave their little flags' for a while, but unthinking loyalty to the monarchy was on the way out. It could attract devotion by being paternalistic. He argued for the new ombudsmen to be located within the Palace, so that people could look to the monarch for redress against grievance. He was, of course, trying to exploit that old asset of the Crown – the popular belief that if only the monarch knew what was wrong it would be put right. Benn said this idea was nonsense. He came away thinking the Duke a brighter man than he had believed, 'but very like a Tory MP, which of course he is'. At that time there was wild talk of military disobedience over Rhodesia, and the eccentric Cecil King solicited Mountbatten's support for a national government. (Subsequently he claimed that the latter told him that the Queen had had more letters of complaint about the government than any previous monarch.)[4] In this climate the Duke's admirers touted him as a possible saviour. The polls always had him high on the list of potential members of a government of national unity. But he stayed silent and took out his dislike of political posturing on safer targets abroad. When the future Chilean president and coup victim Salvador

Allende explained that he was wearing a suit at a white tie reception because his party represented the poor, and did not approve of hiring evening dress, the Duke retorted: 'I suppose you'd wear a bathing suit if they told you to!'[5]

But Philip was not slow to air the royal family's money problems. During a virtuoso performance on *Meet the Press* on US prime-time television in November 1969 he handled with great aplomb questions about the influence of the Beatles, British trade prospects, the relative failure of the 'more rigid' monarchies of Europe, and educational choice. Then he was asked a very unadversarial question: how could the royal family survive on an allowance based on the 1952 Civil List arrangements? Philip replied, 'We go into the red next year . . . which is not bad housekeeping if you think of it.' He detailed accurately what the allowances were, and then continued, with words that raised a storm back home: 'Inevitably if nothing happens we shall either – we may have to move into smaller premises; who knows?' Had he closed down Sandringham, his sympathetic interlocutors asked. He replied: 'No, *not entirely* [authors' italics]. For instance we had a small yacht which we have had to sell, and I shall have to give up polo fairly soon and things like that. I am on a different allowance anyway, but I have also been on it for the last eighteen years.' Was there resistance to an increase? He tilted at his parliamentary critics: 'I suppose so. I mean I don't think anybody likes seeing money being – anybody getting more money, frankly, except the people who are getting it themselves.'

The Cabinet, as its assorted diarists noted, grumbled mightily. 'A sheer piece of exhibitionism, showing off how good he is on TV,' thought Crossman. Even the loyal Wilson complained that 'It takes royalty to assume that all their private income is to be kept to themselves.'[6] 'Why after all should the Civil List be increased to allow Philip to play polo when his wife is one of the richest women in the world?'[7] Barbara Castle asked. The embarrassed Wilson reached for one of his pet placebos – a Select Committee to review the Queen's income. The Civil List was not for polo ponies, but to assist the monarch and her immediate family with the expenses involved in meeting public duties. Just what these were became clear when the Select Committee on the Civil List reported under the chairmanship of the new Conservative Chancellor of the Exchequer in November 1971. The funds invested under the 1952 arrangement as a hedge against inflation had been exhausted by 1970. But for the first time members of the Select Committee, including the Windsors' most vociferous critic Willie Hamilton, raised the question of the Queen's private fortune, which had been accumulating over the generations.

The Lord Chamberlain, Lord Cobbold, handled the Civil List questions with the acumen expected from a member of a great banking dynasty. There was detailed information about trivia such as the financial difference between Princess Alexandra's travelling to an official function by train and by car. There was the information that the Queen Mother's vast allowance, fixed at £70,000 per annum in 1970 prices, meant that she 'naturally retains a rather more elaborate Household'. Lord Cobbold exhorted the Committee to 'think in the Queen Mother's case more in terms of services rendered over the years of peace and war than to try to relate expenditure to the actual official duties of later years'.[8] Twenty-four years later, with the Queen Mother approaching her ninety-fifth year, the consideration for services rendered seemed even more substantial – £640,000. There was some sniping from the Committee at individual royals, particularly Hamilton's *bête noire* Princess Margaret, after Sir Michael Adeane maintained in consecutive breaths that the payments should be considered in the light of the recipients' inability to earn a salary, but that Lord Snowdon did, and should.

The key issue was not the 'pay rise', as the press described it, but the royal exemption from tax. Phillip Hall has shown how much misinformation on this subject had been provided before the 1971 hearings, with official booklets and semi-official spokesmen echoing each other that 'the Queen does not pay income tax on the Civil List but does on income arising from her private estates'.[9]In fact she did not pay tax on her private investment income, nor estate duty on her private properties, nor anything other than the local authority rates on her estates. The Prince of Wales, as Duke of Cornwall, voluntarily remitted half the Duchy revenues to the Treasury, but kept the rest as untaxed income, so that the immunity from tax applied to the sovereign's son as well as herself. Her own immunities went very wide. Why, for example, if the Queen's private estates were notionally open to tax, did she pay no tax on the profits of farming them? asked Joel Barnett. An Inland Revenue official replied that farming profits were treated as trade; trade was not an estate, 'and [the 1862 Crown Private Estates Act] does not say the Queen shall be subject, it says the estates shall be subject'.[10] The Select Committee, mindful of a spate of articles in the press following a polemic in the *New Statesman* entitled 'The Royal Tax Avoiders', by the then leftist firebrand Paul Johnson, tried to establish some facts about the royal fortune. It was not easy. Lord Cobbold simply echoed his sovereign's reported remark that estimates of £50 million were 'wildly exaggerated'.[11]

In the end a Select Comittee majority defeated, on a party vote, a proposal by Douglas Houghton that the expenses of maintaining the monarchy be drawn together under the administration of a Crown Commission, which would meet them from general expenditure. The issue of how reasonable they were would be taken out of the hands of the Palace, and the 'hidden' costs of trains, planes and yachts would be shown where they properly belonged, not lurking in departmental votes. (Willie Hamilton, in his alternative draft report, described this more brutally as 'expenditure upon the Royal Family' but got short shrift. The Committee, he says bitterly, 'didn't so much deliberate as grovel'.)[12] Its majority saw no anomaly in the use of a large staff for overlapping public and private duties. 'The Queen', Cobbold said, 'regards these people as her own servants.'[13] All, it was argued, were upholding the dignity of the Crown. Since Members of Parliament, then and now, have always resisted the idea that their own staff should be controlled and employed by the Fees Office, rather than personally, they were not on the strongest ground in proposing to wind up the Queen's role as an employer.

For the first time there was a lively press debate about the royal tax exemptions. The *Daily Mirror* argued that the proposed increases worked out at 5 per cent per annum over the period since the Civil List was last assessed, but that four questions needed to be asked. How big was the Queen's fortune? Should it be tax-free? Were there too many hangers-on and minor royals? Did the royals live in too much splendour when there were one million people out of work?[14] These questions were not answered, and could not compete with personalized arguments following Willie Hamilton's description of Princess Margaret as a 'kept woman' – but they would come back to haunt the royal family for all that. Hamilton, though publicly mocked, received letters which showed that the *Mirror*'s questions were in many people's minds: 'it is money which is at the heart of British republicanism and money which taints the otherwise total commitment of many loyalists towards their Queen'.[15]

On the principal issue, however, Lord Cobbold had won. The office of Lord Chamberlain was no mere decoration of state; its holder controlled the Palace of Westminster and acted as a censor. Home Secretary Roy Jenkins had accepted a unanimous report that the Lord Chamberlain's powers of censorship over the live theatre should be abolished. But Lord Cobbold lobbied ministers against this decision, and the Prime Minister was soon wilting.

> 'I've received representations from the Palace,' he said. 'They don't want to ban all plays about live persons but they want to make sure that there's somebody who'd stop the kind of play about Prince Philip which would be painful to the Queen. Of course,' he hurriedly added, 'they're not denying that there should be freedom to write satirical plays, take-offs, caricatures; what they want to ban are plays devoted to character assassination, and they mention, as an example, *Mrs Wilson's Diary*.'[16]

This was a shrewd move by the courtiers. The magazine *Private Eye* had mocked Wilson, and all politicians, throughout the sixties, though for a long time it left the royals unscathed. The fictional diary was a tender spot for the Prime Minister, but Jenkins insisted that whatever the Queen thought of her Lord Chamberlain's powers they had to go.

In 1975, when Wilson was back in Downing Street again, a fresh appeal was made to update the Civil List in view of the soaring inflation of the early seventies. The opinion formers of the day were invited to the Palace, where the entire royal family stood beaming at the top of the staircase to greet them. It was 'a great night of royal salesmanship'[17] and it worked on the Labour Party. The Civil List increases were to be agreed on an annual basis, with the Queen herself agreeing, for the moment, to bear the cost of her Gloucester and Kent cousins (£118,000 in 1976) from Duchy of Lancaster revenues. The continued accumulation of her untaxed income and assets, and the steady acquisition of new properties for racing and shooting purposes, went largely unrecorded. *Private Eye* targeted her directly for the first time. WINDSOR WOMAN IN MASSIVE £420,000 POOLS WIN was the cover headline, with the speech bubble from the royal mouth proclaiming: 'It will not change my way of life.'[18]

One projected change might have touched the powerful interests around the throne directly. More than eight hundred peers sat in the Lords by hereditary right, their powers of debate and delay more real than the monarch's. Remove that power, and one of the mainstays of the principle of hereditary succession, embodied in the monarchy, would be gone. Richard Crossman noticed 'a frisson' when the Queen read out Labour's proposals for Lords reform in her speech from the throne at the State Opening of Parliament. The changes would have cut into the Lords' delaying powers, and removed the automatic right to vote possessed by every hereditary peer who could be bothered to take his seat. The issue touched on what was always the conservative argument against change: strip away the basis for one respected authority, and you diminish them all.

But the intended reforms failed in the face of a filibuster by opponents and those who wanted the Lords abolished altogether. For a further quarter of a century the House of Lords has retained a membership the majority of which sits by hereditary right. There were, however, no new hereditary creations after 1964, under either Wilson or his Tory successor, Heath. The marriage of the Queen's daughter Anne to Captain Mark Phillips was not followed by the customary ennoblement. She was the first monarch's daughter since Princess Cicely, 466 years before, to marry a man without a title either possessed or bestowed.

Anne had long been typecast as a sulky and rebellious teenager: 'snobbish, bored, pouting, sullen and disdainful', the *Washington Daily News* had called her. In *Royal Family* she had seemed awkward, a foil to her eager-to-please older brother. Her blunt responses and short fuse marked her as her father's daughter. She competed hard and made sure that she was good at one big thing, rather than flirting with many different ones. The Princess was good enough to represent her country at three-day eventing, and part of the appeal of Mark Phillips (cruelly nicknamed 'Fogg' by her family) was that he could handle a horse even better than she could.

Anne's approach to life was not unlike that of the Prime Minister, Edward Heath, who did not suffer fools gladly. Cecil King, summoned to a musical evening at Windsor, noticed that the Prime Minister 'was seen talking to no one else except Anne'.[19] Each of them would have found the other's lack of small talk a tonic. Small talk, however, was the essence of the sovereign's meetings with her Prime Ministers; with the serious Heath these occasions were less relaxed than with some of the more avuncular incumbents of that post.

Heath had plans for the monarch. With singular determination he had embarked on the parliamentary battle to take Britain into the European Common Market. That meant an aptly timed royal visit to France, to soothe away the bruises of the Gaullist vetoes of the sixties and to prove that Britain was now *communitaire*. (The visit gave the opportunity for her brief visit to the dying Duke of Windsor.) It also meant a flurry of visits to the dominions, to prove to Australia, New Zealand and Canada that the mother country still loved them. The tension arose from a third obligation, deeply felt by the Queen but more of an irritant to Heath – the Commonwealth summits themselves.

At Singapore in 1971 Heath found himself cornered by his fellow Commonwealth leaders over his plans to sell helicopters to the South Africans, in defiance of an arms embargo which Britain had supported. The Queen was upset by his 'undisguised disrespect for the institution in general and most African leaders in particular.'[20] There was still a high tide of optimism about the emergent black African states in the Commonwealth secretariat, and the Queen sensed it. 'The Queen in Singapore was very troubled . . . it was a younger Africa then, much more optimistic about the future, much more principled in their whole outlook on international affairs. This issue looked like taking sides with apartheid, and the Queen was never for that.'[21] Ironically one of the African leaders, Milton Obote of Uganda, was overthrown by Idi Amin's coup while he was in Singapore.

The next Conference was to be held in Ottawa. The Canadian Premier, Pierre Trudeau, had disliked the stiff formalities of Singapore. He wanted a more informal gathering, and he wanted Heath to come too. But Heath was put out because he had not been consulted about the timing. Secretary-General of the Commonwealth Sonny Ramphal remembers: 'Ted was committed to not showing up, and I know that Trudeau worked very hard . . . and (it can only be a suspicion) that he worked very hard through the Queen.' In the end 'Ted made his point by not staying for the whole of the meeting, but he was there.'[22] This was an advance on his initial view that if he did not go, nor need she. From Ottawa onwards no one would have any doubt that the Queen intended to be a permanent fixture at these regular events, and was not bound to take advice on them from her British Prime Ministers. Over the years the core of her relationship with the Commonwealth has been her deep knowledge of the independence leaders of sixties' vintage, many of whom are, in a sense, her contemporaries.

Elsewhere in the world, however, the Queen was badly let down by a representative acting in her name. In 1975 Gough Whitlam's Labour government ran into trouble when the Senate, in which his party did not have a majority, blocked the Budget. The Governor-General, Sir John Kerr – a Whitlam appointee – took it upon himself to dissolve both Houses and to appoint the opposition Liberal leader, Malcolm Fraser, as caretaker Prime Minister since Whitlam would not call an election. A furious Whitlam told a hurriedly convened press conference that if he had had any inkling of what was afoot he would have asked the Queen to dismiss the Governor-General.[23]

Malcolm Fraser, dubbed 'Kerr's cur' by Whitlam when he won a landslide victory in the subsequent election, argues that what happened strengthened the monarchy. He had been tipped off. 'I had a telephone call from John Kerr at eleven in the morning, and – this was Sir John's prudence – he protected Her Majesty absolutely throughout this whole interview. He kept her informed but never asked her advice on any matter at all. The Queen would have been infinitely more damaged if it became known that the monarch's representative had deliberately refused to use the reserve powers [to dissolve Parliament] written into the Australian constitution.'[24]

The Queen was protected by Kerr from what would have been an insoluble dilemma had Whitlam got to her first. Was she constitutionally obliged to accept the advice of her Prime Minister, or to endorse the action of her representative? In the event she did not have to choose. What the incident did highlight was the tenuous nature of being 'Queen of Australia' while being resident in London. Malcolm Fraser was keen to involve the royal family more closely in Australian life, and suggested to the Prince of Wales that he should 'buy a country property and either breed horses and race them on the Australian circuit, or cattle and show them. People would have been delighted if the Prince's bull won the Grand Championship in Sydney or if the Prince's horse won the Melbourne Cup. But he wasn't sufficiently interested or concerned, I think, to continue with that particular proposal.'[25] Fraser's notion fell on diplomatically deaf ears. Much later, when Prince Charles wanted to be Governor-General, the option of an Australian identity in any form had closed.

The Queen had just opened the Australian Parliament in February 1974 when she was called back to London by a constitutional crisis at home. Britain had been convulsed by the miners' strike and the proclamation of a three-day week. Edward Heath's embattled government had sought a way out of the confrontation by calling a 'Who Governs?' election. Heath and his ministers were exhausted. The most senior civil servant, Sir William Armstrong, had collapsed. 'He lay on the floor talking wildly about moving the Red Army from here and the Blue Army from there' before he was 'taken away for a rest'.[26] The election was a disaster for Heath, with his bitterest Tory critic, Enoch Powell, calling for a Labour vote. The most remarkable feature was the high Liberal vote. 'The electorate was trying to tell us something. But was anyone listening?'[27]

Labour ended up with four more seats than the Conservatives, but the latter had won more votes. Heath sat tight in Downing Street and attempted to interest the Liberal leader, Jeremy Thorpe, in a coalition. Thorpe might have taken a post if his colleagues would have allowed it, but the message they told him to convey was 'while it wasn't clear who had won the election, it was quite clear who'd lost it'.[28] Throughout the weekend Palace staff kept in touch with Heath, uneasily aware that if the crisis went on for too long he could be seen as kept in office by royal tolerance. On the Monday he went to see the Queen and resigned. Had he asked for a dissolution, so that a clear mandate might come out of a second election, the Queen would have been advised by her Private Secretary to call on Harold Wilson first to see if he could form a government – as in the end he did, requesting the dissolution himself in the following October, when he won a tiny overall majority.

For the Queen, the return of a mellow Wilson must have had the comfort of slipping on an old shoe. He was more garrulous now. At Downing Street, and where permitted in the audiences with the Queen, there was a certain 'lingering over the spirit bottle'.[29] Joe Haines, his factotum, recalls him returning from the Palace a trifle tipsy, and proud of the Queen's interest in the gossip he could relay.[30] Personalities were safer to discuss than policies and principles, and much more fun. At one of their early meetings Wilson confided to the Queen that he would retire before long. 'I've told her the date,' he would tell his cronies during his last administration, 'she's got the record of it so that no one will be able to say afterwards that I was pushed out.'[31] The date was never vouchsafed, and he went on throughout 1975 in his new role as 'the sweeper not the striker', slowly becoming more of a part-time Prime Minister, while the economy began the slide down to the International Monetary Fund crisis of 1976.

In March 1976, on the eve of Wilson's sixtieth birthday, his own backbenchers were in bitter revolt over proposed cuts in public expenditure. The Prime Minister tipped off James Callaghan, whom he expected to succeed him, that he would resign the following week. On 16 March he went unnoticed to the Palace, and returned to give a stunned Cabinet the news. He had gone on long enough: there were other talents that should be given their opportunity before the run-in to the next election. The Queen thus said farewell to her sixth Prime Minister, whom she made a Knight of the Garter.

While Wilson's dramatic resignation occupied the media, on 19 March a brief announcement was put out from Kensington Palace: 'HRH The Princess Margaret, Countess of Snowdon, and the Earl of Snowdon have agreed mutually to live apart. The Princess will carry out her public functions unaccompanied by Lord Snowdon. There are no plans for a divorce.' The Palace hoped that Wilson would steal all the headlines, but it underestimated how big this royal news was. The Snowdons' marriage had gone from passionate to semi-detached. For a while they had amused themselves with other companions, content to do anything that did not frighten the horses. As Snowdon's career as photographer and documentary maker blossomed, the Princess seemed to be in sharp decline. Her sparse official engagements were mocked. She was the butt of Willie Hamilton's personal attacks, which, as an added indignity, he later claimed the Queen had encouraged because she was 'very disturbed about the behaviour of her sister'.[32] He named a Tory MP, Alan Clark, as the messenger; Clark today insists he was joking: 'I might have said to Willie as a sort of aside – you know, here's something you can really get your teeth into – but I would never go up to [him] and say the Queen wants you to do something.'[33] Margaret was in her early forties, still attractive and sensual. As Snowdon looked elsewhere, and sequestered himself in his own rooms at Kensington Palace, the couple either sulked in private or rowed in public. She felt he was 'hurling her royal rank back at her without reason', she told her biographer. Soon she found a haven elsewhere, a new love. She told Christopher Warwick that she 'was filled with a renewal of spirit, maybe the Holy Spirit'.[34] If so, the Holy Spirit can seldom have found a stranger place to manifest itself.

The Princess had been given a plot on the Caribbean island of Mustique by her friend Colin Tennant, and it was here that she brought Roddy Llewellyn, an amiable young man seventeen years her junior, with more social connections than talents. 'The budding romance hit exactly the right note the first evening,'[35] according to gossips in the know. As it came into the public prints, accompanied by photographs of the couple together (cropped from larger group pictures), Lord Snowdon let his indignation be known. On 14 March the *News of the World* followed up its stories of the Princess's visits to Roddy's commune, where she 'slept in the only furnished room', with a profile of 'That Angelic Rodders, By His Ex-Flatmate'. Snowdon, who had been more discreet about his own relationship with Lucy Lindsay-Hogg, now had his opportunity to exhibit innocence. After the separation was announced Snowdon gave an affecting show of grief when he landed in Sydney, and wished the Princess well 'in a halting voice'.[36] 'I've never seen such good acting,' the Princess said.[37] By contrast Roddy got a terrible press; 'Margaret's Darling Angel On The Dole' summed up the mood. For a while the story competed for prominence with the election of Wilson's successor, James Callaghan.

The press hostility further damaged the already unpopular Princess. Hamilton's book, published the year before, had savaged 'her expensive, extravagant irrelevance'[38] in familiar style. There was a good deal of evidence that the public agreed with him. In Philip Ziegler's exhaustive analysis of the letters that Willie Hamilton received 'there are 550 hostile references by name to members of the royal family . . . of which Princess Margaret and Princess Anne account for 323 or 58%'.[39] Editorials, MPs and bishops pronounced that she should consider whether her public position was tenable any longer. Because Margaret's spats with the press and reported extravagances coincided with a period of severe economic hardship and calls for sacrifices elsewhere, they did more harm to the royal family than any scandal since the time of her uncle Edward VIII. Her sister felt obliged to consult with the spiritual and temporal authorities, who duly proffered the advice she had been expecting; the forced retirement of the

Princess would be a greater disaster than her soldiering on. This she did, enduring divorce, serious hepatitis and some savage treatment by *Private Eye*, before a slight rally when some commentators belatedly discovered that 'while [she] plays hard she works hard too'.[40]

If no one ever found the answer to the question 'What is Princess Margaret for?', this was not because the question was unanswerable. As the sovereign's only sister she needed the protective hauteur that nonplussed her friends, but it kept her talents enclosed rather than letting them out. Snowdon had been able to dip in and out of being a royal, at some profit to his own career. She never could. There was no serious competitor for the Bad Girl role in her generation of royals until the appearance of Marie-Christine Von Reibnitz, whose marriage to Prince Michael of Kent in 1978 gave the press a new target – 'Princess Pushy'. Margaret would lose her prominence as the younger members of the family filled the gossip columns, fading as gently from them as the diaphanous Roddy Llewellyn did from her own life. It was a final irony that she was always destined to act as counterpoint to her sister's successes, a dire reminder that the accident of primogeniture allows one life to glitter with achievement while another set of talents moulders away. Margaret's misfortunes in 1976–7 simply provided the dark background for Queen Elizabeth's achievements around her fiftieth year, which augmented the reputation of the monarchy.

Royal stamina took the Queen through her Jubilee year of 1977, which did not seem the happiest of times for a national party. Welsh and Scottish nationalism, and the torments of Northern Ireland, seemed to be pulling the United Kingdom apart. It had a *de facto* coalition government, struggling with the ravages of inflation, industrial disputes that were sometimes violent, and economic decline from wider causes. The Queen's youthful effigy had appeared in 1952 on a solid array of pennies, sixpences, shillings, florins and half-crowns, unchanged in appearance since her great-great-grandmother's time. Now all this had gone with decimalization, widely viewed as a hidden devaluation. As the *Times* morosely noted, the pound note now had a purchasing power only one quarter of its 1952 value.

The Queen's husband made his own views on the state of the nation clear with a commissioned article that seemed to echo the views of the new Leader of the Opposition, Margaret Thatcher. He argued 'that we have been driven too far along one road; that we have got to come back a little and not concentrate so heavily on the unfortunate, the underprivileged, but try to create a situation where the enterprising can make their contribution'.[41] This enraged Labour backbenchers but left their leader unmoved. Prime Minister Callaghan was trying to invoke a world of order, discipline and standards. For his embattled government, renewed royal pageantry was an unlikely but real solution. Provided the expense could be moderate, and much of the activity self-generating within local communities, it could do nothing but good. The country would identify with the Queen, its one symbol of survival and continuity. The Cabinet agreed to give the Queen an antique coffee pot as a commemorative gift, and sat back to enjoy the general bonhomie.

The Jubilee was a hit with the British people and the Commonwealth nations of the southern hemisphere. With seasonal serendipity the Queen and Prince Philip visited the Pacific islands of Western Samoa, Tonga and Fiji, whose easy graces she had always enjoyed, and then New Zealand and Australia, still murmuring from the dismissal of Gough Whitlam. Then she returned to Britain with the swallows, and began a summer tour of the home island in the new walkabout style. The Celtic nationalists were put in their place by a speech in Westminster Hall, where the Queen took a highly political note on a matter of current controversy: 'I cannot forget that I was crowned Queen of the United Kingdom of Great Britain and Northern Ireland. Perhaps this Jubilee is a time to remind ourselves of the benefits which union has conferred at home and in our international dealings, on inhabitants of all parts of this United Kingdom.'[42] The speech was made on the day after the Scottish Nationalists had made major gains in the Scottish local elections, but, by coincidence or not, that was the high point of their advance.

When the Queen arrived in Scotland on 17 May the SNP led the polls with 36 per cent of the vote. Nationalists dreamed of 'Embassy Row springing up somewhere in the terraces of Edinburgh', and their defence committee was 'designing epaulettes and badges for the regiments that would be taken out of the British Army'.[43] But the royal tour awakened a ral enthusiasm for this symbol of unity. Royalist Scots felt rejuvenated. In both Scotland and Wales the royal progress was unconfined, and the centripetal powers of the monarch were confirmed as a dynamic of togetherness. Eighteen months later devolution failed to find a sufficient majority in Scotland, and was defeated by a 4:1 margin in Wales. Secession seemed a very remote option indeed. Only in Northern Ireland, which the Queen insisted on visiting despite the risks, was there a sullen indifference in the Catholic and Republican enclaves, fitfully illuminated by the bonfires and fireworks of their 'loyalist' neighbours.

In England itself, enthusiasm for the Jubilee had been a slow burner. 'By the end of March', Ziegler noted, 'it was possible to detect a mood, not so much of enthusiasm as something close to resignation.' Then, slowly, the enthusiasm took off, climaxing with a chain of bonfires across the land on 6 June, and a procession through London the following day. The State Coach, with the Prince of Wales riding behind it as Edward VII had ridden behind his mother's coach in 1897, went this time to St Paul's Cathedral. The walkabout that followed, as the Queen progressed to the Guildhall, was designed to be seen as a popular re-coronation by acclaim – by the British, of the British, for the British. A public holiday and good weather guaranteed the success of thousands of street parties. Even the most clamantly left-wing of the London boroughs, like Barking, were swept along by the feeling that it was time for a tired people to have a party – a mood closer to VJ Day than to the coronation of 1953. An older England briefly re-awoke: every village had its own sports day, ox-roasting, social evening or garden party.

Dissidents from this mood did not have a happy time of it. The anti-Jubilee issue of the *New Statesman* sniped at Prince Philip but funked the republican case. The one constitutional historian it mustered mildly observed that 'the Crown provides just the right amount of historical therapy to be tranquillising without being harmful. . . . For the sake of a democratic Britain, perhaps even a democratic socialist Britain, now is institutionally the time to conserve. The monarchy, historic incubus though it may be, is a part of that process.'[44] It was easier to peddle 'Stuff the Jubilee' badges or buy the Sex Pistols' record, which its admirers believed had 'all the force of a hand-grenade tossed into an arrangement of gladioli':[45]

> God save the Queen
> A fascist regime
> Made you a moron
> A potential H-Bomb.

The Sex Pistols sang that the Queen 'ain't no human being', but the nation disagreed. This was a substantial and successful relaunch of the Windsors.

For Elizabeth II it was a time to be reminded that she was esteemed for herself, as symbolic survivor, national icon, and, with the pregnancy of Princess Anne, new role player as future indulgent granny. The Callaghan government, too, had good cause to be satisfied. The Jubilee met its political agenda of quietism and safety-first admirably. It conjured up a renewed patriotic endeavour, never better seen than when Virginia Wade, the quintessential well-bred British loser, won the Wimbledon tennis title in Jubilee Year. And it provided exactly the right mix of 'historical therapy' at insignificant cost. In David Cannadine's irresistible paradox: 'it was an expression of national and imperial decline, an attempt to persuade, by pomp and circumstance, that no such decline had taken place, or to argue that, even if it had, it really did not matter'.[46]

That there *had* been such a decline, and that it could be reversed by drastic methods, was the credo of the Leader of the Opposition. Whereas Callaghan was a natural conservative leading a radical party, Thatcher was a radical, almost a revolutionary, who meant to drag the grandees and crypto-social democrats of her own party behind her chariot. Her relations with the Queen merit a chapter in themselves, but it should be recorded at the outset what these two women had in common, besides their age and sex. Mrs Thatcher meant to tackle the kind of agenda that was never far from Prince Philip's speeches – bad industrial relations, entrepreneurial timidity, welfare state mollycoddling. There would be no trouble for the Prime Minister from that quarter. She treated the monarch with almost exaggerated deference. And the shadow of IRA violence lay across both their lives. Margaret Thatcher's close political ally, Airey Neave, had been blown to pieces in New Palace Yard by a terrorist bomb at the beginning of the 1979 election campaign. Then in 1980 Lord Mountbatten, sailing near his Irish holiday home of Classiebawn Castle with members of his family, was blown up by the IRA. Five of the eight on board, including one of his twin grandsons and an Irish boy of the same age from the village, were killed. His daughter Countess Mountbatten, who survived with her husband and her other twin reflects that 'the fact that we were all together in this little thirty-foot fishing boat was in a way comforting, because he was with his family, doing what he loved doing. . . . He went out like a shooting star and that's perhaps the way he would have chosen – perhaps not an IRA bomb, but that sort of a death, rather than lingering disabled into old age.'[47]

Mountbatten had been a port of call for the younger royals for two generations. He had recently advised Prince Michael of Kent on how he could surmount the obstructions to his marrying the Catholic divorcee Marie-Christine Von Reibnitz. He was rumoured to have one of his own granddaughters in mind as a suitable bride for Prince Charles, and he had always been the Prince's closest confidant in the royal circle. He had a wider range of contacts, and more eclectic interests, than anyone else within it. At Mountbatten's spectacular funeral – planned, by himself, many years earlier – the anguish of the Prince of Wales was very apparent. In the next decade, when social and political divisions widened, and where neither he nor his mother would be welcomed as moderating influences by the denizen of Downing Street, the young man would have to find his own way.

10

TWO QUEENS IN THE HIVE

Margaret Thatcher began her remarkable autobiography with the words 'We knew we had won . . .' but passed on at once to make a reference to the sole contest, always undeclared, in which she was never an outright winner – that with another woman who was head of her profession in Britain, the Queen. 'Although the press could not resist the temptation to suggest disputes between the Palace and Downing Street, especially on Commonwealth affairs, I always found the Queen's attitude to the work of the government absolutely correct.'[1] What will not be clear until the state papers are disclosed is how correct the Queen found Mrs Thatcher. The new Prime Minister had a direct manner and bustling style which contrasted starkly with the careful ambiguities of courtiers. At home and abroad, this was not to be an administration dedicated to making the complacent comfortable.

Within months of taking office Mrs Thatcher stood up in the House of Commons and named Sir Anthony Blunt as a former Russian agent. Her hand had been forced by a book, Andrew Boyle's *The Climate of Treason*, which made it clear that his name would come out under cover of parliamentary privilege. The Prime Minister was advised against making her statement by Cabinet Secretary Sir Robert Armstrong, on the basis that, as her biographer puts it, 'literally anything out of the mouth of an informed minister was likely to shed a ray of light into corners best left publicly dark'.[2] No corner had been darker than the art historian's Palace connection. It had been Blunt's bastion: the position from which he had been able to protest his innocence, and even to threaten writs, right up to the time of Mrs Thatcher's statement.

On that very day, as though the Queen had just heard of this scandalous state of affairs for the first time, Blunt was stripped of his knighthood. Royalty shuddered and cast him out, having known all along (if Adeane's admission to Peter Wright is to be believed)[3] what manner of man he was. The news caused outrage on the Right. Alan Clark found it all 'disreputable; one of those episodes that indicate a kind of closed society in the Palace circle that regards itself as immune from the norms of appropriate behaviour. . . . My view is that Anthony Blunt should have been executed because he had contributed by his action to the deaths of our agents.'[4] Mrs Thatcher's action had unwittingly exposed the involvement of the Palace in a very British piece of humbug. It was not an auspicious start.

Abroad, the Queen had already come to the aid of her new Premier. After fifteen years of defying sanctions and world opinion the Smith regime in Rhodesia had been pushed into an 'internal settlement' which provided a compromise black prime minister, Bishop Muzorewa, after an election which the African parties fighting the guerilla war had not been able to contest. In the politically charged atmosphere of the time, Murzorewa was widely seen by black Africa as a front for Ian Smith. With a Commonwealth Heads of Government Conference scheduled for Lusaka, the Zambian capital, in July 1979, the issue was explosive. The Queen was advised by the Prime Minister not to go. 'The Queen dismissed [talk of danger] with absolute scorn,' Sonny Ramphal remembers.[5] The response of the Palace was that she was going as head of the Commonwealth, and that she had visits to Tanzania and Malawi to perform first. The Queen therefore went to Zambia well ahead of Mrs Thatcher, who arrived to a hostile press. Donning dark glasses, she said to the astonished Foreign Secretary: 'I am absolutely certain that when I land in Lusaka they are going to throw acid in my face.'[6] In fact she found the atmosphere more exuberant than offensive, although she was taunted in the newspapers as a bigot who lacked 'the extraordinary loving heart of the Queen'.[7] The Prime Minister was a tyro in African affairs. The Queen was not, and the difference showed.

Like Mrs Thatcher the Queen had close relations whose instincts were well to the Right, and who sympathised with the Rhodesia lobby. She nevertheless listened hard, both to her Zambian host Kenneth Kaunda and to the Australian Prime Minister Malcolm Fraser. The latter had already tried to persuade Thatcher not to accept the Rhodesian internal settlement, after being warned by Lord Carrington that 'she'll never change her mind about anything if there are more than two people in the room'. Fraser found the Queen more pragmatic:

> With Her Majesty there wouldn't have been any argument because she had a sense of these things, knew what it was all about from a very long involvement in the affairs of the Commonwealth . . . and an innate instinct for justice, for what had to happen, if you like. So [there were] two enormously different people with enormously different reactions, and you know one of the difficulties for Her Majesty must be the convention under which the monarchy operates in Britain to be living alongside at times a head of government with which one disagrees. A lot of that is assumption . . . I come to personal conclusions about her instincts, none of it based on anything which she's ever said to me.[8]

The Commonwealth leaders swiftly concluded that 'it was perfectly clear that the Queen was for a compromise. . . . To respond to the situation [there had to] be movement away from UDI, away from racism, to independence, to freedom for Zimbabwe.'[9] Mrs Thatcher, to her credit, saw a way to emerge from all this with concessions but without surrender. The British offered a constitutional conference in London, leading to free elections involving all factions, including the Patriotic Front guerillas. There would be no recognition of Muzorewa as the interim authority. There would be a return to the responsibilities of the colonial power first, not to some nebulous Commonwealth body. Observers thought the Prime

Minister downcast at the end of the Lusaka Conference as she read the statement drafted by the Foreign Office. Her voice 'lacked its usual timbre.'[10] The Queen, in contrast, seemed moved and elated when she said farewell to Lusaka. The subsequent Lancaster House Conference in London did bring the warring factions to agree on elections, which were held under the supervision of a British Governor, Christopher Soames, acting in the Queen's name. The Marxist Robert Mugabe won majority support, and kept Zimbabwe in the Commonwealth. It was a success of real substance for Margaret Thatcher and the Foreign Office which she so despised. What was less noticed at home was how much of the indispensable groundwork, and the creation of a confidence-building atmosphere, had been done by the Queen.

But not all trips carried out for the good of the state had such a happy outcome. The monarch's overseas tours had always been, in part, an instrument of foreign policy. In 1980 Elizabeth II was subjected to unaccustomed indignities when a state visit to Morocco, where a sizeable construction contract was in the offing, fell foul of the eccentric King Hassan II. The Queen and her entourage had just been warmly received in Algeria and Tunisia, but in Morocco the Commander of the Faithful kept the Defender of the Faith waiting while he played golf. He turned a trip to Marrakesh into a sinister farce by insisting on half a dozen changes of limousine as a precaution against assassins. At a tented rendezvous in the Atlas Mountains the King left his guest waiting for the welcoming feast while he refreshed himself in an air-conditioned caravan nearby. Michael Shea, the Queen's press secretary, watched journalists waiting to see if the Queen would explode with rage. She did not. 'The Queen was an island of peace and tranquillity compared to what was happening round about her.'[11]

The Queen does not get mad when she has a chance to get even. At the final reciprocal banquet aboard *Britannia* Hassan arrived late, ignored the benign pleasantries of the Foreign Office minder, Douglas Hurd, and attempted to leave after half an hour. On a ship this is not an easy task, and Hassan was kept aboard, in the politest way, to watch Beating the Retreat on the quayside. Every arcane moment of the ceremony was inflicted on the descendant of the Prophet before he was able to disembark. Watching British journalists noted that his hostess did not come on deck to wave him off after a 'frosty, almost cursory leave-taking'.[12] As the British royals flew back to London with an anguished Douglas Hurd trailing in their wake, they left a message for the King: 'We have been especially touched by the way in which Your Majesty took such a personal interest in our programme.' The much-vaunted sense of humour does sometimes show through.

The Moroccan trip was a break in the monotony of the Queen's life as she came to the end of her third decade on the throne. In the drabness of Britain, now suffering from heavy unemployment and the rapid destruction of one fifth of its manufacturing base, the royal routines offered no major diversion to a sharply divided nation. Indeed on one occasion the divisions intruded on the routines. As the Queen rode towards Horse Guards Parade for Trooping the Colour in June 1981 a youth fired six shots at her from close range. They were blanks. The Queen, like her uncle Edward VIII on a similar occasion many years earlier, quickly calmed her mount and rode on. But the plunging horse, briefly glimpsed on television, became one more unnerving fragment in the mosaic of royalty. These images soon merged with others. There were hunger strikes to the death in Northern Ireland, and ferocious urban riots in some of Britain's cities. The emollient or 'wet' faction of the Cabinet was squeezed dry by a Prime Minister who proudly proclaimed that she was not for turning. Then out of all this wasteland grew the tall flower that was Diana Spencer. Prince Charles was to have a wife at last.

The turn of the decade had been a difficult time for the Prince. He had passed his thirtieth birthday knowing he might be only a fraction of the way through a lifetime's preparation for a few years on the throne. As the historian David Cannadine puts it: 'Monarchy is a very brutal institution. The heir to the throne has no job until either his mother or his father dies. It's the institutionalization of an oedipal trauma.'[13] This Prince, moreover, still had low self-esteem. It stemmed largely, according to one of his biographers, from Prince Philip's being a 'curious combination of someone who cares a great deal about his children but expresses that in a rather tyrannical and difficult way . . . he is still capable of reducing his son to tears by carpeting him over some public gaffe or a speech that he felt misjudged'.[14] The Prince had thus come to lean on his 'honorary grandfather', Lord Mountbatten. Whereas the dynasts in the royal family fretted that the Prince was not disposed to an early marriage, Mountbatten, the arch-dynast, had given different advice: 'I believe, in a case like yours, a man should sow his wild oats and have as many affairs as he can before settling down, but for a wife he should choose a suitable, attractive and sweet-natured girl *before* she met anyone else she might fall for.' Women, he argued, had to 'remain on a pedestal after marriage'.[15]

The Prince had circled around attractive aristocrats like Jane Wellesley, but such young women knew that marriage to him would mean a life sentence of glamour in aspic. He had had racy friends whose looks were inverse to their eligibility. Some had pasts which were an open book; some had their pasts revealed when they moved into royal favour. Married women made safer confidantes, and discreet companions. The sweet old-fashioned virgin proved hard to find. Mountbatten's daughter could see the Prince's difficulties. He was 'unlucky to strike a period of history when girls, women in general, had become so liberated and had led such free and independent lives. It was quite difficult to face up to the tremendous loss of liberty and restrictions if they did marry the Prince of Wales.'[16]

The assassination of Mountbatten in 1979 was a shattering blow to the Prince. 'He was the one person who understood him,' argues the Earl's old friend Barbara Cartland, 'and understood that he was a brilliant person having had a very difficult father. I'm not being unkind, but I mean he is German. . . .'[17]Prince Philip feared that Mountbatten's influence would overshadow Charles, and was arguing against his son accompanying the ex-Viceroy on a trip to India, when fate and the IRA intervened. Mountbatten may have schemed that his granddaughter Amanda Knatchbull, whom he had intended should accompany them to India, would catch Charles's eye. The purchase of Highgrove House in

Gloucestershire suggested that he was nest-building. Early in 1980 Mrs Thatcher had chaired a small Cabinet committee set up to examine the implications of his marrying a Catholic – Princess Marie-Astrid of Luxembourg had been a press fancy three years before. Its members recall 'the extreme anti-Catholicism' of the Prime Minister's approach.[18] Fortunately, when the Prince's choice was announced to the world it seemed impeccably safe.

Diana Spencer was the youngest daughter of a former royal equerry, 'Johnny' Spencer, the 8th Earl, and his former wife Frances, herself the daughter of the Queen Mother's friend Lady Fermoy. She had five bloodlines of rampant Stuart genes going back to Charles II, but was (as her relatives tactlessly boasted) free of previous sexual liaisons, being but an artless teenager. As she emerged from puppy fat into a tall and lissom young woman she caught the fancy of the Prince of Wales. There were danger signs, but he ignored them. Diana was the child of a broken marriage. Her father guiltily doted on her, but was managed by a new wife, Raine, whom his children loathed. So Diana craved affection, and could scheme to get it. She first touched the heart of the Prince of Wales by telling him how forlorn he had seemed at Mountbatten's funeral. He needed someone to look after him, she said. Charles had mother-figures in plenty, and saw this uneducated girl, thirteen years his junior, in quite another light. She was *tabula rasa*, and could be written into an important part of his life, while the rest of it, including his mother/lover figure Camilla Parker-Bowles, went on as before. Diana was infatuated. 'He was her knight in shining armour,' says one confidant, 'and I do believe that at some stage love was returned.' Marriages have been made on much less, but few could expect the tests to destruction that inevitably went with this one.

Diana duly underwent her baptism of fire from the media. She was stalked by royal sleuth James Whitaker as she watched the Prince fly-fishing in September 1980. Even then she showed a streetwise awareness: 'All I could see was a green-booted wellington sticking out behind a pine tree . . . then I saw this person had a make-up mirror in her hand and was looking back across the river through it to see who or what was there.'[19] A little later Whitaker and his peers turned up at the kindergarten where Diana worked, securing the notorious see-through photograph of her cotton skirt against the sun. 'She learned a lesson that day. However nice people are, the one thing a journalist wants is a picture and a story.' It was not the only thing Diana learned. 'She always knew she looked very good in front of a camera. She enjoyed the attention of the photographers and she was always flirtatious.' Few saw it at the time, but Diana had had a forerunner inside the Palace – the Queen Mother. Penny Junor, after watching her for ten years, concludes:

> Diana and the Queen Mother have a great deal in common. They both married into the royal family and they have this unique ability, which I think goes beyond anything that any blood royal has, of communicating with people. Blood royals have a problem with the press. They fundamentally don't like them. Diana, and the Queen Mother too, will say hello. The camera loves them. They give this coquettish little look – and behind it is pure steel in both cases, I think.[20]

The steel in Diana was not at first apparent. Her mother, by this time Frances Shand Kydd, wrote to the press asking that jounalists should leave her alone. One piece of press intrusion upset her for deeper reasons. The *Sunday Mirror* published a story that Diana had made a secret visit to the royal train when the Prince was aboard one night. The story was indignantly denied by the Palace. The editor, Bob Edwards, checked his reporters' story. Diana had dined at the Parker-Bowles' house and left afterwards for London. Edwards still believes that she ended up in sidings in Wiltshire, although he later received a card from a well-connected columnist which simply said: 'It wasn't Diana. It was Camilla.'[21] Andrew Morton has documented Diana's slow realization that wherever she turned it was always Camilla, the object of the Prince's affection, trust and, it seems, perennial desire. Another authority, who wishes to remain anonymous, says that even beforehand there were signs that the marriage would not work, but it went ahead 'because the tea towels had already been embroidered'.

All these forebodings were put aside on the day. The

government, eager for diversion and pageantry, declared it a public holiday and the massed royals drove in open carriages to St Paul's. Johnny Spencer stood in uneasy proximity to his ex-wife, while Raine Spencer watched him anxiously. Her mother, the romantic novelist Barbara Cartland, now step-granny to a real princess, consoled herself for the absence of an invitation by dressing up in a St John's Ambulance Brigade uniform and toasting the bride and groom on television. Soap opera and royalty once more came dangerously close. So completely did Diana seem to fit the bill for Palace, press and public that Barbara Cartland said, 'It's the first time the [next] Queen of England has been chosen by referendum.'[22]

But the Princess's dress designer found herself puzzling on the great day that 'Diana had lost an awful lot of weight', so that they had had to keep taking her dress in.[23] The danger signs of the Princess's eating disorders were already there. She had received inadequate help in adjusting to the iconic family with whom she now stood on the Palace balcony. Later she denied that she had been schooled in royal ways by the Queen Mother: 'When I started carrying out official engagements I hadn't a clue what I was doing. It was dreadful. I know that people think that all sorts of people gave me lessons. But they didn't. Just nobody helped me at all.'[24] Within the Palace she failed to pick up the rhythm of the secret hierarchies. The wisest of the old courtiers had some sympathy for her: 'She wasn't used to the formality which is inseparable from the royal family, even at Balmoral. . . . I think she found it difficult to sit next to frightful old bores. . . . I was brought up knowing how to behave in front of servants, how to make conversation at lunch and at dinner with whoever I was sitting next to. And I don't think people have this knowledge now.'[25] On the wedding day, however, most people felt as Charteris did: 'I saw nothing but sunshine and happiness for them. I'm only sad I was wrong.'

On one occasion the Queen did intervene on her daughter-in-law's behalf. Press secretary Michael Shea called in the nation's newspaper editors to plead for privacy for the now pregnant Princess of Wales. After an exchange of pleasantries he played his big card. The Queen walked in, awash with corgis. The *News of the World*'s editor, asked her why, if Princess Diana felt harassed, she did not simply send out a footman to buy her wine-gums. 'What a pompous man you are, Mr Askew,' replied the monarch, and the press pack fell gratefully on their wounded colleague. The hapless man lost his job within a month. Few noticed that his basic question – why was Diana always backing into the limelight? – would one day need an answer. For the moment the superstar could do no wrong: she produced an heir, Prince William, within a year of her marriage.

However, the Queen's gift for repartee deserted her when she suffered a more direct intrusion in 1982. An unemployed labourer, Michael Fagan, twice broke into Buckingham Palace. On the first occasion he was content to make off with a bottle of wine. On the second he strolled round at his leisure, unchallenged, and finally discovered the Queen's bedroom. She was woken by him slamming the door. 'I drew back the curtains and looked at her face. She spun round and said, "What are you doing here?" So before I had a chance to speak she's hopped out of bed. . . . There wasn't any shock on her face; a very cool lady. She just walked out of the room, and said "Get out" two or three times.'[26]

Later the Queen told Michael Mann, 'The thing I was really worried about was that Prince Philip was going to bust in, and all hell was going to break loose.'[27] Fagan unwittingly did the Palace a favour. He hugely embarrassed the Home Secretary, William Whitelaw, who offered to resign at this revelation of the lax policing at the Palace. The Queen had pressed every alarm bell in sight – without getting a swift response. Fagan had triggered alarm systems, had been seen as he wandered the corridors barefoot – nothing had been done. Had he been a deranged killer instead of a harmless eccentric she would have stood no chance.

Another member of the royal family had been at serious risk that year. When the Argentine invasion of the Falkland Islands drew a combative response from Mrs Thatcher, the primary responsibility rested on the fleet. Prince Andrew was a helicopter pilot aboard the carrier *Invincible*, the pride of the hastily assembled task force. There were those in government who felt that a young royal was too great a risk in this hazardous venture. The Queen's chaplain recalls that 'there was considerable suggestion that Prince Andrew shouldn't go, because of his position in the royal family. The Queen over-ruled that. She said, "No. He's a serving officer. He must take his turn with the rest."'[28] For the Palace, therefore, this drama was more than a great affair of state. The Prince saw action at sea, as his father and grandfather had done before him. His moment of maximum danger came on the Argentine national day, 25 May, when their depleted Air Force launched a last, furious, all-out attack. When an Exocet missile hit the container vessel *Atlantic Conveyor*, for a while there were excited rumours from Buenos Aires that it was the *Invincible* which had gone down.

'With hindsight', say historians, '25 of May [was] the turning point of the war at sea.'[29] Prince Andrew had his part in it, scattering decoy chaff from his helicopter as the attack came in. His mother had referred to him on that day, saying, at an engagement at Alnwick Castle: 'Our thoughts are with those in the South Atlantic, and our prayers are for their safe return to their homes and loved ones.' After a moment's silence she added, 'Ordinary life must go on.'[30] This sombre approach puzzled some of the Prime Minister's more brash admirers:

> The Queen's attitude during the Falklands War was something of a mystery to many of us. She was not nearly as forthright at the outset as one might have expected. . . . She was perhaps also, by then, a little wary of the role that Mrs Thatcher was assuming. She was not gung-ho at all, whereas George VI would have been totally gung-ho, and so would George V; no question about that. As for Victoria, she'd have actually been at sea with the task force, stood off with *Britannia*.[31]

Alan Clark was expressing the romantic rage of the supporters of a warrior queen that the real queen was somehow not quite on side. It was one of the embarrassments of the war for royal apologists that not only the Queen but also *Britannia* never put to sea. Despite all the arguments that it could be a hospital ship in time of war it turned out to use the wrong kind of fuel – incompatible with the rest of the fleet. As Phillip Hall says,

'It is odd that such an oversight should have occurred when the Duke of Edinburgh was a frequent user of the ship, and had spent twelve years in the Navy.'[32]

On the evening of 14 June Mrs Thatcher went into the House of Commons to announce that white flags were flying over Port Stanley. No one had better cause to rejoice than she, who had been firm throughout and 'was now elevated to a new level of public esteem, hitherto untouched'.[33] In this spirit of exaltation the Prime Minister did not conceal her disapproval of what she thought were milksop sentiments expressed by the Archbishop of Canterbury at a special thanksgiving service in St Paul's. Relations with the Church of England, of which the Queen was Supreme Governor, became glacial. Later Mrs Thatcher put her own interpretation on the war, telling a Guildhall banquet that to be proud of the task force was to be proud of being British. She presided – in the absence of members of the royal family – at an ostentatious City salute to the task force. The sight of her taking the salute with her military leaders drove home a point not lost on either woman, and summed up by David Cannadine:

> It was Thatcher's war. She was responsible for the military direction of the war – so to the extent that the nation rallied, it rallied behind her rather than the Queen. The Queen was curiously low-key, an absentee. Precisely why that was we don't yet know. . . . Thatcher as warrior queen, the very emblem in her own person and often in her own clothes of Britannia, very much upstaged the Queen.[34]

From that day forward the Prime Minister was to grow in self-confidence and a sense of her own rightness on every issue. It would dismay some of the advisers of the real monarch, as they watched what they saw as the rival queen in the hive spreading her wings.

Opponents were swept aside in turn. The Labour Party of 1983, led by the venerable Michael Foot, recorded its worst election performance since 1918. The Prime Minister's stellar reputation seemed to carry all before it. Even those who had suffered from her policies murmured, 'She's wrong but she's strong.' Old scores were settled elsewhere. Union membership was banned outright at the government's security listening centre, GCHQ in Cheltenham. A compromise which would have traded membership for a no-disruption pledge, negotiated by Cabinet Secretary Robert Armstrong, was brushed aside by the Prime Minister. She listened instead to her press secretary, Bernard Ingham, who produced the one line always likely to get a conditioned reflex from her. 'It will look like a U-turn,' he said. 'It will *be* a U-turn.'[35] The deep resentment at GCHQ lasted for a decade, with some staff disaffected at the way their civil rights had been treated. When the later bugging of the royal family was slyly revealed to the world in 1992, one of the reasons why the electronic eavesdroppers fell under immediate suspicion was that, by then, old loyalties had been eroded by new resentments.

The National Union of Mineworkers, which had helped to bring down Edward Heath in 1974, was now drawn into an unwise confrontation. The NUM president, Arthur Scargill, as militant and unyielding as Thatcher herself, was the perfect opponent for a government which had reorganized the police, ensured that coal stocks were high, prepared the industry and had the media on side. The Prime Minister's comparisons were crude but effective. 'We had to fight an enemy without in the Falklands,' she orated. 'We always have to be aware of the enemy within, which is more difficult to fight and more dangerous to liberty.' In her memoirs, the NUM strike is not described in these terms. It becomes, even more luridly, 'Mr Scargill's Insurrection'. Insurrections have to be put down, and the NUM were ground down over a bitter and barren year.

At the end of 1984 Mrs Thatcher had a brush with a more vengeful antagonist. During the Conservative Conference at Brighton she had narrowly escaped death from an IRA bomb. Five delegates were killed, and two of her key ministers seriously injured. Assassination, the frequent curse on kings, had been aimed at her personally. Shaken but resolute, the Prime Minister said simply: 'Life must go on.' She appeared on her conference platform on time. From this moment onwards, her status abroad had the glamour and instant recognition previously enjoyed only by Churchill in the fullness of his achievements. Foreign statesmen were mesmerized by what Mitterrand called 'the eyes of Caligula and the mouth of Marilyn Monroe'. As she swept down one aircraft stairway after another, from Tokyo to Tbilisi, she was dressed more and more regally – 'like a Holbein portrait,' the fashion writer Brenda Polan noted.[36] She began to refer to 'my government' in queenly style, and to use the royal plural – as in 'We are a grandmother.' No disaster was safe from her instant and ministering presence. The real Queen was slow off the mark at such times, fearing she would be a distraction – even a further hazard. No such scruples troubled Mrs Thatcher. Instructions were given that she was not to be upstaged by those lesser royals who did turn up in the disaster areas. The Queen bore all this with fortitude and exemplary correctness; but there were mutterings at the Palace.

Alan Clark picked up these bad vibrations. 'Mrs Thatcher was always a very strong monarchist. . . . It was always said that she curtseyed very, very low and this was an object of private mockery at the Palace. . . . Mrs Thatcher's personal charisma and glamour and the deference which she was accorded on the global stage . . . were certainly bitterly resented.' In response to pressure from the Palace, the Foreign Office sent out instructions that the Prime Minister should not be greeted with the National Anthem when she landed on foreign soil. 'I'm afraid there were periodic attempts to humiliate her,' says Clark, 'to cut her down to size.'[37] There were early stories that the weekly meetings between monarch and Prime Minister were 'dreaded by at least one of them'.[38] When Mrs Thatcher asked if she should ensure that her apparel did not clash with Her Majesty's, she was firmly snubbed. The Queen, came a message from the Palace, never notices what other people are wearing – an incredible denial of three generations of Windsor clothes-consciousness. But the Queen has always had a capacity to live within her role and let the Premier of the day make the running. She is capable of laughing about herself. When she dined with Mrs Thatcher and her five living predecessors, Macmillan, Home, Heath, Wilson and Callaghan, she was seen to make a mock deferential bob for the photocall.

Queen Elizabeth II by Cecil Beaton, 1955.

Princess Margaret and Lord Snowdon, 1962.

Queen Elizabeth opens the Victoria Underground Line, 1969.

Charles's Investiture as Prince of Wales, 1969, complete with transparent canopy for the TV cameras.

Prince Charles with Lord Mountbatten, 1979.

Lady Diana Spencer, pursued by the press, 1980.

The wedding of Prince Charles and Princess Diana, 1981.

Queen Elizabeth II and Prime Minister Margaret Thatcher, 1979.

Australian Prime Minister Paul Keating puts a protective arm round the Queen, 1992.

Prince Andrew and his wife Sarah, the Duke and Duchess of York, 1986.

Prince Edward engaged in amateur dramatics, 1986.

Prince Charles and his young family on holiday in Italy, 1985.

The marriage of Prince Charles and Princess Diana looks close to collapse, 1992.

Windsor Castle in flames, 1992.

The fact was that for most of the time the two women co-existed well enough within their respective roles. On some things they shared a common outrage. When President Reagan sent troops to the Commonwealth country of Grenada to mop up a small leftist clique which had liquidated the charismatic leader Maurice Bishop and was thought to be under Cuban influence, he did not consult the head of state (the Queen) and was not entirely open with his closest political ally. The Prime Minister had cabled Reagan in the early hours of 25 October 1983 to say that military action by the USA would be seen as 'intervention by a western country in the affairs of a small independent country, however unattractive its regime'.[39] By then the operation was in full swing. The Queen and Mrs Thatcher both woke to pictures of excited, almost hysterical marines hustling the unprepossessing revolutionaries aboard their helicopters. The Queen saw her Governor-General, Sir Paul Scoon, uneasily validating the invasion, *ex post facto*, and was 'deeply offended', as the Commonwealth Secretary-General soon discovered.[40] The Prime Minister was summoned to an immediate audience – said to be the only one in her eleven years in office at which Mrs Thatcher was not invited to sit.

President Reagan, whose knowledge of the constitutional status of Grenada was flimsy, soon charmed Mrs Thatcher back on to his side, telling her that when he next dropped in on Downing Street he would be careful to throw his hat through the door first.[41] Others were not so easily appeased. It was true that Grenada's Commonwealth neighbours in the Caribbean approved. But in the wider Commonwealth those governments which feared destabilization by powerful neighbours, such as Zimbabwe, argued forcefully that the United States should have been denounced publicly as well as chastised privately. The next Commonwealth Heads of Government Meeting in New Delhi was soured by these resentments, which were put to the Queen. One observer there saw her being corralled for a photocall with Mrs Thatcher and the Indian Prime Minister, Indira Gandhi. She 'felt she was being used a little bit in a political context and would have nothing to do with it'.[42] An eye-witness noted that she 'dismissed the idea with a flick of the wrist and Mrs Thatcher looked at her as black as thunder'.[43]

New Delhi was nothing compared to the next meeting, at Nassau in the Bahamas. At this Commonwealth Conference the British Prime Minister was totally isolated on the issue of sanctions against South Africa. She was opposed to them, and said so volubly. The secretariat saw the unanimity of the opposition which this aroused. 'She had worked herself into the position where people were beginning to identify her not with anti-sanctions but with pro-South Africa . . . it was as though she was more opposed to sanctions than to apartheid.'[44] Matters were not helped by the fact that Mrs Thatcher and her travelling court – advisers like Charles Powell and Bernard Ingham – were impatient of the attitudes struck by Commonwealth leaders. Alan Clark recalls that 'she was pretty scornful of it all. She and Charles Powell had a translation for the acronym CHOGM (Commonwealth Heads of Government Meeting). Their translation was Compulsory Hand-outs for Greedy Mendicants. It was kept quite private, but that was the attitude.'[45] With such a viewpoint the British Prime Minister was unlikely to be moved by what she saw as moral posturing.

The Queen's position was different. She had gone to Nassau on the *Britannia* and remained aboard throughout. Observers noted visible irritation as she went through the ritual of photocalls and dinners – when a boat-load of delegates turned up late, she drummed her fingers on the rail in a manner reminiscent of her great-grandfather. She had been left in no doubt that many delegates believed that Britain was close to forfeiting its special place in the Commonwealth. Rajiv Gandhi, whose mother had hosted the last CHOGM in New Delhi before her assassination, talked of the danger that the whole institution would come to an end. Much the same was said by a succession of African leaders in their routine twenty minutes with the monarch. 'Why can't you talk to her?' was the theme. It was Bob Hawke's first conference as Australian Premier. He was soon attuned to the strained atmosphere: 'I was well aware that you wouldn't describe the relationship between Her Majesty and her Prime Minister as one of extreme cordiality. In a formal sense there was a respect and acknowledgement of the role and importance of the other, [but] it's fair to say that the Queen didn't have a great affection for Mrs Thatcher. She had the odd expression about her which I found rather fascinating.'[46]

What happened was a stand-off. Though outnumbered 48:1 Mrs Thatcher would not yield to secure unanimity, and appeared on television dramatically illustrating with finger and thumb how tiny and insignificant the agreed sanctions were. But she had to agree to a Commonwealth study being undertaken by what was inelegantly described as the Eminent Persons Group. It recommended sanctions, which Mrs Thatcher continued to denounce as 'repugnant'. But the Commonwealth had been preserved intact, and the Queen was credited with a major role in this. Sonny Ramphal believes that 'if the Queen hadn't been there, we might have gone on the rocks. . . . Mrs Thatcher became an aberration, and added to that by not caring.'[47] In part it was a difference of personal chemistry. One woman had a lofty, perhaps exaggerated, view of what the Commonwealth stood for. The other saw only its sanctimonious verbosity. The difference came through in personal behaviour. 'Put Mrs Thatcher in a jeep driving down a country road in Tanzania or Jamaica, and put the Queen in the jeep, and they're two different people,' says Ramphal. 'One is an observer, the other a friend come to visit.' For the bustling Prime Minister it was all an interruption from the real world; to the Queen it *was* the real world.

The differences should not be exaggerated. Both women behaved with absolute propriety. Their personal relations, in the United Kingdom context, seem to have been unruffled. Yet it was in that context that their real or assumed distance was remarked. In June 1986 the Commonwealth Games in Edinburgh were hit by a boycott caused by Thatcher's adamant stand on sanctions. Just before the Games the *Sunday Times* printed a front page sensation: 'Queen dismayed by "uncaring" Thatcher'. The article was claimed to be the result of 'several briefings by the Queen's advisers, who were fully aware that it would be published'. It then made four points: (1) The Queen believes that the Thatcher government lacks compassion and should be more 'caring' towards the less privileged in British society; (2) The Queen feared during the year-long miners' strike of 1983–4 that long-term damage was being done to the country's social fabric; (3) Her Majesty had reservations about Thatcher's decision to use British airbases for their raid on Libya last April; and (4) The Queen fears that the whole thrust of the Thatcher government's policies threatened to undermine the consensus in British politics which she thinks has served the country well since the Second World War.

There was nothing here about the Commonwealth connection, but the article went on to say that 'the Queen is said to feel duty-bound to do everything she can – short of speaking out in public – to save the Commonwealth'.[48] The article caused uproar. The *Sun* pitched in with 'Stop Your Meddling, Ma'am'. Its rival, the *Daily Mirror*, delighted in a lurid rewrite of the original story, innocent of fresh facts: 'Queen and Charles Loathe Thatcher'. Facts, indeed, were in short supply, as elusive as the advisers who had allegedly briefed the *Sunday Times*. What was the truth of the matter? Andrew Neil, the editor, defends the story as it stands.

> There was a whispering campaign orchestrated by the Palace . . . to do down the Thatcher government. This began to appear in a whole host of stories done very subtly, never sourced to the Palace . . . that Mrs Thatcher was upsetting the royal family in general and the Queen in particular. There was a four-page article published in the *Economist* about the Prince of Wales's attitude to the Trident missile. It was never revealed in the *Economist* that [it] had been prompted by an interview by Prince Charles himself.[49]

Neil was not acting out of solicitude for the sensibilities of the Palace. He attributed his story directly enough to cause trouble. 'We didn't play by the Palace's rules – we sourced it to the Palace, and that's what caused the furore. They were perfectly happy to see these kinds of stories in the British press provided they weren't in the frame.' The man in the frame turned out to be Michael Shea, the Palace press secretary. In the week before the fateful article, he had addressed a meeting at the Palace on relations with the press, and some who heard him said that he believed it would prove to be a model of his art.[50] He must have been sadly disillusioned at the betrayal of confidences, and the way in which the piece built up a picture of total breakdown. He says: 'Certain facts about the Commonwealth or the coal strike or whatever were blown up out of all proportion and made into a package that suggested there was rivalry where none existed.'[51]

It was left to Sir William Heseltine, in a letter to the *Times*, to set out what the Queen's prerogative was vis-à-vis the politicians. The sovereign 'had a right – indeed a duty – to counsel, encourage and warn her government. She is thus entitled to have opinions on government policy and express them to her chief ministers.'[52] Nevertheless, he argued, the sovereign must act on advice, and keep all communications entirely confidential. This she always did. Heseltine did not deny that the Queen had views; he simply said that they could never be known. The result of the alleged leak was a bad few days for the real or imagined rivals. Mrs Thatcher was heard to say that it was the worst twenty-four hours of her premiership. Her supporters, like Alan Clark, believed that the briefing 'must have been a put-up job to cut Thatcher down to size'. Relations with the the Queen were cooler, and with the heir they perhaps never recovered. The Queen also showed the strain: as a result of the stress she had a heart check-up.

Yet those who prized the Thatcherite project were more alarmed than those who blenched at it. Hugo Young writes that 'it seemed to these fevered minds as if a great populist leader and her great populist campaign for national recovery were about to be subverted by a kind of trick'.[53] But despite the Thatcherite alarm Mrs Thatcher herself was too happy playing Elizabeth I to be disconcerted too long by Elizabeth II. And her instinctive deference to the monarch held her back from a confrontation. As another ex-*Sunday Times* journalist, Anthony Holden, puts it: 'The interesting thing about House of Windsor plc is that it represented everything Mrs Thatcher loathed. It was a flabby, over-costed, ineffective, unproductive organization that needed asset-stripping, cutting, chopping, perhaps even abolishing, and she did nothing about it at all except give it the best financial arrangements it had had in its entire history.'[54] The Grantham alderman's daughter was, in the end, a product of the generation that identified with the dutiful monarchy of the war years, with Spitfires and ARP helmets and deep, unquestioning patriotism.

The Thatcherite press was not like this. It was strident in its contempt for outdated institutions that might hold back the new meritocracy in its ravenous desires. A wimpish monarchy, shrinking from hard choices, nostalgic for the very consensus which it believed had held back Britain since the war, was a legitimate target for it. This happily combined with the new prurience, which flourished on the principle that scandal and sensation sold more papers. Both strands were interwoven in the powerful press empire of Rupert Murdoch, an Australian outsider with a substantial contempt for ancient British deference. The Queen herself would not be a target. There was no need. Her sons and their wives were to make targets enough.

The Prince of Wales was now approaching his fortieth year. His marriage had liberated him from one kind of speculation, only to invite another. If he had misgivings about the glamorous wife for whom the crowds always clamoured, he at first passed them off as a joke. It was clear that the couple had few interests in common beyond their two sons. Diana was said to have purged the Prince's household of more than forty retainers at different levels, but this merely increased his isolation. In the words of his biographer, 'she had liberated Charles to be himself: a tortured, self-doubting, almost monkish introvert, a man of ever more furrowed brow, bowed down by the accident of his birth, born in a century which he increasingly mistrusted'.[55] He had set out to mitigate the divisions of the eighties. His conference at Windsor in 1984, bringing together leading businessmen and articulate, frustrated young blacks, led to his being appointed president of Business in the Community (BiC), a body dedicated to bringing enabling funds to the regeneration of local enterprises in inner city areas. Perhaps unwittingly he seemed to represent an alternative and sympathetic face of the Establishment, and the fact did not go unnoticed in the Prime Minister's praetorian guard. One who saw him lingering in an Inner London probation centre with young offenders, incubating one of his public speeches which linked unemployment and urban neglect with social ills, remembers that it was immediately after this that the image of 'loony' Charles, mooning round Scottish islands and talking to his plants, began to be formed in the press.[56] Charles's private views were sometimes expressed more vividly by others than by himself. The community architect Rod Hackney, one of his circle of unofficial advisers, came away from a dinner with the Prince in expansive mood. He told the *Manchester Evening News* that, in their words, 'the biggest fear of Prince Charles is that he will inherit the throne of a divided Britain . . . split into factions of "haves" and "have nots"'.[57] Accurate or not, this was perceived to be the Prince's position.

In other areas he lashed out more wildly. He had long been a supporter of alternative medicine, to the disquiet of the British Medical Association. Then he turned on the architects, choosing the 150th anniversary of the Royal Institute of British Architects to attack the proposed National Gallery extension in Trafalgar Square as a 'monstrous carbuncle on the face of a well-loved friend'. This pre-empted a ministerial decision, and wrecked the career of the architect concerned, Peter Ahrends. It also shocked his audience to the marrow. He had been invited to present the RIBA Gold Medal to a distinguished Indian architect, Charles Correa, for work with the homeless of the third world. Maxwell Hutchinson, later president of RIBA, was in the audience: 'He never mentioned poor Charles Correa . . . but started to dish out the vitriol, telling us that we'd got everything wrong and, what was worse that we were to blame for everything, for housing ills, social ills, planning ills, highway ills. And it gradually rose to a huge climax and left us numb.'[58]

The architects felt mightily ill used, especially when Charles's populist language evoked a huge public response. They felt that he was getting off cheap shots, because they guaranteed him the front page publicity that had been stolen away by his wife. 'He was in the gossip columns. His wife wasn't,' says Hutchinson. 'He used the simile [but] he didn't ever say critically why something was good or bad . . . the Royal National Theatre was like a nuclear power station; Peter Palumbo's building at No. 1 Poultry was like a 1930s' wireless set; the British Library at St Pancras was like a training school for the secret police. But he was never able to explain *why* it was good or bad.'[59] The Prince had many defenders. Some of them were architects, able to offer neo-Palladian visions which appealed. More were ordinary mortals who, like his friend Nicholas Soames MP, felt 'relieved that he had spoken up against the tyranny of modern architecture'.[60] The Prince seemed to provide something of substance to outface his critics when he launched another new scheme – Inner City Aid, for the rejuvenation of community housing 'from the bottom up'. Backed by Rod Hackney, it would need the kind of nurture which Charles gave to his Highgrove plants. The problem for the Prince was that his ambitions always moved on. He craved offices of state and became distrated from inner city wastelands.

In 1988 he met Mrs Thatcher, who had now been Premier for almost half his adult life, to discuss a wider role. He wanted to be able to deliver the Queen's Speech at the State Opening of Parliament if his mother was abroad. He desperately needed co-partnership with the Crown. A visit to the Australian bicentennial celebrations that January had stirred other hopes when he had been sounded out 'by a previous Governor-General [Sir Ninian Stephen] to consider the possibility of succeeding him during the 1988 bicentennial year'.[61] The Prince badly wanted the job, but his appointment needed bi-partisan support. 'It was never on the cards,' recalls Bob Hawke, then Australian Prime Minister, who vetoed the notion. 'The Governor-General must be an Australian. Silly as they were in some ways, my conservative predecessors shared that view.'[62] The only distant prize proffered by Mrs Thatcher (perhaps in the belief that she would be around to deliver it) was that the Prince might be the last British Governor of Hong Kong before it reverted to Chinese sovereignty, as his great-uncle Mountbatten had handed over India. In all these hopes Charles was frustrated. And there was worse to come: a full-scale criticism of the Prince from one of Mrs Thatcher's closest intimates, now brooding in isolation after leaving the government. Norman Tebbit reacted harshly on *Panorama* when the Prince's well-publicized views about inner cities were raised. It would be dangerous for the monarchy, Tebbit said, if the Prince went too far. 'I suppose the Prince of Wales feels extra sympathy for those who've got no job because in a way he's got no job, and he's prohibited from having a job until he inherits the throne.'[63]

The public views of the Windsors, mother and son, with a few splenetic contributions from Prince Philip, never provoked anything approaching a constitutional crisis, though on both sides of the divide there were those who would not have been averse to it. The real tribulations of the royal family came from quite another quarter: its own proliferation, and the opportunity it afforded the press to pry into private lives and to mock what it found there. That tendency was on the increase with the decline of deference, but now the family helped it along. Its members did not merely pull the wooden horse into the citadel; they built the steed from scratch. And if there was one occasion which marked the beginning of that process, it was the wedding in 1966 of the Queen's amiable second son, Prince Andrew, to a Miss Sarah Ferguson.

11

FAMILY AFFAIRS

> A certain family has been segregated; bred with a care lavished only up on race-horses; splendidly housed, clothed, and fed; abnormally stimulated in some ways, suppressed in others; worshipped, stared at, and kept shut up, as lions and tigers are kept, in a beautiful brightly lit room behind bars. The psychological effect upon them must be profound; and the effect upon us is as remarkable. Sane men and women as we are, we cannot rid ourselves of the superstition that there is something miraculous about these people shut up in their cage. . . . Now one of these royal animals, Queen Marie of Roumania, has done what has never been done before; she has opened the door of the cage and sauntered out into the street.[1]

Virginia Woolf was writing about the first of Queen Victoria's grandchildren to become an international celebrity for what she did, rather than for who she was. Marie, daughter of Alfred, Duke of Edinburgh and later of Coburg, wrote her memoirs, was immortalized in one of Dorothy Parker's best-remembered poems, and generally behaved with unroyal gusto. In the last decade a number of the key young Windsors have done a Marie. They have opened the cage and sauntered out into the street, as ordinary in their pleasures and follies as the next man or woman, extraordinary only in how those pleasures and follies can be indulged – and exposed. This has caused people to question the cost of barriers and the value of protocols which help to keep royalty a thing apart.

This questioning spirit did not begin with the egregious 'Fergie', but she particularly provoked it. Sarah Ferguson, the daughter of Prince Charles's polo manager, Ronald Ferguson, was introduced into the royal circle on the initiative of Princess Diana in Ascot Week, 1985. She shared with Diana Stuart royal blood, a runaway mother and a strong, wilful character. But she did not have the unsullied past which had been deemed essential for Diana. At the time of the invitation to join the royal party she was living with an ex-racing driver and advertising salesman twenty-two years her senior, Paddy McNally. But if she had a past so did Prince Andrew, whose long liaison with the actress Koo Stark had been very much in the public domain.

Once it became clear that there was a strong physical affinity between Sarah Ferguson and the Prince, the match gained the Queen's blessing. Andrew and his fiancée came across in television and press interviews as relaxed, hearty, and absorbed in each other. It was time for more Abbey spectaculars, commemorative stamps and titles. On his wedding day the Prince was created hereditary Duke of York by his mother. This was the first new hereditary dukedom since his youngest great-uncle had been created Duke of Kent, and it accorded with Mrs Thatcher's reintroduction of hereditary titles for exceptional service.

Prince Andrew had in fact rendered no exceptional service to the state, but he was brave, uncomplicated, and had kept out of serious trouble. Now he had a wife who seemed so like him as to be a chum. One of the key problems about the dysfunctional marriage of Charles and Diana seemed to have been avoided. The question was rather whether the press would give this unusual new Royal Highness a chance, and how she would adapt to royal status. She provided one early clue by gate-crashing Andrew's stag night with Diana – both dressed in police uniforms. Then she slipped out of Clarence House on the eve of the wedding to mingle with the crowds. The bars of the cage would not mean much to her. Initially the new Duchess was a boon for the moody and isolated Diana. Her no-nonsense image as the Sloane next door, as happy as Diana in the world of jokes and japes and gold-plated Sony Walkmen. Neither young woman received much help from appalled courtiers. They offered the secret casket of royal mystery; the Duchess wanted to parlay it into a good time. The veteran courtier Lord Charteris recalls that 'I was very fond of her. I thought she was a splendid girl, but basically unsuited to the task of being a royal princess – in any time, not only modern times.'[2]

Things rapidly went wrong for the Duchess. Her inelegant style was the subject of bitchy comment from female columnists. The tactless decision to build a huge ranch-style mansion at Sunninghill, near Windsor, opened up endless mockery of its *Dallas*-style splendours. It was dubbed South York, in imitation of the fictional Ewing mansion, Southfork. That it cost £5 million of the Queen's money, and that it had been built in a protected area where no other house would have been allowed, added to the criticisms. Fergie was drawn to showbiz superstars and oil billionaires. Her behaviour in the USA with and without the Duke was profoundly unroyal. 'She came over as a clown,' recalls American-born writer Susan Crosland. 'The lavish evening dress, and the jewels. And then this person jumping boisterously around pulling faces, and people think: "Oh, that's a royal prince; that's his wife, HRH. Good grief!"'[3] The need for cash led to deals which were lucrative but questionable. There was a photo spread in *Hello*! magazine, rumoured to have attracted a fee of £250,000. There was a book, *Budgie the Helicopter*, dashed off by the Duchess after she had qualified as a pilot. *Private Eye* cruelly revealed the existence of another great work, *Hector the Helicopter*, not a million miles away in its plotline. By now the Duchess was reaping the whirlwind. She was attacked for abandoning her new-born daughter Princess Beatrice while she went to join the Duke at the Australian bicentennial celebrations, and the numbers of her ski trips and 'freebies' were meticulously catalogued. The editor of *Private Eye* is clear about her cardinal error:

> She was having too much fun, which people don't like in the royal family. [They] want them to go and be cold in Scotland and get wet in Balmoral, and traipse around in ill-fitting, uncomfortable clothes. . . . When they start going to the Caribbean and going skiing and doing things that we want to do, then people get rather irritated. And Fergie was the ultimate in that. She seemed to be on holiday all the time.[4]

An early public glimpse of the new Duchess came when Prince Edward organized the younger royals to take part in a special *It's a Royal Knockout* on television. Four teams wearing mock-medieval costume competed in messy, knock-about antics, all for charity, in an attempt to woo the mass media. Edward had shown pluck in walking out of the Royal Marines' training course (to the rage of his father) to try to be something in showbiz. He needed rather different skills to make a success of this bizarre parody of pageantry. From the first appearance of the contestants – with Fergie and her cohorts chanting frenziedly, 'We're the best blue bandits in the world' at football commentator compere Stuart Hall – it was a hideous embarrassment. Princess Anne alone behaved with a kind of desperate dignity on the tawdry set; she was, she told Hall, leading 'the strong silent team'. Andrew Morton remembers 'one of the coldest, most unpleasant days of my life. . . . We watched as Prince Andrew and the Duchess of York were throwing fruit at each other . . . and we said, "My God, what are these people doing to each other?"'[5] When Prince Edward got a surly response from the assembled press who had watched on closed circuit television he 'flounced out', Morton added, 'like a ballerina with a hole in her tights'.

It's a Royal Knockout was damaging because for once the young royals had nobody to blame but themselves. It established a picture of fun-loving, raucous young tearaways, and the good intentions and the money raised for charities popular with the Windsors were quickly forgotten. The Dean of Windsor, Michael Mann, watched the programme on television: 'I think it was a disaster. . . . The thing that came over to me was that it was actually pulling the whole of the royal family down. . . . It was making it a clown affair, and that is not the right way to win respect.'[6] A series of similar unflattering snapshots of the new generation appeared over the next two years as their marriages came apart.

Princess Anne, however, had won her way back into public favour. Very much her father's daughter, she had a brusque, no-nonsense way with the press, telling them to 'Naff off' if they got too close. Also like Prince Philip, she compelled admiration by choosing comparatively few charitable outlets but sticking with them for the long haul. As a hard-working President of the Save The Children Fund she won worldwide acclaim – enough to justify her creation as Princess Royal in 1987 on grounds of merit. The problem was her husband. A shared love of horses was not enough to keep the marriage together. Mark Phillips would have needed versatility, wit, patience and a very thick skin to keep pace with a princess of the blood royal. He had none of them. The couple formally separated, and the theft of a batch of love letters in 1989 from the Princess Royal's briefcase broke the news that she was in love with one of the royal equerries – Tim Laurence, five years her junior. Laurence had made the jump from serviceman to courtier as easily as Peter Townsend before him. But this time there was no royal ostracism when the relationship became known. Princess Anne in her fortieth year was a much tougher cookie than Margaret at twenty-five. Laurence waited in the wings until the opportune moment for marriage. It was Mark Phillips who vanished back into the obscurity from which he had been summoned by trumpets fifteen years before.

The marriage of the Prince and Princess of Wales was also unravelling. The couple had been on holiday together, skiing at Klosters, when they were scarred by a personal tragedy that might have brought them closer together, but did not. Prince Charles had taken a party off-piste when an avalanche swept away two of them. Major Hugh Lindsay was killed instantly, while the party's hostess, Patti Palmer-Tomkinson, had her legs crushed. Charles turned for consolation not to Diana, but to the older married women who had always been his confidantes, and in particular to Camilla Parker-Bowles.

The unglamorous Camilla was an unusual royal paramour, far older than the Prince's wife. She had known Charles for twenty years, and had a shrewd idea of what and where the Prince liked to be. He was godfather to her son, and he had bought Highgrove in part because it was near her home. Her husband, Brigadier Andrew Parker-Bowles, was appointed Silver Stick in Waiting in 1987, bringing the pair formally into the royal circle. Thanks to the revelations given to Andrew Morton by Diana's friends and relations, the series of snubs which the Princess felt she suffered at the ceaseless exchange of gifts and messages between her husband and Camilla have entered the public domain. Their abiding affection is clear from the notorious taped conversation of 18 December 1989. No one should have to endure the intimate moments in an illicit relationship being paraded as these were – the collusion, the alibis, the longing of two lonely people for physical intimacy. Charles's bizarre views on his reincarnation as a tampon matter less than the couple's mundane concerns – she is worried about children's birthdays and the unexpected return of her husband; he is worried about his latest speech for Business in the Community – and the evidence of old and lingering loyalties:

> *Charles*: 'I love you.'
> *Camilla*: 'Love you too. I don't want to say goodbye.'
> *Charles*: 'Well done for doing that. You're a clever old thing. An awfully good brain lurking there, isn't there? Oh, darling, I think you ought to give the brain a rest now. Night, night.'
> *Camilla*: 'Night darling, God bless.'
> *Charles*: 'I do love you and I'm so proud of you.'
> *Camilla*: 'Don't be silly. I've never achieved anything.'
> *Charles*: 'Yes you have.'
> *Camilla*: 'No I haven't.'
> *Charles*: 'Your greatest achievement is to love me.'

Charles's marriage was a forlorn shell, and looked it. Diana could upstage the Prince effortlessly whenever she was with him, and highlight his apparent indifference by the mournful splendour of her solo appearances. Charles was not used to such treatment. As one close observer recalls, he 'was playing second fiddle [and] anyone coming to work for a member of the royal family is told: "Beware, these people are stars."'[7] Loyal biographers like Penny Junor insisted that 'their union has not only survived the rigours of a decade but has come out at the other end stronger than ever.'[8] But whether it was Diana cornered with one of her military beaux in some Chelsea mews, tearfully begging the cameraman for his film, or Charles happening to turn up at some foreign resort where Camilla was lurking, the true message got across: these were separate lives. When the couple met to take Prince William to his first day at Ludgrove School in 1990 journalists present duly noted that 'their meeting, which lasted for a total of thirty minutes, would be the last time they would see each other for thirty-nine days'.[9]

Nevertheless, Charles and Diana seem to have provided a happier home for their children than the Prince's forbears. The foundress of the Hanoverian line, the Electress Sophia, wrote in her remarkable memoirs of her mother: 'Her Majesty had her whole family brought up apart from herself, preferring the sight of her monkeys and dogs to that of her children.'[10] Similar attitudes had been perpetuated down to his own generation. But the Princes William and Harry were brought up differently, especially by their mother. Her own misery as the child of a broken home shaped her thinking in this as much as did her interest in the marriage guidance organization Relate. 'I want to give my children security, I hug them to death,' she says.[11] The little boys went to school in Berkshire, and there is no talk of their going on to chilly Gordonstoun. They saw both worlds: their father dressed them formally and took them shooting and fishing, while their mother dressed them in jeans and headed for Disneyland. Only in the perpetual civil war of their parents did they lose out. There, all the small dramas of childhood became part of a larger crisis. When Prince William was hit on the head by a golf club and rushed to hospital

Diana stayed with him, while Charles left for the Royal Opera House and an engagement with visiting EC officials. He was rewarded with barbed headlines: 'What kind of a dad are you?' It is too early to tell what burden of confusion and guilt the boys will carry from their exposure to the ceaseless coverage of their parents' difficulties over the past few years.

By the end of the 1980s there was unremitting hostility to many of the royals, though not all of it was justified. John Grigg puts it succinctly: 'People say that the minor royals have been letting the side down. Actually the minor royals have been doing very well. It's been major royals who have let the side down.'[12] Their behaviour was no worse than the commonplace activities of the sons of George V, but those young men had never operated under the pitiless glare of the press, forever trapped on stage. The young Windsors were ground small by the tabloids and the satire mill. *Spitting Image* had had a spoof Queen, as the only remaining root-and-branch opposition to Thatcherism, selling the *Socialist Worker*. What the royals were unwittingly doing was selling millions of copies of the *Sun*, the *Daily Mirror* and the *Daily Star*. The press could be self-righteous about it. Andrew Neil of the *Sunday Times* invoked all his Presbyterian contempt for empurpled fecklessness:

> In the build-up to the Gulf War . . . what did I see in the papers every day? I saw one young royal dressed as a transvestite at some party, Prince Andrew playing golf in Spain, Prince Philip and Prince Charles going round shooting defenceless animals in the countryside, and the Duchess of York giving parties at Annabel's . . . and I did not think the royal family was behaving in the way that I and the country expected it to behave. There seemed to be a kind of upper-class decadence taking over.[13]

With the war in full spate Neil wrote an angry editorial, attacking the royals for 'insensitivity which disgusts the public and demeans the monarchy'.[14] His fellow editors chided him, but within a week it was clear that anger at the young royals' style of life had become widespread. The ineffable Fergie was chronicled on her trips around London nightspots, trailing 'a group of socialites . . . all hoping in equal measure to pick up some social cachet as she trips in and out of their salons'.[15] Neither did it help that the Duchess's circle included a young American, Steve Wyatt, whose family did big business with Saddam Hussein. March 1992 brought the discovery in a London flat of photographs of her and Wyatt together. In the wake on the storm of publicity which ensued it was announced that the Duke and Duchess of York were to separate. The Queen's press secretary, Charles Anson, offered his resignation (which was not accepted) for the blindingly obvious statement that Fergie was 'unsuitable for royal and public life'.

Prince Charles as an individual – let alone as a partner in a failing marriage – seemed to have lost his way by the end of the 1980s. In the years since the Jubilee he had set up a cat's cradle of overlapping trusts, many brought together under the aegis of Business in the Community. There had been well-publicized inner city visits and initiatives in London, Yorkshire and elsewhere. The largely voluntary helpers who staffed the committees saw the Prince occasionally, admired his unstuffy attitudes, and knew that he had faced opposition because of the wide range of people he was trying to assist. One local organizer remembers:

> He's interested in architecture, he's interested in homelessness, he's interested in the young blacks, he's interested in nature conservancy, and he's serious about all of them. . . . When they first saw the people he was bringing back to the Palace to a meeting, his advisers and courtiers were very disturbed. They didn't think these were the sort of people he ought to be associating himself with. I think he had quite a battle.[16]

But the charge of dilettantism was made by others who wished him well. 'He's tended to have a horse in every race. Expressing opinions on practically every subject under the sun can be counter-productive,' John Grigg argues.[17] And the biographer Anthony Holden claims that, even in the field where he has been most outspoken over the longest period, 'the really interesting thing about Charles and architecture is that with all that money he hasn't commissioned a single building'.[18] Royal patronage may yet give the lie to the quip that all the Prince has ever achieved is to put turrets on Tesco supermarkets. But no sign of an emerging Nash or Paxton can be seen in the Prince's coterie.

Charles's days as a social reformer were drawing to a close even before his strained meeting in 1988 with Mrs Thatcher. He had allowed his cherished Inner City Aid project, which he had launched with Rod Hackney, to run down over the years 1986–8, despite desperate pleas from the organizers. His homilies on ecology, and the resources lavished on his Highgrove organic farming, sometimes made him seem like Marie Antoinette playing at milkmaids. It was noted that his liking for crofters' cottages, ox-drawn ploughs and straw-fired central heating did not stop him using wasteful and polluting methods of travel. One of his assiduous biographers, whose succeeding tomes on the Prince had been first respectful, then thoughtful, and finally sulphurous, declared that 'Renaissance Man had become the pub bore.'[19] A number of key advisers left his employ. Those who stayed found compliance the best policy.

At the very end of 1988 Alan Clark, Minister for Trade, was summoned to dinner at Highgrove. He recorded in his diary what happened when he arrived late. 'As I entered the "businessmen" (who else?) stopped talking and looked at me. Some feigned indignation. Most were complacent: "Hur, hur, he's already blotted his copybook." The Prince, on the other hand, did not stop talking.' As the dinner went on the Prince 'hit the table, not authoritatively but petulantly: "*Why* can't something be done?"' The subject was the inability of managers to communicate in other languages. Clark said cruelly that in thirty years the Japanese would be dominant, and so would their language. 'The businessmen glowered at me through the cigar smoke. HRH looked uneasy.' Clark reflected that 'the trouble that affects all attempts by royalty to "inform" themselves is that the other participants are mainly, no, solely interested in scoring goodboy points and ingratiating themselves with the Royal

Chair'.[20] He sympathised with the Prince's determination to be useful despite being hemmed in by sycophants. What he did not see was 'any continuity of conviction'[21] or the inner strength apparent in the Prince's father. Well-known psychiatist Anthony Clare, also summoned to Highgrove at an inconvenient rush hour time, simply didn't go. 'Most people did go, so Prince Charles can't begin to imagine disadvantages of that kind, because his schedule is carefully arranged.[22]

The year of the fortieth anniversary of his mother's accession, itself a bitter-sweet reminder of how long he must wait for the throne, proved to be Charles's undoing. The celebrations and the television documentary *Elizabeth R* were intended to make this the Queen's triumphant year, but the searchlight was never off her children, her problems and her wealth. Two very different royal books were published in 1992. One was a piece of inside gossip, deplored in advance but shown to be well researched from impeccable sources; the other was a piece of long-term financial investigation which managed to bring about, at one or two removes, a complete change in the way the world saw the Windsors: their fortunes plummeted as speculation about their fortune grew.

Andrew Morton had for some years been a middling member of the pack of royal-watchers and *soi-disant* confidants. When the manuscript of his account of Diana's marriage began to circulate it was immediately apparent that was not based on casual gossip and speculation; *Diana: Her True Story* did indeed ring true. The Princess's family and friends had plainly collaborated with the author. Morton had met one of the circle for a routine interview and was flabbergasted by what he got. 'In a greasy spoon restaurant in north Ruislip this astonishing tale poured out about Di and how she suffered from bulimia, how she's made various failed suicide attempts, how Charles had been consumed by a passion for Camilla, which had in Diana's eyes been the cancer at the heart of their marriage. When I walked away I thought: this can't be true.'[23]

Was it true? The book was serialized in the *Sunday Times*, not in the tabloids. Editor Andrew Neil had originally decided not to publish. But then

> we took out all the named quotes and we went to the people who'd been named and said, 'Look, you've been quoted as saying this – did you say it, and if you did say it will you stand by it?' To a person they did. We decided it was accurate and of constitutional importance as well. It was an amazing story and blew the fairytale apart. As journalists who had conspired with the fairytale in years gone by, now we'd found out the truth we ought to publish that.[24]

The initial reaction to the serialization was bitterly hostile. Lord Macgregor, Chairman of the Press Complaints Commission, rushed out a statement that the press was 'dabbling in the stuff of other people's souls'. Only much later, when the full extent to which Morton had been used to put forward Diana's case was uncovered, did the Commission admit that it had gone too far. One of those who drafted the original statement concedes that 'if we had known then what we know now we wouldn't have made the statement in the same words'.[25]

In one sense it is not surprising that the Commission was misled. There *was* a grossly intrusive press, and no royal had ever before used a journalist in such a blatant way to pursue a partisan quarrel. Princess Diana was out of the gilded cage for good. The savage portrayal of her husband as cold and selfish, a poor parent infatuated with another woman, was intended to contrast with her own innocent misadventures, eating disorders, suicide bids and search for tenderness. Among the book's abundant photographs from the Spencers' archives, testifying to her love of the camera since childhood, there was only one dour snap of Prince Charles – in black and white, with Camilla Parker-Bowles, in front of a tree on which someone had carved a heart and the initials CR – the royal cipher, Carolus Rex, which he might never achieve.

The Princess implicitly endorsed the book by openly visiting one of the named sources, Carolyn Bartholemew. The picture it painted seemed to be accepted by the public. Diana soared in public esteem. A third of all those polled believed her to be the most popular royal, as compared to a derisory 9 per cent for the hapless Charles.[26] Curiously, most of the incidents of neglect, sickness and despair retailed in Morton's book had taken place some years before. Since then Diana had assiduously played the part of the Princess Alone, posing in front of the Pyramids and the Taj Mahal. Charles had attracted ridicule by taking television journalist Selina Scott with him to film his 'solitude' on a Scottish island. His wife had a surer touch. Journalists saw Diana lead a vast array of photographers around the Taj Mahal to find the perfect spot for an image of desertion, but they did not give the game away. Diana, by contrast with her husband, appears to have cheerfully given the admiring cameramen what they wanted. The Princess, who happily described herself as 'thick as two planks' and conversed in disco-speak, proved to be the greatest image-maker in the history of the Windsors.

The Prince's friends thought he had been betrayed. There were times when he had had to put duty not merely before pleasure but also before the demands of paternity. Now he was pilloried for it. Friends like Nicholas Soames MP regarded Morton's book as 'a turning-point in royal reporting . . . it enabled a period of unrestrained, undisciplined and completely disgraceful reporting. The press had lost any difference between public and private life.'[27] One of the regular biographers of both Prince and Princess, Penny Junor, believes that Diana had been incensed by 'people reading my book and believing she was happy'. Morton's book was 'a complete revelation' but 'deeply unfair to the Prince of Wales: the way it was serialized verged on the wicked'.[28] For many years *Private Eye* had run a fictional 'Heir of Sorrows' column featuring a mournful Prince, older than his mother in outlook and appearance, whose schemes forever go wrong, and his airhead wife, who calls him Chazza and appears to have been born wearing a Walkman. The editor had to stop running the column: the harsh facts (or faction) had outrun what now seemed gentle satire.

There was worse to come. Rumours had circulated for some time that many of the young royals had been secretly bugged, and that samples of the tapes were in newspaper safes. No one knew for sure. Then in 1992 Fergie and Di both hit rock bottom. The Duchess was secretly filmed with another American fixer and man-about-town, Johnny Bryan, at a villa near St Tropez. The children of the broken marriage played happily in the pool while their mother flirted topless with her bald 'financial adviser'. A hundred other pools would have shown a similar scene, but they would not have made a splash in the *Daily Mirror*. It happened on the day after Fergie arrived at Balmoral to join the royal party, bringing her daughters to see their grandmother. Bryan had tried to get an injunction to stop publication, on the grounds of invasion of privacy, but a High Court judge declined to oblige. The timing maximized the Duchess's embarrassment; it was a chastened Fergie who fled Scotland by the first scheduled flight, leaving little of her last terse conversation with the Queen to journalistic imagination.

The use of a royal person in what the Windsors' most faithful biographer called 'shifting images of mild pornography'[29] became even more voyeuristic as the press circulation war intensified. The Murdoch conglomerate, News International, had for several years been sitting on what it believed was a tape of an intimate conversation between the Princess of Wales and one of her gallant young troupers. The conversation had been recorded on New Year's Eve, 1989. One of the speakers was at Sandringham, the other on a carphone in an Oxfordshire lay-by. One version had already been published in the American *National Enquirer*, while copies of the tapes had been hawked around British newspapers for more than a year. They had originally been received with incredulity. One who heard them then says 'they still thought, "Well, this is unbelievable."' And at that stage, early in 1992, the idea of publishing such a transcript was almost inconceivable. 'What changed it all? Morton changed it all. That book changed the entire climate of reporting of the royal family.'[30] To the Morton book were added the Fergie photographs, a mighty blow in the press circulation war. Then five days after their appearance the *Sun* finally used a bowdlerized version of the tapes.

The man addresses his friend as 'Squidgy' and 'Darling Squidge' throughout; thus these became the Squidgygate tapes. The initial printed version revealed a lonely woman surrounded by an overpowering family, suspicious that 'I'm going to do something dramatic because I can't stand the confines of this marriage.' Her husband's relatives are 'distancing themselves' from her because she can go out and 'conquer the world'. His grandmother 'is always looking at me with a strange look in her eyes. It's not hatred. It's sort of interest and pity rolled into one.' She sees herself as 'a wise old thing' with healing powers which churchmen humbly acknowledge. Until legal restraints prevented it, the *Sun* provided a premium-rate telephone line for the public to listen to the conversation – not in full, for the explicit exchanges about sexual fantasy only appeared later. Nevertheless this, like the Fergie photographs, was an instance of the press using evidence of the young Windsors' relationships as a form of pornography.

The cumulative effect of these revelations was to sap the prestige of the royal family and the monarchy. *Spitting Image* included a bare-breasted Fergie puppet in its opening titles. *Private Eye*'s front cover used the St Tropez photographs with the caption, 'I have to warn you that some things can go down as well as up.' In fact, royalty got the kind of press it had not endured since George IV's divorce from Queen Caroline. Candid friends of the monarchy, like Alan Clark, concede the damage: 'It's quite unnecessary to single out particular individuals and scandals: everyone will have their own most disappointing episode. But the total effect of this has been to reduce their standing, not just of the individuals but of the institution.'[31]

The irony was that the actual embodiment of the institution, Elizabeth II, had continued to accrue respect in her fortieth year on the throne. The television biography *Elizabeth R* concentrated on the Queen; her husband and eldest son barely featured. A picture emerged of a woman of animation, mental and physical. She scuttled about at the Derby, with the game old Queen Mum at her side, breaking into a canter in her eagerness to see her sweepstake entry, Generous, win the race. She teased Sir Edward Heath, for whom it has truly been said that a joke is no laughing matter. When Heath lectured US Secretary of State James Baker, saying that he could have gone to Baghdad to confront Saddam Hussein 'as I did', the Queen broke in with, 'Ah, but you are expendable.' She shouted into Ronald Reagan's deaf ear, peered from a helicopter at the H-Blocks on her first visit to Northern Ireland for fourteen years, and said nervously to the resident of one old people's home: 'You have a room of your own here? That must be rather nice.' Many of her own rooms in her many mansions were on display.

The film will stand the test of time. A generation hence it will be the classic snapshot of the royal family as it wished to be seen: the four harmonious generations, the pattern of the seasons; duty and domesticity nicely balanced. 'In this existence,' said the Queen, sounding rather like the Dalai Lama in her choice of noun, 'the job and the home go together.' *Elizabeth R* ended spectacularly at the Ghillies' Ball at Balmoral, with the ninety-two-year-old Queen Mother joining the dancing alongside her children and grandchildren. Over the film, the Queen mused about duty. 'If you live this sort of life, which people don't very much, you live by tradition and continuity. I find that people don't take on jobs for life. They try different things. You know, as far as I'm concerned I know exactly what I'll be doing two months or a year hence. And I think this is what the younger members find so difficult: the regimented side of it.'

There once was a time when this powerful mixture of sentiment and duty, embodied in a person for whom the nation felt genuine affection, would have carried her through the anniversary year. The smiling faces of the young royals in the film, however, belied what the public had come to know as the truth. The Ruby Year was also one in which the cost and ownership of the rubies – and everything else – was questioned as never before. Phillip Hall's book *Royal Fortune* provided the bedrock of research for media willing and able to play to public discontent about royal extravagance at a time of prolonged recession. He began with the assumption that the Queen's investment portfolio, shrewdly invested, would have risen from £20 million in 1971 to £341 million two decades later. Since she paid no tax on it, an annual income of some £18 million was accruing to the royal coffers – in tax savings alone around £20,000 per day.[32] Hall pointed out that the income was there to be reinvested, since the Queen also received over £2 million each year from the Duchy of Lancaster, after meeting the running costs of those of her family who were not provided for by the Civil List.

When these figures were added to the other tax exemptions (including exemption from the hated Poll Tax) and grant applications relating to the royal estates, and to guesstimates of the value of private possessions, from jewels to racehorses, there was enough to fuel a continuing public debate throughout 1992. One of Mrs Thatcher's last services to the monarchy had been to push through a review of the Civil List in 1990. The principal members of the royal family were awarded large sums for their expenses, with surpluses in the early years allowing for a rise by 7.5 per cent annually until the year 2000 – substantially above the rate of inflation for the first three years of the deal. It was inevitably contrasted with the government's attitude to all other pay claims. Even admired royals seemed to be getting too much – the nonagenarian Queen Mother was receiving over £600,000 annually; those less admired were begrudged anything at all. The hidden subsidies for the operation of the monarchy also came under Hall's scrutiny. In a normal year the questions might have been contained, and the calumnies rejected, but in 1992 every extravagance of the young Windsors seemed to be matched by an example of insensitive greed. A (perfectly legal) application from the Balmoral estate for a £300,000 Forestry Commission grant to fence in young plantations vulnerable to red deer sat ill with the conspicuous display and tax-free luxury of the family who gathered at Balmoral every summer.

The guests that September included the Prime Minister, John Major, newly strengthened by an election victory that few had expected him to win. Major knew there were rumbles on his own benches about the scandals of the summer. He came armed with the simultaneous declaration by the most aristocratic of his backbenchers that 'there is a strong case for the public purse to recompense members of the Royal Family according to the specific duties they perform on what amounts to a *pro rata* basis'.[33] The Prime Minister returned to London with a royal concession: the Queen would take over responsibility for the remaining minor royals on the Civil List, at a cost of £1.4 million a year. There was, however, no plan for her to pay tax. This information was discreetly slipped out as a written parliamentary answer by the Chancellor of the Exchequer, Norman Lamont, on 3 November, a day of high drama elsewhere. But it was not overlooked. The *Daily Mirror*, in the most savage personal attack of the reign, dubbed the Queen 'H. M. Tax Dodger'. Opinion polls throughout the year suggested that around 80 per cent of her subjects believed she should pay tax.[34] Then, while the public soaked up more press gossip about the Prince and Princess of Wales, pictured on their last disastrous overseas tour together in Korea, the tax issue was forced by an unexpected catastrophe.

On 20 November, the Queen's forty-fifth wedding anniversary (which Prince Philip spent in Argentina), a fire devastated Windsor Castle. It was undergoing substantial restoration at public expense under the auspices of English Heritage, and hangings near the restoration work caught fire first. The flames gutted St George's Hall, then raced through the Brunswick Tower and some of the private apartments. No one was killed, as had happened during the blaze at Hampton Court six years earlier, but similar questions were asked. Why was the building not properly insured and inspected? How much did English Heritage actually know about what was going on there? Initially there was sympathy for the Windsors themselves. This was the building from which they had taken their name. Since George IV most of them had put their stamp on it, and could call it home. Prince Andrew was on hand, and active in a rescue operation which ensured that only one picture of any merit was lost. The Queen came out from London, a small distraught figure in a headscarf, inspecting the soaked artefacts laid out on the wet grass.

But personal sympathy vanished when the Secretary of State for National Heritage, Peter Brooke, blundered on stage. He announced that the government (and therefore the taxpayer) would foot the entire bill for the restoration of the Castle – said on a facile estimate to be £60 million. For the second time in a month the Queen and her close advisers had entirely misread the public mood. Given what was believed to be her wealth, and the public/private ambivalence about the furnishings of Windsor, some thought should have been given to a royal contribution. It was not. Public fury on this occasion was spontaneous. Anthony Holden picked up the mood: 'Why should we pay for a palace that we're not allowed into, that we pay to maintain? She didn't take out fire insurance? If my house burns down and I haven't taken out fire insurance is the Queen going to pay for it? No way.'[35] Others complained that when Windsor was standing it belonged to the Queen; when it burned down it belonged to the public. Over the weekend the Queen, hoarse from the chill she had picked up on the damp Windsor lawns, thought harder than ever before about the institution she embodied.

She was to speak on Monday, 23 November at a Guildhall banquet to celebrate her forty years on the throne. Sombrely dressed, her voice an octave lower than the fluting tones that had so upset her early critics, she borrowed a phrase from a letter which she had just received from the veteran courtier Sir Edward Ford. He had written immediately after the fire, to say that she deserved an *annus mirabilis* for her forty years of service, but had got an *annus horribilis* instead.[36] The words, instantly translated by the *Sun* as 'One's Bum Year', summed up the rueful nature of the speech. All institutions, including the City and the monarchy, must be able to face criticism, she said, but it ought to be tempered 'with a touch of gentleness, good humour and understanding'. One of her most sympathetic listeners, Lady Longford, noted that 'it was the first time that most people could remember Her Majesty speaking of "criticism" and "change" in the same approving breath'.[37] For a woman who had never embraced change it was as courageous as it was individual. Countess Mountbatten, her near contemporary and cousin by marriage, reflected that 'It was marvellous, and great that she'd taken the bull by the horns and hadn't pretended that she'd had a marvellous year.'[38] The historian who had written perceptively about the creation and re-creation of the royal image, David Cannadine, thought it 'one of the most remarkable speeches since Edward VIII [the abdication broadcast] – talking about personal problems, the nature of the institution, and her place within it . . . The normal rule for monarchs is never apologise, never explain.'

The biggest change of the reign came just three days later. It was announced in Parliament that the Queen, as well as paying all Civil List expenses except those of herself, her husband and her mother, would in future voluntarily pay income tax, as would the Prince of Wales. The Prince, like the Queen, would be exempted from inheritance and capital gains taxes. So his situation was not be significantly different. If he now pays 40 per cent tax on his Duchy of Cornwall income, he will still receive roughly the same as when he made a voluntary contribution to the Exchequer of 25 per cent. He made it clear in an interview with Lady Longford that if the royals came off the Civil List they would earn money and claim expenses elsewhere: 'there is never something for nothing'.[39] 'The announcement was badly timed,' judges another royal cousin, Lord Harewood, 'coming straight after the Windsor fire.'[40] But most veteran courtiers, while deploring the fact that the Queen appeared to have been forced into her 'voluntary' decision, felt there was no option. 'The advice she was given was that the announcement should be made then. It was unfortunate timing because the Queen got no credit for it.'[41] The critics argue that a tax bill which may not reach seven figures represents only a minute fraction of the costs of the royal lifestyle. A critic tots up the bill:

> The world's biggest private yacht, used for thirty-seven days last year at a cost to the taxpayer of £363,000 per day it was in use – some of that for a private holiday by Prince Philip. The Royal Train [the Queen has never travelled by British Rail],[42] £67,000 per outing. The Royal Flight, three jets, six helicopters, £2000 per hour. . . . The *Wall Street Journal* recently calculated that the British monarchy costs the British taxpayer almost double the combined cost of every other European monarchy. Now that is something going to have to change.[43]

The debate about change was to start almost at once. It was announced on 9 December, before the *annus horribilis* had run its course, that the Prince and Princess of Wales were to separate. To cries of astonishment John Major added that this did not change the Princess's right to be crowned Queen Consort in due course. It was soon to be clear, however, that the Princess did not have this particular right in mind. She was intent upon challenging the Windsors' concept of how they did their job, in a year in which Prince Charles would see his reputation reach rock bottom with revelations that seemed to disqualify him from the kind of coronation his mother had had, and perhaps even from the throne itself.

12

AFTER THE FIRE

Until the beginning of 1993 none of the blows suffered by the House of Windsor had shaken it fundamentally. Its finances had only been touched at the margin. The weak sisters among the younger royals might yet be shrugged off. What the monarchy found harder to combat was the covert operation aimed at undermining the whole family – whether for financial gain or warped reasons of state has not yet become clear. The bugging operation which had secured compromising tapes of the Prince and Princess of Wales and the Yorks had been known about for some time. A press gripped by circulation warfare was hungry to use them. The Murdoch newspapers, some thought, had additional motives beyond circulation-building. Sir Edward Heath believes that 'that part of the press which is owned by a renegade Australian is determined to destroy the monarchy if it can, and we must be aware of that'.[1] The so-called Squidgygate tapes had been published in August 1992. Throughout the year Prince Charles knew in general and probably in particular what was on the tapes of his 1989 conversations with Camilla Parker-Bowles, and that some of them were in the hands of the press. As with the Watergate tapes, all the agony of waiting could not prepare the principal for the pain of revelation. On

Wednesday, 13 January 1993 faxes of a transcript just published in Australia began to zip between business and media offices in London. It was an open dare to the warring London tabloids. They had a strong motive to hold back: this was a critical week in the deliberations of the Calcutt Committee, which editors feared would propose fierce curbs on the press. But the pressure to steal a march on rivals was overwhelming and one of them was bound to publish. Five days later the *Sunday Mirror* obliged. 'Just when we thought things couldn't get any worse!' the Queen is quoted as saying to her private secretary after he broke the news.[2]

If genuine, the so-called Camillagate tape, or tapes, put the Prince at a huge disadvantage. His defenders, like Lord St John of Fawsley, immediately insisted on television that no one could rush to judgement, and that in any event adultery could not be committed over the telephone. But the press and the public drew their own conclusions. A mocking *Sun* cartoon showed the plants in the royal greenhouse imploring their royal owner to 'Talk Dirty to Us!'[3] The paper's editor, Kelvin Mackenzie, told a Commons Select Committee that there was a public interest in knowing if 'the Defender of the Faith cuckolds someone else's wife'. A Gallup poll showed that the number of those who rated him as most popular member of the royal family had fallen even lower – to 5 per cent. Diana rated 22 per cent, the largest score of the entire family.[4] Charles had to face headlines ('I'll Never Be King, Sobs Charles') which suggested, wrongly, that his family had despaired of him and that he would be passed over for a regency, exercised by the Princess Royal on behalf of his son William.

The Church of England prelates were put on the spot. Faced with what appeared to be the sins of this putative Defender of the Faith, where did they stand? They had to say that they did 'expect our leaders at every level to embody Christian values'.[5] But they were uneasy about making their fears and criticisms specific. It was left to a lesser cleric, the Ven. George Austin, Archdeacon of York, to say what many traditional Anglicans were thinking:

> Charles would become king when the Queen dies. The problem is the Coronation service, I think. If it were proved beyond doubt that he had gone into the marriage in an adulterous relationship, taken vows in church which were solemn vows before God to be faithful to another woman, and had then continued his unfaithfulness, then I believe it calls into question the taking of oaths before God in church.[6]

The Prince's champions took issue with Austin. Nicholas Soames MP has denounced his criticisms as 'perfectly disgraceful, untrue, inaccurate . . . a gross thing to say'.[7]

Others have said, more mildly, that most monarchs throughout history had been adulterers, and none the worse for it as rulers. Uxorious monarchs like Henry VI, George III and Charles I had had a poor success rate compared to many of the more libidinous ones. The problem was that the family image of the monarchy, so assiduously cultivated by the Windsors through three generations, was eclipsed by the images conjured up by the tapes. After their revelations a sacramental coronation would seem a kind of sacrilege. Even those close to the Prince wondered 'if there'll ever be a coronation like the last one, partly because of those tapes'.[8] This is made more likely by the situation of the Church of England itself. It faces defections to Rome from within its own ranks, including that of the Duchess of Kent. And Britain is now a multi-cultural society of many religions, so the Established Church is further than ever from being the nation at prayer. It therefore looks possible that Disestablishment, breaking the link between Church and State, may come well before the reign of King Charles III. Then, just as royal remarriages would be civil rather than religious (although Princess Anne had found a Scottish church in which to tie her second knot), so the sovereign might take a civil oath as Defender of the Constitution, rather than a religious one as Defender of the Faith.

A second question raised by the Camilla tapes, little noted in the plethora of prurient gossip, was what kind of constitutional state Prince Charles stood to inherit. The bugging of his and his wife's and brother's telephones was a far more complex affair than at first appeared. A number of recordings had been made in a short period in 1989. Some have been published; some have not. The first indication of their existence came when a retired Abingdon bank manager with a scanner aerial in his back garden contacted the *Sun* with the tape of his eavesdroppings. 'I switched it on, and I had hardly got down to listening when I heard Diana's voice.'[9] Cyril Reenan took his tape to the *Sun*, was paid £1000, and told that it would be lodged in the vaults. He was promised a great deal more money if the story ever came out. When Morton's book was published he called his contact and was told: '"Mr Reenan, your tape was worthless to me." He said, "We managed to get another tape from a girl in Oxford. She didn't let us have it until a year after yours."' Mr Reenan, who was to regret his paltry earnings when his identity and snooping became public knowledge, realized that he had overheard not a conversation but a recording of a conversation. 'Squidgy' and her friend had talked on New Year's Eve, 1989. The Oxford radio ham, Janet Norgrove, *had* heard a part of the conversation, on a weaker signal, at the time. Reenan picked up a longer version, much more clearly, four days later.

It is therefore clear that someone, somewhere, was recording, re-editing and regularly rebroadcasting the tapes to be picked up by radio hams – not for personal gain, but out of mischief or malice. The recordings of Charles's conversations, within the same narrow time period, may not come from the same expert source. Harry Arnold of the Mirror Group said in an Australian television documentary that it had been recorded by 'an ordinary person' with a scanner.[10] The programme produced expert evidence to back him up. But the picking up of these conversations does not appear to have been a chance affair. It seems much more as though someone had pilfered and recycled the audio-record of a routine, if covert, bugging. The security services know the risk of assassination which hangs over the royal family. The more elusive the young royals were in their movements, the more secretive was the intelligence gathering which enabled their unwelcome protectors to 'follow from in front'. As Prince Charles's biographer puts it:

> To me it seems beyond doubt that people at GCHQ . . . whose job it is to monitor senior public figures, were initially responsible for the taping of those conversations. . . . By the same token, if the Prince of Wales begins to make regular visits to the home of a Gloucestershire housewife it's the job of the security services to protect him, to make that house secure.[11]

It was a view supported by the doyen of espionage fiction, John Le Carré, in the press. 'Eccentricity at GCHQ', he wrote, 'is part of its self-image, just as great secrecy is part of its arrogance, its clubbishness and unreality.' Within that world it was easy to find 'a solitary GCHQ man or woman possessed of secret fantasies [or] two or three similarly deranged souls who have found each other and are having fun'. Le Carré dismissed as 'baloney' the emphatic ministerial denials that there had been wire-tapping. 'The question is whether, having intercepted the phone calls, GCHQ's servants leaked them. On present evidence there are too many indications that they did.'[12] Indications are one thing; hard evidence is another. Press enquiries have not turned up mad, disaffected or venal intelligence personnel among their hidden informants. Fake tapes began to flood the market, while real ones were held back. In what former ministers describe as a 'bizarre' decision, the government refused to hold any kind of enquiry. The trail went cold. 'We know that on one occasion it wasn't a mobile phone, it was a landline involved. We've got as far as we can go: this is a very secretive society,' Andrew Neil concedes. 'Until some Deep Throat comes forward . . . we've hit a dead end.'[13]

Prince Charles stood to lose his strongest card – his ability to mobilize Establishment opinion – if the secret state was out of control. If those who began by thinking they protected him ended by betraying him, whether for money or malice, his position would be totally undermined. In *To Play the King* novelist Michael Dobbs set a concerned, solitary new monarch, separated from his scheming wife, appalled by the poverty and breakdown of the inner cities, in direct confrontation with a government prepared to use the secret service against him.

Although Dobbs's book and its television adaptation were fiction, they left the public in no doubt about the odds against a well-meaning but maverick monarch if the real wielders of power grew tired of him.

Charles also appeared impotent against two other power centres – the Princess and the press – which fed off each other. As long as she continued to carry out public engagements the Princess of Wales seemed made for the tabloid press, with its insatiable appetite for trivia about royalty. In coping with the press she had received no assistance from courtiers, whom she found stiff, protocol-ridden, prone to back-biting and intrigue. Other members of the family had been more helpful but they had never really accepted as one of themselves a starry-eyed girl whose first ambition was to iron her husband's shirts and who did not instinctively recognise journalists as the enemy. Initially Princess Diana, though naturally wary on account of her history of rejection, liked the press. Later she begun to feel that she had no existence of her own but had to live up to the idealised image of herself which appeared in print. She became still more vulnerable when the great rift occurred. It made marvellous copy. A 'shadow court' of friends grew up around her, feeding the newspapers stories about her martyrdom and her future reincarnation as the Princess Mum, mother of the King-in-Waiting, William V. They stressed her ability to break out of the straitjacket of royal ways:

> Diana has begun to pioneer the kind of monarchy Britain wants to see in the twenty-first century. Not merely does she travel by public transport rather than by privately subsidized jets, trains, and planes; not merely does she support charities that are of social relevance and urgent issues; she makes her children stand in line at Marks and Spencer's in Kensington High Street.'[14]

Even some admirers of the Prince, like television journalist Clive James (who had introduced himself to 'Charles Charming' with a book of loyal doggerel), felt that he could make an effort to see what she achieved. It was 'the key to those qualities she has more of than he does. The reaction she gets in the hospitals and the hospices is no mere contrivance.

The wounded and the lonely spot her immediately as one of them.'[15]

What did she spot in herself? She was the heroine of the mini-series *Diana: Her True Story*, which featured a savage caricature of Prince Charles. She was immortalized by Camille Paglia as the archetype of feminine achievement. She met Mother Teresa, and the poor and the sick of Nepal and Zimbabwe. She effortlessly upstaged the Windsors by telephoning the grieving parents of the victims of the IRA Warrington bombings to sympathise – 'I've got children of my own, and I understand' – and to let the world know that she was not allowed to go to the funeral in person.

Throughout all this the Prince was said to be planning his counter-attack; it could not happen if he was competing for the limelight. Diana's status as a semi-detached royal, carrying out her own engagements with her own staff, but dependent on the funding of her husband's Duchy since she was not on the Civil List in her own right, was fragile. Key staff began to be reassigned. Life became a little harder. A curious set of pictures of her exercising in a leotard in a health club, taken by stealth to make money for its owner, shook her self-confidence. Apparently she would cry for hours after her engagements, so much so that the Palace considered her to be emotionally unstable. Proposals were made behind the scenes. The way should be left clear for the rehabilitation of Charles in the Silver Jubilee year of his investiture. On 3 December 1993 she bowed out of public life with an unexpected announcement at a charity lunch, disappearing from view (temporarily) in appropriate manner to the sound of 'Lady in Red' at a promotional launch for Virgin Airways, while being ecstatically hugged by Richard Branson.

Rehabilitation, not reconciliation, has been marked out for Charles. From his appearance with his sons at the Queen Mother's Birkhall estate in August 1993, enjoying 'delightful family moments to restore his battered public image', the cameras have been compiling a new record.[16] The Prince has his Boswell in Jonathan Dimbleby, who produced both book and film for the anniversary of the investiture. Photo-opportunities have been lavish but have occasionally misfired

– such as when the Prince let it be known that he and his sons would queue for a ski-lift like everyone else, only to grow frustrated after a couple of minutes and pull rank. There have been well-placed interviews hinting that the Prince feels his efforts for British business overseas go unappreciated, as well as newspaper features singing the praises of his network of trusts. 'There is an annoyance, his aides say, that all the other things – the tittle-tattle – get covered and the rest get very little attention.'[17] This is a relaunch, not a reinvention. Will it work? Some of those who wish the Prince well have their doubts: 'The sort of repackaging job done by a lot of slick PR people. [It gets] that is absolutely hopeless, getting down to the very level from which they've got to extricate themselves, namely the PR soundbite.'[18] Alan Clark puts his faith in 'a period of withdrawal and asceticism as probably the best way of recovering the mystique on which actually a monarchy is based'. Charles, says the editor of the *Sunday Times*, looks too much as though he is running for president. 'It's a sign of the weakness of the monarchy that the heir to the throne has to do that.'[19]

Part of Prince Charles's rehabilitation has involved visiting Australia and New Zealand, and surviving a demonstration in Sydney which looked for a moment like an assassination attempt. In 1988 Charles had been the principal royal figure at the bicentennial celebrations. Now he returned to find the country convulsed by the debate about a republic. The Australian Premier, Paul Keating, has seized the republican issue and run with it to an election victory which many thought out of his reach. For his alleged familiarity towards the Queen on her last visit the British tabloids had dubbed him the 'Lizard of Oz'. The British monarchy never put down roots in Australia when it had the opportunity. As the old Anglophile Australians die off the House of Windsor seems increasingly vulnerable to the tyranny of distance. 'The idea that the Crown is some single sacred silken thread, which if tugged from the garment of our constitution will cause the whole thing to fall in tatters at our feet, is too ridiculous. The case against the monarchy in Australia is a simple patriotic one: the Queen is not Australian,' argues the chairman of the republicans, Malcolm Turnbull.[20] Novelist Thomas Keneally, who helped to launch the movement after the bicentennial, adds that the 'pyramidal nature of the British caste system' is at odds with the impulses of Australian egalitarianism. Here 'ministers travel in the front seat of their limos . . . and the King is the person who made the last million'.[21] The Prince could make no headway against the tide of the future.

Furthermore he had to cope with the prurient interest in his own misfortunes. Bob Hawke, a passive republican, thinks the anti-monarchical cause has been advanced by the 'meanderings and philanderings of the clan. The debate has been: "The Queen, yes; but this bloke who has expressed some strange views about what he'd like to come back as – you know, *him* – King of Australia?"'[22] By the millennial year the Queen will be so close to her own Golden Jubilee as Queen of Australia that the republicans may let her see out her span. Turnbull admits that there are 'many more Elizabethans than there are monarchists'. Prince Charles joined the debate with courtesy, saying that Australian wishes must be paramount. But he can have come home to Britain with no illusions about the sentiments of the country which he regards as a second home.

All his restless activity reflects the fact that has to *do* something, whereas his mother only has to *be* something. Her path was always easier than his. She began with glamour and the promise of youth. She did not need a raft of achievements or committees. The men who served her, like Martin Charteris, fell for her on the spot and have always carried the torch for her. She has stoically carried on through middle age. In *Elizabeth R* she quoted the soldier's explanation for the gallantry for which he had been decorated: 'It was the training'. She had the royal training, and it has prepared her to continue playing her part into majestic old age. Then, in Suzy Menkes' words, 'she'll be venerated for standing up for values that perhaps we'll come back to, values of certainty; for not playing to the camera; for not being always available'.[23] Temperamentally the Queen is very different from her heir. As Professor Anthony Clare says, she has been 'an anodyne monarch. She doesn't ruffle, she smoothes. [She is] not a catalyst, [but] a bringer together.

The Prince of Wales won't be that kind of monarch, has more opinions, sees his role as a catalyst.'[24]

Like her father and grandfather, she shows no signs of giving up. Her cousin by marriage, Pamela Hicks, watched her come through the *annus horribilis*:

> Obviously one's heart goes out to Prince Charles, but I think it's the Queen that one's so desperately sorry for, because she's a very private person, not gregarious like her mother is. . . . It's difficult for her to understand somebody who doesn't have a sense of duty, and for her to experience unkindness is something that's quite new. Everyone thinks what fun to be the Queen if you can be Queen for a day: but for a lifetime. . . .[25]

Her reign has already stretched out for more than half the span of the Windsor dynasty. One grey October day in Glasgow must do duty for ten thousand others. The Queen has come down from Balmoral to the Fairfield Yard. She was here before, in the glad confident morning of the 'Elizabethan Age', to launch the *Empress of Britain* for Canadian Pacific Railways. Govan has seen many false dawns since then. This yard was eventually taken over by the Kvaerner Group from Norway in 1988. Norwegian enterprise now harnesses Scottish skills, and the Queen is here to launch the *JO Selje*, first of a series of stainless steel chemical carriers. It wallows in the Deep Basin, against the Scandinavian pastels of the construction sheds and the porridge- and hash-coloured bricks of the Glasgow tenements beyond. Frogmen fuss round the boat on a security check.

The crowd is small, respectful. Oily water has gathered on the plastic covers which sheath the traditional red carpet. The trick is to remove the cover just in time for the royal foot to be the first to mark it, but this never works. Scottish Office flunkeys are scrubbing at it when the Queen appears, a small figure in a deep crimson coat and hat. She is forty yards down the ramp before she essays a brief tennis-elbow wave at the cheering schoolchildren on the quayside. A small child slithers down the concrete with a bunch of blue irises. The Queen clutches them briefly and passes them to a muscular lady in waiting. There is a dour blessing from a preacher. Craftsmen, he says, are diligent in their work. Without them, the nation cannot be established. The Queen, diligent in her turn, replies.

There is a mistake in her speech, as handed out to the press. She does not spot it, ploughs on through the text, but pronounces *JO Selje* perfectly and takes a skittish delight when the bottle fails to break on the stainless steel hull. She leaves past a noisy group of disabled adults, looking blankly past their wheelchairs as Princess Diana would never do. But in the afternoon, over in Motherwell where she had arrived late to open a new industrial unit, she realizes that the hundred or so schoolchildren have been soaked to the skin while waiting. Their home-made Scottish flags are drenched, a little forest of wilting saltires. They get a small walkabout while the VIPs wait in their turn. Then the bulbous Rolls sweeps her away. The child's irises from Govan are still on the back seat. The banality of this life, far from either luxurious ease or majestic state, is the norm. As she moves from factory to factory, plants sapling after sapling, she adds to the tally of forty-one years. Another five score children will be able to tell *their* children that they once saw the Queen of Scots.

What the Queen offers, year in year out, is dignity rather than magic. It is the reason why courtiers all fervently say, when the question of the succession comes up: 'I hope the Queen lives forever.' If she lives to her mother's present age with equal energies she will still be on the throne in 2020, with her son a sad septuagenarian. In its sheer length such a lifespan would pass beyond the current debate about the Established Church's links with the Crown. The Church of England will be a Church in England, and better for it. By the second decade of the new millennium the notion that a whole family, to the uttermost generation, has to be set aside to symbolize the Protestant hegemony in the realm will seem ridiculous. The restraints of the Royal Marriages Act and similar absurdities will go, freeing royal descendants to live out their lives as they will. In theory a monarchy no longer bound by the Act of Settlement need not even be the Windsors, whose Hanoverian ancestors got the job because of their religion. Believers in heredity – who have, by definition, long memories – may look back nostalgically at this time to the Stuart dynasty, whose members came to the throne through their descent and lost it through their religion. There are Jacobites still in Scotland who say with simple conviction: 'The wrong family are on the throne . . . when Queen Anne died there were fifty-seven claimants with a better claim than George I'.[26] The gates of Trequair in Scotland have been locked since the Earl rode off to join the 1715 Jacobite rising, and his descendants say they will not be unlocked until there is a Stuart on the throne once more.

An independent Scotland, should it emerge in the next quarter-century, might share the view that the Windsors are Hanoverian/Scots hybrids, faking it up in kilts at Balmoral. But its likely egalitarianism would accord ill with the hereditary claims of the Stuarts. Similarly, independent-minded Wales, where a BBC poll on the anniversary of Charles's investiture showed that only 47 per cent of the population thought they needed a Prince at all,[27] may have no more time for him when he becomes King. Nor is there much future for the scheme trailed mischievously by A.N. Wilson that an alternative successor should be trained up, who is 'not a vulgarian whose wife likes posing for the television cameras, but is a decent quiet sort, preferably someone in whom it is not possible to take much interest'. (He proposed the Queen's shy cousin, Richard Duke of Gloucester, a trained rather than an amateur architect:[28] it is a notion as absurd as the wartime suggestion, which convulsed the House of Commons, that the Duke's bibulous father, Henry, should be made Commander in Chief of the Army.) It is more realistic to suppose that, if the Queen is not succeeded by her son or grandson, it will be because the British state has opted for a non-hereditary figurehead. The powerful presence across the Irish Sea of Mary Robinson, a president who owes nothing to the shop-soiled hierarchies of the Irish political parties and defeated one of the then Taoiseach's close colleagues to get the job, shows that grace and dignity do not need centuries of hothouse cultivation.

Republican partisans have been encouraged by the shambles of the Windsor family saga. Tony Benn, who took great pleasure in telling the Queen at his farewell audience that his family were hereditary politicians,[29] has introduced a Bill to turn Britain into a 'democratic, secular, federal Commonwealth of the British nations' with a president elected by a two-thirds majority of the members of both Houses. The House of Lords would previously have been replaced by an elected House of the People. Benn's target is the Crown privilege which is exercised in government, the courts and the armed forces in the Queen's name. The Bill would leave the dispossessed royals living in whichever residences, with whatever compensation, Parliament saw fit to award. The new head of state would be a president elected for not more than two three-year terms. All this comes up against the fact that there is a head of state already, with the kind of personal approval ratings that most politicians can only dream of. Benn concedes a continuing role for the Queen as Head of the Commonwealth, a title she could keep.

> The title, whatever it was, might remain but it would provide no legal cover for what is an authoritarian, secretive and centralized system of government. That is why I think it's so important to differentiate between the two. India became a republic, but still recognized the Queen as Head of the Commonwealth. We could become a republic and recognize the Queen as Head of the Commonwealth.[30]

This process is indeed under way in the Commonwealth. Yet the great debate in Australia may not end in the precipitate removal of the monarchy. Referenda, as Mr Benn has discovered here, have an odd habit of being as much about those who propose them as about the subject to be decided. A referendum disposing of the known quality of the Queen on the proposal of Mr Keating might turn into a vote about him, not her. However, the long-term trend is ominous. The Queen told her Commonwealth leaders in Cyprus in October 1993 that the next forty years of the organization would be as eventful as the first, although she and the Duke would not be around to see them, and that few of the nations over which she reigned would keep the monarchical system. She has mourned the losses, like the secession of Fiji, and rejoiced in the proposed return of South Africa and Namibia. But the future is not secure. If her heirs and successors cease to be heads of state in Great Britain, as Benn proposes, their entitlement to be recognized as Head of the Commonwealth will vanish too. What would happen then is anybody's guess. That title might be passed around the Commonwealth heads of state according to length of service, starting with the great Kamazu, Dr Hastings Banda, President for Life of Malawi.

If Britain has suffered a sea change in its relationship with its maritime Empire-turned-Commonwealth, it has had a no less profound land change in its relations with the Europe of Maastricht and the Single Act. Romantic republicans, like Mr Benn, think the evils of European supra-federalism can only be kept at bay if sovereignty in the name of the people is restored to a Commonwealth of Britain. Others reckon that the gradual cession of sovereignty to Brussels will produce exactly the written constitution which Britain needs. That need was pointed up during the long arguments about what was permitted and when, under the present muddled system, during the Maastricht debate itself. Then John Major confronted his dissidents with the threat that he would seek a dissolution from the Queen if he was defeated in Parliament. Many felt that she would have no obligation to grant it under these circumstances, but the arcane precedents offered no real guide. 'We live under a system of tacit understandings. But the understandings themselves are not always understood,' wrote one authority at the turn of the century.[31] The understandings which relate to the monarch's role in the political process were last written down in 1949;[32] they were discovered in a box in the Public Record Office entitled 'British Constitutional System' by the assiduous Professor Hennessy in 1993. The box contained nothing of present interest or relevance. No one knows what has passed between the monarch and any of her nine prime ministers. Her role remains shrouded in mystery, as well as mystique, and it may well be that the breeze from Europe will dispel it.

Shrewder republicans certainly reckon that the old constitution, hidden away, is not a jewel but a vapour. They yearn for something more substantial.

> Britain is a country without a written document, and in search of one. This the union treaty, providing a fundamental framework for rights, laws, and the political legitimacy of institutions, provides. . . . Institutions that were hitherto unaccountable, limited not by law or constitution but only by 'good sense' history and what the constitutional sages said they could get away with, can now be restrained by constitutional means.[33]

Professor Stephen Haseler sees this new Europe of clear checks and balances as an alternative to 'the London-based, centralised, and tightly controlled Leviathan that is Her Majesty's royal-state'. It will have its rotating federal head of state. The hereditary monarchies and grand duchies within it will have no status other than as the voluntarily retained symbols of national identity. From this, republicans argue, as well as from the absence of virtue in the hereditary system and the cadet members of the royal family, it will be best to drop the Windsors, symbols of the worst of the old Establishment. Australians want to patriate their head of state; British republicans want to democratize it.

Facing this challenge, a challenge more dangerous even than that of 1917, the Windsors will need to reinvent themselves once more. The Queen has immense personal capital invested in the hearts of the British over forty years. As her reign approaches that of Victoria in length, however, the anachronisms of hereditary courtiers, gradations of rank, and the contrast between the way the media portray her children's lives and the platitudes of the Court Circular have had a corrosive effect. In part this is bad luck. Elizabeth II does not have Victoria's way with a word, any more than her son has the Widow of Windsor's artistic talent. But she has been dutiful. Where Victoria hid at Balmoral in ostentatious bereavement and sabotaged uncongenial prime ministers, Elizabeth has evidently behaved with perfect propriety. She has kept their confidences, known their weaknesses. 'Some things stay there, and some things go out of the other ear, and some things never come out at all,'[34] she has said. If there were an election for president, she – more than any russet-coated captain wistfully desired by Mr Benn – would surely get the two-thirds majority stipulated in his Bill.

It is external circumstances of the two reigns which have been so different, as David Cannadine points out:

> The present Queen's reign is very much Queen Victoria's reign, but in reverse. When Victoria came to the throne the monarchy wasn't very rich, wasn't all that popular, wasn't very imperial, and wasn't very ceremonially grand. By the end of her reign it had become very rich, very popular, very imperial and very ceremonially grand. Roughly speaking, that amalgam lasted through until the beginning of the present Queen's reign. It began very grand and it's becoming smaller and smaller, but making things smaller is much harder than making things bigger, and that's the problem with which the present British monarchy is faced.[35]

This shrinkage is inexorable. It is a shrinkage of things, as well as expectations. There will not be another ocean-going liner misnamed the royal yacht, upon which the royal family always have first call as though it was their personal plaything. Trains and planes will come from stock, rather than being unique to the sovereign. Ceremonial will survive because the tourists love it and the British are good at it. The royal family itself will get the hint that it cannot win long-term acclaim by playing to the soap opera appetite for what Lord Charteris calls 'the continuing story of *Peyton Place* . . . births, deaths, marriages'. It must achieve by reticence what it is now denied in magic. The eventual demise of the Queen Mother will be a moment of national mourning which will erase for a period the endless speculation about her grandchildren.

After that, with Elizabeth II now the family matriarch in her turn, the Windsors will have an opportunity to refashion themselves for a less deferential age. Democratic monarchy may be a contradiction in terms, but accountable monarchy is not. The monarchy can and should be accountable for monies and deeds. The republican arguments have made such headway because they have been stoked up by anger and envy. A new monarch who makes it plain that, instead of defending the Established Church and the established order, he will take an oath to defend the constitution and to be its faithful liegeman against all manner of folk, could have the vision for 2020. He would be Const. Def., not Fid. Def. In the long period before then it is not necessary to 'run for office', nor to espouse celibacy, nor indeed to undermine the standing of Diana as a media celebrity and national comforter. The best way for Charles to prepare for the throne, and to ensure that there is still a throne to prepare for, is to behave as though that distant destiny is only a small part of a fulfilled life.

Meanwhile, there is no mechanism to stop the Queen from going on. Maybe she is not immune to the sycophancy which surrounds presidents as well as princes, but she is a heroine to her servants. After a lifetime of courtiership Lord Charteris sums up his boss: 'I really can't think of any occasion when I've not felt better for doing business with her. She's a stiffener of backs. She is realistic. She is as honest as the day is long, and she's humble. A very good egg.'[36] Above all, the Queen has made a virtue out of transcendent ordinariness, a virtue which she must hope that her descendants will emulate. This has been the secret weapon of the dynasty – of George V, George VI and Queen Elizabeth – and royals such as Edward VIII, who eschew it, do so at their peril. It encourages subjects to identify with sovereigns while also revering them. Thus, it seems, will the Windsors continue to link the glories of the nation's past with its aspirations for the future.

[illegible]

5 M. [illegible]
6 [illegible]
7 [illegible]
8 E. Thompson [illegible]
9 P. Burke [illegible]
10 W. [illegible]
(1984), pp. [illegible]
11 D. Cannadine [illegible]
Ritual: the British [illegible]
c. 1820-19[illegible]
[illegible]
12 D. [illegible]
13 E. E. [illegible]
March 1991 [illegible]
14 [illegible]
15 A. [illegible]

Notes

These references are, in effect, a running bibliography, so we have dispensed with a separate booklist. The references are given in full when first cited and abbreviated thereafter. The place of publication is London unless otherwise stated.

Chapter 1

1 P. Vansittart, *Happy and Glorious* (1988), p.171.
2 *Review of Reviews*, July 1891.
3 A. Holden, *The Tarnished Crown* (1993), p.50.
4 *Times*, 23 January 1901.
5 R. Blake, *Disraeli* (1967 edn), p. 562.
6 M. Fowler, *Below the Peacock Fan* (1987), p.194.
7 J. Lees-Milne, *The Enigmatic Edwardian* (1986), p.58.
8 D. Thompson, *Queen Victoria: Gender and Power* (1990), p.132.
9 P. Burke, *The Fabrication of Louis XIV* (1992), p.4.
10 W. Bagehot (ed. R.H.S. Crossman), *The English Constitution* (1964), pp.16–24 and passim.
11 D. Cannadine, 'The Context, Performance and Meaning of Ritual: The British Monarchy and the "Invention of Tradition", c. 1820–1977', in E. Hobsbawm and T. Ranger (eds), *The Invention of Tradition* (1983), p.128.
12 H. Nicolson, *George the Fifth: His Life and Reign* (1952), p.142.
13 E.E. Morison, *The Letters of Theodore Roosevelt*, VII (Cambridge, Mass., 1954), p.142.
14 R. Rhodes James, *Albert, Prince Consort* (1983), p.89.
15 A. Palmer, *The Kaiser* (1978), p.141.

16 A.C. Murray, *Master and Brother* (1945), p.80.
17 E. Hughes, *The Prince, the Crown and the Cash* (1969), p.17.
18 Kenneth Rose denies that George V was racially prejudiced. But on his accession Diana Cooper wrote that she heartily disliked everything about him 'except that I thank God he hates the Jews'. P. Ziegler, *Diana Cooper* (1981), p.29.
19 Private information: Nigel Nicolson.
20 Private information: Nigel Nicolson.
21 D. Bennett, *Queen Victoria's Children* (1980), pp.48–9.
22 Princess Marie Louise, *My Memories of Six Reigns* (1965), p.48.
23 Princess Alice, *For My Grandchildren* (1966), p.123.
24 Interview: Lord Dudley.
25 Interview: Nigel Nicolson.
26 L. Westminster, *Grace and Favour* (1961), p.103.
27 F. Hardie, *The Political Influence of the British Monarchy 1868–1952* (1970), p.143.
28 B.J. Hendrick (ed.), *The Life and Letters of Walter Hines Page*, III (1925), pp.53–7.
29 J. Pope-Hennessy, *Queen Mary* (1959), p.451.
30 Gore, *George V*, p.433.
31 Interview: Kenneth de Courcy.
32 J.M. McEwen (ed.), *The Riddell Diaries* (1986), p.70.
33 K.O. Morgan (ed.), *Lloyd George Family Letters 1885–1936* (1973), p.159.
34 A. Ponsonby, *R.A. Ponsonby* (1989), p.64.
35 E. David (ed.), *Inside Asquith's Cabinet* (1977), pp.146–7.
36 A. Palmer, *Crowned Cousins* (1985), p.210.
37 K. Wilson (ed.), *The Rasp of War* (1988), p.188.
38 D. Winter, *Haig's Command* (1991), p.277.
39 R. Rhodes James (ed.), *Memoirs of a Conservative* (1969), p.55.
40 K. Young (ed.), *The Diaries of Sir Robert Bruce Lockhart*, I (1973), p.246.
41 Interview: Kenneth Rose.
42 Interview: Lord Houghton.
43 W. Thorne, *My Life's Battles* (1925), p.195.
44 *Times*, 4 April 1917.
45 H.G. Wells, *Mr Britling Sees It Through* (1968 edn), p.405.
46 *Times*, 21 April 1917.
47 Nicolson, *George*, p.308.
48 *New York Times*, 16 May 1917, quoting the *Penny Pictorial*.
49 *Times*, 18 July 1917.
50 M. and E. Brock (eds), *H.H. Asquith Letters to Venetia Stanley* (Oxford, 1982), p.285.
51 K. Rose, *King George V* (1983), p.226.
52 P. Brendon, *Our Own Dear Queen* (1986), p.93.
53 *Times*, 12 November 1918.
54 S. Weintraub, *A Stillness Heard Round the World* (1986), p. 263.
55 E.S. Turner, *Dear Old Blighty* (1980), p.262.

Chapter 2

1 J.W. Wheeler-Bennett, *King George VI* (1958), p.160.
2 J. Vincent (ed.), *The Crawford Papers* (1984), p.397.
3 *Herald*, 16 November 1918.
4 T. Morgan, *FDR* (1985), p.195.
5 Interview: Lord Boyd-Carpenter.
6 Nicolson, *George*, p.337.
7 Lord Beaverbrook, *Men and Power 1917–1918* (1956), p.388. The words were Lord Curzon's but, as Lloyd George inferred, the argument came from the King.
8 Mabell Countess of Airlie, *Thatched with Gold* (1962), p.142.
9 M. Gilbert, *Winston S. Churchill*, IV (1975), p.276.
10 Lees-Milne, *Enigmatic Edwardian*, pp.309 and 311.
11 Airlie, *Thatched with Gold*, p.143.
12 R. Blythe, *The Age of Illusion* (Harmondsworth, 1963), p.20.
13 S. Hynes, *A War Imagined* (1990), p.280.
14 J. Lees-Milne, *Harold Nicolson*, II (1981), p.235.
15 R.S. Churchill, *Lord Derby* (1959), p.159. Kenneth Rose coasts doubt on this story, which may have improved in the telling. But it is, surely, an accurate representation of King George's parental attitude.
16 Lord Harewood tells this story in his autobiography but P.N. Furbank, Forster's official biographer, believes it to be apocryphal.
17 Interview: Kenneth de Courcy.
18 O. Sitwell, *Queen Mary and Others* (1974), p.28.
19 R. Gray, *The King's Wife* (1990), p.333.
20 Nicolson, *George*, p.342.
21 Interview: Suzy Menkes.
22 S. Menkes, *The Royal Jewels* (1985), pp.52–3. Apparently the present Queen has reimbursed the descendants of the Romanovs.
23 Interview: Countess Mountbatten.
24 Private information.
25 Interview: Sir Steven Runciman.
26 Interview: Philip Ziegler.
27 Jones, *Ponsonby*, p.64.
28 Interview: Philip Ziegler.
29 J.A. Frere, *The British Monarchy at Home* (1963), p.85.
30 P. Ziegler, *Edward VIII* (1990), p.85.
31 Interview: Barbara Cartland.
32 Duke of Windsor, *A King's Story* (1951), p.136.
33 F. Donaldson, *Edward VIII* (1974), p.74.
34 Michael Thomas Papers.
35 Michael Thomas Papers: Stamfordham to Thomas, 20 September 1920.
36 Interview: John Grigg, quoting his father.

37 Windsor, *King's Story,* p.163.
38 Interview: Sarah Bradford.
39 Interview: Sir Dudley Forwood.
40 Thomas Papers, 15 April 1927.
41 Ziegler, *Edward VIII,* p.165.
42 Interview: John Grigg, quoting his father.
43 D. Hart-Davis (ed.), *In Royal Service: Letters and Journals of Sir Alan Lascelles* (1989), pp.15 and 65.
44 J. Morgan, *Edwina Mountbatten: A Life of Her Own* (1991), p.105.
45 Private information.
46 Interview: Lady Alexandra Metcalfe.
47 Interview: Peter Townsend.
48 Private information.
49 Bagehot, *The British Constitution,* p.85.
50 K. Roby, *The King, the Press and the People* (1975), p.128.
51 Ziegler, *Edward VIII,* p.172.
52 Frere, *British Monarchy,* p.99.

Chapter 3

1 A.J.P. Taylor, *English History 1914–1945* (1967), p.378.
2 W.H. Hancock, *Smuts,* II (Cambridge, 1968), p.55.
3 A.J. Sylvester, *Life with Lloyd George* (1975), p.180.
4 McEwen, *Riddell Diaries,* p.168.
5 Beaverbrook, *Men and Power,* p.204.
6 Winter, *Haig's Command,* p.328.
7 Interview: John Grigg.
8 Beaverbrook, *Men and Power,* p.337.
9 J. Ramsden (ed.), *Real Old Tory Politics* (1984), p.203.
10 K. Middlemas and J. Barnes, *Baldwin* (1969), p.170.
11 D. Dilks, *Neville Chamberlain,* I (Cambridge, 1984), p.360.
12 E. Longford (ed.), *Darling Loosy: Letters to Princess Louise 1856–1939* (1991), p.297.
13 M. Secrest, *Kenneth Clark* (1984), p.116.
14 C.L. Mowat, *Britain Between the Wars* (1978 edn), p.169.
15 *Daily Herald,* 4 January 1924 and 24 December 1923.
16 R. Postgate, *The Life of George Lansbury* (1951), p.251.
17 McEwen, *Riddell Diaries,* p.339.
18 J.R. Clynes, *Memoirs,* II (1937), p.230.
19 Rhodes James, *Memoirs of Conservative,* pp.177–8.
20 Interview: Philip Ziegler.
21 M. Muggeridge, *Chornicles of Wasted Time,* I (1972), p.49.
22 A. de Courcy, *Circe* (1992), p.188.
23 E.S. Turner, *The Court of St James's* (1959), p.362.
24 N. and J. MacKenzie (eds) *The Diary of Beatrice Webb* (1985), *Diary of Webb,* p.254.

25 P. Snowden, *An Autobiography*, II (1934), p.662.
26 *Daily Herald*, 2 January 1924.
27 Clynes, *Memoirs*, II, pp.240 and 55.
28 Pope-Hennessy, *Queen Mary*, p.516.
29 J. Symons, *The General Strike* (1957), p.118.
30 H. Hearder, 'King George V, the General Strike, and the 1931 Crisis', in H. Hearder and H.R. Loyn, *British Government and Administration* (Cardiff, 1974), pp.239–41.
31 Windsor, *King's Story*, p.218.
32 Interview: Julian Ridsdale.
33 Hart-Davis, *Royal Service*, p.51.
34 M.S. Lovell, *Straight On Till Morning* (1987), p.88.
35 E. Trzebinski, *Silence Will Speak* (1977), p.286.
36 Hart-Davis, *Royal Service*, pp.109 and 103.
37 Thomas Papers, February 1929.
38 *Sphere*, 12 January and 16 February 1929. 'Cosmopolitan' was evidently the journal's euphemism for American rather than Jewish.
39 Thomas Papers, February 1929.
40 J. Bryan III and C. Murphy, *The Windsor Story* (1979), p.103.
41 R. Rhodes James, *Anthony Eden* (1986), p.130.
42 D. Marquand, *Ramsay MacDonald* (1977), p. 635.
43 Rose, *George V*, p.378.
44 H. Laski, *Parliamentary Government in England* (1938), p.396.
45 S. Koss, *The Rise and Fall of the Political Press in Britain*, II (1984), p.536.
46 Cambridge University Library, Baldwin Papers, Vol.9, f.272.
47 *Times*, 12 November 1932.
48 P. Hall, *Royal Fortune* (1992), passim.
49 Interview: Sir Steven Runciman.
50 A. Allfrey, *Edward VII and His Jewish Court* (1991), p.195.
51 F.M.L. Thompson, *English Landed Society in the Nineteenth Century* (1969 edn), pp.330 and 344.
52 Interview: David Cannadine.
53 *Sphere*, 16 February 1929.
54 J. Curran and J. Seaton, *Power Without Responsibility* (1981), p.153.
55 *Daily Mail*, 27 December 1932.
56 Interview: John Grigg.
57 Interview: Sir Steven Runciman.
58 Thomas Papers: Prince of Wales to Thomas, 19 September 1934.
59 Interview: Kenneth de Courcy.
60 Thomas Papers, 1930.
61 Thomas Papers.
62 *Documents on German Foreign Policy* Series C, IV (1962), p.49.
63 Interview: Diana Mosley.
64 C. Higham, *Wallis* (1988), p.16.

65 Interview: Kenneth de Courcy.
66 Interview: Barbara Cartland.
67 J. Pope-Hennessy, *A Lovely Business* (1981), p.211.
68 Interview: Lord Dudley.
69 Interview: Kenneth de Courcy.
70 Inverview: Veronica Maclean.
71 Interview: Kenneth de Courcy.
72 S. Menkes, *The Windsor Style* (1982), p.159.
73 M. Bloch, *Wallis and Edward* (1986), pp.148 and 139.
74 H. Vickers, *Cecil Beaton* (1985), p.193.
75 Private information.
76 Thomas Papers: Halsey to Thomas, 10 January 1935.
77 Thomas Papers, 22 April 1935.
78 *New York Times,* 7 May 1935.
79 *Illustrated London News,* 11 May 1935.
80 *New York Times,* 6 and 7 May 1935.
81 Interview: Nigel Nicolson.
82 F. Watson, 'The Death of George V' in *History Today,* December 1986, p.28.
83 Interview: Sarah Bradford.

Chapter 4

1 Interview: Barbara Cartland.
2 Windsor, *King's Story,* p.282.
3 Interview: Enoch Powell.
4 P. Gibbs, *Ordeal in England* (1938), pp.12 and 14.
5 A. Briggs, *The Golden Age of Wireless* (1965), p.266.
6 Interview: Frank Giles.
7 F. Donaldson, *Edward VIII* (1974), p.181.
8 *Documents on German Foreign Policy*, C, IV, p.1024.
9 *Documents on German Foreign Policy*, C, IV, p.1063.
10 *New York Times*, 3 February 1936.
11 *Documents on German Foreign Policy,* C, V, p.193.
12 Interview: Sir Steven Runciman.
13 Interview: Reinhard Spitzy.
14 H. Hardinge, *Loyal to Three Kings* (1967), p.69.
15 Interview: Kenneth de Courcy.
16 Interview: Philip Ziegler.
17 Interview: Julian Ridsdale.
18 Interview: Sir Dudley Forwood.
19 Interview: Nigel Nicolson.
20 Interview: Philip Ziegler.
21 E. Wrench, *Geoffrey Dawson and Our Times* (1955), p. 339.
22 J. Charmley, *Duff Cooper* (1986), p.95.
23 Interview: Nigel Nicolson, quoting his father's diary.
24 Lord Birkenhead, *Walter Monckton* (1969), p.128.

25 Bloch, *Wallis and Edward*, pp.174–6.
26 Interview: Lord Hardinge.
27 *New York Times*, 16 October 1936.
28 *We saw it happen* by Thirteen Correspondents of 'The New York Times' (1939), pp.174 and 171.
29 P. Brendon, 'Amendment Envy' in *Columbia Journalism Review*, November–December 1991, p.68.
30 Interview: Philip Ziegler.
31 H. Wickham Steed, *The Press* (1938), p.76.
32 T. Jones, *A Diary with Letters 1931–1950* (1954), p.277.
33 *Washington Post*, 17 October 1936.
34 *New York Times*, 16 October 1936.
35 A. Chisholm and M. Davie, *Lord Beaverbrook* (New York, 1992), p.338.
36 Lord Beaverbrook, *The Abdication of King Edward VIII* (1966), p.30.
37 J. Gunther, *Inside Europe* (1937), p.242.
38 Koss, *Political Press,* II, p.542.
39 Interview: John Grigg.
40 R. Rhodes James (ed.), *Chips: The Diaries of Sir Henry Channon* (1967), p.77.
41 Jones, *Diary*, p.291.
42 R. Payne, *The Civil War in Spain 1936–1939* (1963), p.153.
43 Donaldson, *Edward VIII*, p.226.
44 *Daily Herald,* 20 November 1936. There are several versions of this pronouncement, but the *Herald* said that it was quoting the King's 'exact words'.
45 O. Woods and J. Bishop, *The Story of The Times* (1983), p.288.
46 Interview: Van Lockhead.
47 J. Pope-Hennessey, *A Lonely Business* (1981), p.219.
48 B. Inglis, *Abdication* (1966), p.257.
49 Rhodes James, *Chips*, p.84.
50 Interview: Kenneth de Courcy.
51 Interview: Kenneth de Courcy.
52 J. Barnes and D. Nicholson (eds), *The Empire at Bay: The Leo Amery Diaries 1929–1945* (1988), p.433.
53 Middlemas and Barnes, *Baldwin*, p.995.
54 C. Stuart (ed.), *The Reith Diaries* (1975), p.190.
55 *History of The Times*, IV (1952), p.1036.
56 M. Stannard, *Evelyn Waugh: No Abiding City* (1992), p.359.
57 *Daily Herald*, 5 December 1936.
58 Interview: Philip Ziegler.
59 Interview: Julian Ridsdale.

Chapter 5

1 Thomas Papers: Duke of York to Thomas, 25 November 1936.

2 Interview: Philip Ziegler.
3 Interview: Sir Dudley Forwood.
4 Interview: Lord Eccles.
5 D.B. Schewe (ed.), *Franklin D. Roosevelt and Foreign Affairs*, 2nd series, IV (New York, 1980), p.150.
6 Interview: Sir Steven Runciman.
7 *Nation*, 19 December 1936.
8 Interview: Sir Steven Runciman.
9 *Annual Register for 1936* (1937), pp.107–8.
10 Clynes, *Memoirs*, II, p.242.
11 A. Roberts, *'The Holy Fox': A Biography of Lord Halifax* (1991), p.4.
12 S. Bradford, *George VI* (1989), p.119.
13 A. Howard, *RAB: The Life of R.A. Butler* (1987), p.66.
14 J.M. Golby and A.N. Purdue, *The Monarchy and the British People* (1988), p.111.
15 Interview: David Metcalfe.
16 M. Bloch, *The Secret File of the Duke of Windsor* (1989), p.135.
17 I. Seward, *Royal Children* (1993), p.23.
18 Interview: Peter Townsend.
19 N. Hartnell, *Silver and Gold* (1955), p.94.
20 Roy Strong, 'Fitting Image' in *Sunday Times*, 30 May 1993.
21 Interview: David Cannadine.
22 *Herald*, 11 December 1936.
23 Gibbs, *Ordeal*, p.23.
24 *Documents on German Foreign Policy*, C, IV, p.1024.
25 *Times*, 11 May 1937.
26 Stuart, *Reith Diaries*, p.198.
27 K. Martin, *The Crown and the Establishment* (1962), p.124.
28 *Times*, 12 May 1937.
29 J. Flanner, *London Was Yesterday* (1975), p.78.
30 Interview: Lady Longford.
31 *Herald*, 12 May 1937.
32 Sylvester, *Lloyd George*, pp.193 and 181.
33 *Herald*, 10 May 1937.
34 H. Jennings and C. Madge (eds), *May the Twelfth 1937* (1987 edn), pp.272, 305 and passim.
35 *Daily Mirror*, 6 March 1937.
36 *Times*, 11 May 1937.
37 Jennings and Madge, *May*, p.303.
38 Schewe, *Roosevelt and Foreign Affairs*, V, p.329.
39 *New York Times*, 10 May 1937.
40 Bryan and Murphy, *Windsor Story*, p.314.
41 O. Sitwell, *Rat Week* (1986), p.61.
42 Hall, *Royal Fortune*, p.81.
43 Bloch, *Wallis and Edward*, p.233.
44 Interview: Sir Dudley Forwood.
45 Ziegler, *Edward VIII*, p.361.

46 Vincent, *Crawford Papers*, p.618.
47 Rhodes James, *Chips*, pp.125 and 130.
48 Interview: Peter Townsend.
49 Interview: Frau Elbing.
50 *New York Times*, 23 October 1937.
51 Interview: Sir Dudley Forwood.
52 *New York Times*, 7 November 1937.
53 Interview: Sir Dudley Forwood.
54 Schewe, *Roosevelt and Foreign Affairs*, VII, p.174.
55 P. Schmidt, *Hitler's Interpreter* (1951), p.74.
56 Schewe, *Roosevelt and Foreign Affairs*, VII, p.172.
57 Interview: Kenneth de Courcy.
58 *New York Times*, 12 December 1937.
59 D. Dilks (ed.), *The Diaries of Sir Alexander Cadogan* (1971), p.202.
60 O.H. Bullitt, *For the President: Personal and Secret Correspondence between Franklin D. Roosevelt and William C. Bullitt* (1973), p.310.
61 Secrest, *Clark*, p.119.
62 Wheeler-Bennett, *George VI*, pp.348 and 396.
63 Interview: Sir Steven Runciman.
64 K. Feiling, *The Life of Neville Chamberlain* (947), p.378.
65 Interview: John Grigg.
66 D. Reynolds, 'FDR's Foreign Policy and the British Royal Visit to the USA 1939', in *The Historian*, XLV, August 1983, p.465 and passim.
67 J.W. Pickersgill, *The Mackenzie King Record*, I (Toronto, 1960), p.255.
68 Reynolds, *Historian* (August 1983), p.462.
69 T. Evans (ed.), *The Killearn Diaries* (1972), p.107.

Chapter 6

1 Wheeler-Bennett, *George VI*, p.467.
2 Interview: Lord Charteris.
3 M. Gilbert, *Finest Hour: Winston S. Churchill 1939–1941* (1983), p.700.
4 M. Bloch, *Operation Willi: The Plot to Kidnap the Duke of Windsor* (1984), p.86.
5 Tom Harrisson Mass-Observation Archive, Microfiche 2290.
6 Interview: John Grigg.
7 Dilks, *Cadogan*, p.215.
8 Interview: Kenneth de Courcy.
9 Interview: Lady Hambleden.
10 Mass-Observation Archive, Microfiche 247.
11 T. Harrisson, *Living through the Blitz* (1976), p.164.
12 Mass-Observation Archive, Microfiche 1392.
13 F.J. Corbitt, *Fit for a King* (1956), p.162.

14 Hartnell, *Silver and Gold*, p.102.
15 Roberts, *Halifax*, p.292.
16 R. Keyes, *Outrageous Fortune: The Tragedy of Leopold of the Belgians 1901–1941* (1984), p.408.
17 Interview: David Cannadine.
18 Interview: Veronica Maclean.
19 Pickersgill, *Mackenzie King*, I, p.694.
20 P. Brendon, *Ike* (1986), p.113.
21 H. Macmillan, *War Diaries* (1984), pp.122 and 120.
22 J. Harvey (ed.), *The War Diaries of Oliver Harvey* (1978), p.275.
23 Interview: Peter Townsend.
24 M. Panter-Downes, *London War Notes 1939–1945* (1972), p.376.
25 Mass-Observation Archive, Microfiche 2221.
26 Interview: Frank Giles.
27 Gilbert, *Finest Hour*, p.984.
28 Bryan and Murphy, *Windsor Story*, p.364.
29 Interview: Philip Ziegler.
30 Roberts, *Halifax*, p.291.
31 Interview: Barry Sainsbury.
32 Interview: Kenneth de Courcy.
33 Private information.
34 Pickersgill, *Mackenzie King*, III, p.240.
35 B. Pimlott, *Hugh Dalton* (1985), pp.645, 408 and passim.
36 Wheeler-Bennett, *George VI*, p.732.
37 W. Hamilton, *My Queen and I* (1975), p.108.
38 Interview: Tony Benn.
39 Rhodes James, *Chips*, p.463.
40 P. Ziegler, *Mountbatten* (1986 edn), p.406.
41 Interview: Alastair Forbes.
42 Interview: John Grigg.
43 Bradford, George VI, p.399.
44 Interview: Lady Pamela Hicks.
45 Interview: Peter Townsend.
46 Interview: John Grigg.
47 Interview: Veronica Maclean.
48 R. Lacey, *Majesty* (1977), p.121.
49 Interview: Lady Elizabeth Cavendish.
50 Interview: George Hadley.
51 Interview: Lady Hambleden.
52 B. Castle, *The Castle Diaries 1964–70* (1984), p.421.
53 Interview: Lady Longford.
54 M. Crawford, *The Little Princesses* (1950), p.33.
56 F. Rocco, 'Duty before Happiness' in *Independent on Sunday*, 3 October 1993.
57 Interview: William Evans.
58 Interview: Lady Patricia Mountbatten.
59 Princess Alice, *For My Grandchildren*, p.281.
60 B. Boothroyd, *Philip: An Informal Biography* (1971), p.27.

Chapter 7

1 J. Colville, *The Fringes of Power* (1985), p.640.
2 Interview: Lord Charteris.
3 C. Warwick, *Princess Margaret* (1983), p.97.
4 Interview: Lady Pamela Hicks.
5 Colville, *Fringes of Power,* p.646.
6 Colville, *Fringes of Power,* p.641.
7 Private information.
8 Boothroyd, *Philip,* p.50.
9 PRO Prem. 11/247.
10 Interview: Lord Charteris.
11 Howard, *RAB,* pp.276–7.
12 *Daily Mirror,* 9 February 1960.
13 M. Gilbert, *Never Despair: Winston Churchill 1945–64* (1988), p.826.
14 P. Townsend, *Time and Chance* (1978), p.229.
15 Hall, *Royal Fortune,* pp.93–112.
16 Ziegler, *Edward VIII,* p.539.
17 Rhodes James, *Chips,* p.437.
18 Interview: Lord Charteris.
19 Private information.
20 J. Morgan (ed.), *The Backbench Diaries of Richard Crossman* (1981), p.231.
21 Ziegler, *Edward VIII,* p.540.
22 J. Colville, *Footprints in Time* (1976), p.249.
23 E. Shils and M. Young, 'The Meaning of the Coronation' in *Sociological Review,* I, No.2 (1956), pp.63–81.
24 *The People,* 14 June 1953.
25 Crawford, *The Little Princesses,* p.97.
26 Townsend, *Time and Chance,* p.346.
27 D. Keay, *Elizabeth II* (1991), p.80.
28 Interview: Lady Elizabeth Cavendish.
29 G. Payn and S. Morley (eds), *The Noël Coward Diaries* (1982), p.254.
30 Payn and Morley, *Noël Coward Diaries,* p.236.
31 *Times,* 24 October 1955.
32 A. Duncan, *The Reality of Monarchy* (1970), p.124.
33 Interview: John Grigg.
34 Interview: Anthony Craxton.
35 Morgan, *Crossman,* p.483.
36 Interview: Eileen Parker.
37 Interview: Penny Junor.
38 Boothroyd, *Philip,* p.
39 Interview: Eileen Parker.
40 F. Rocco in *The Independent on Sunday,* 13 December 1992.
41 Interview: Mike Parker.
42 Interview: Enoch Powell.

43 Sir R. Menzies, *Afternoon Light* (1967), p.256.
44 Ziegler, *Mountbatten*, p.539.
45 Interview: Lord Hailsham.
46 Interview: Sir Edward Heath.
47 Rhodes James, *Anthony Eden*, p.496.

Chapter 8

1 Interview: Lady Elizabeth Cavendish.
2 K. Amis, *Memoirs* (1991), p.188.
3 C. Warwick, *Princess Margaret* (DATE), p.97.
4 M. Muggeridge, *New Statesman*, 20 July 1956.
5 *Reynolds News*, 12 November 1959.
6 *National and English Review*, Vol.149, No.894, August 1957.
7 Interview: John Grigg.
8 J. Murray-Brown (ed.), *The Monarchy and Its Future* (1969), p.51.
9 Interview: Sir Edward Ford.
10 Interview: Lord Charteris.
11 Interview: John Grigg.
12 Gilbert, *Never Despair*, p.1330.
13 H. Evans, *Downing Street Diary* (1981), p.171.
14 A. Horne, *Harold Macmillan II: 1937–1986*.
15 Interview: Sir Edward Ford.
16 PRO 1963.
17 PRO PREM 11 4368.
18 PRO CAB/128/37, 12 June 1963.
19 *Daily Mirror*, 23 June 1963.
20 J. Parker, *Prince Philip* (1990), p.206.
21 Morgan, *Crossman Diaries Vol II*, p.442.
22 Horne, *Macmillan*, pp.485–6.
23 Horne, *Macmillan*, p.533.
24 Horne, *Macmillan*, p.582.
25 Thames TV, *The Day Before Yesterday 6: The Rise and Fall of Supermac*, October 1970.
26 M. Butler, *August and Rab: A Memoir* (1987), p.81.
27 Horne, *Macmillan*, p.564.
28 Horne, *Macmillan*, p.565.
29 H. Macmillan, *At the End of the Day* (1973), p.515.
30 Howard, *RAB*, p.319.
31 Interview: Lord Hailsham.
32 Interview: Enoch Powell.
33 Howard, *RAB*, p.322.
34 Lord Home, *The Way the Wind Blows* (1976), p.218.
35 A. Boyle, *The Climate of Treason* (1980 edn), p.476.
36 Bradford, *George VI*, p.426.

37 P. Wright, *Spycatcher* (New York, 1987), p.223.
38 A. Summers and S. Dorrill, *Honeytrap* (1987), p.229.
39 Interview: Lord Charteris.
40 *Dictionary of National Biography, 1981–85,* pp.41–3.
41 R.H.S. Crossman, *Diaries of a Cabinet Minister,* I (1975), p.29.
42 Castle, *Diaries 1964–70,* p.48.
43 Interview: Tony Benn. The biography of Benn by Jad Adams (*Tony Benn,* 1993) makes it clear that this is a romantic précis of events that stretched from 10 March to 2 November 1965.
44 Keay, *Elizabeth II*, p.140.
45 Interview: Lord Harewood.
46 Interview: Lord Charteris.
47 A. Holden, *Charles, Prince of Wales* (1979), p.114.
48 Howard, *RAB*, p.351.
49 J. Pearson, *The Ultimate Family* (1986), p.174.
50 Interview: Lord Brabourne.
51 Interview: Hywel Jones.
52 Pearson, *Ultimate Family,* p.197.
53 T. Nairn, *The Enchanted Glass* (1988), p.230.

Chapter 9

1 Castle, *Diaries 1964–70,* p, 421.
2 C. King, *The Cecil King Diary, 1965–70* (1975), p.20.
3 T. Benn, *Diaries Vol.II: Office Without Power, 1968–72* (1987), pp.38–9.
4 J. Parker, *The Queen* (1991), p.186.
5 Duncan, *The Reality of Monarchy,* p.73.
6 Crossman, *Diaries,* III (1977), pp.723–4.
7 Castle, *Diaries 1964–70,* p.728.
8 *Report of the Select Committee on the Civil List,* Session 1971–2, p.73.
9 Hall, *Royal Fortune,* p.114.
10 *Select Committee on the Civil List,* p.42.
11 Howard, *Crossman,* p.353.
12 Interview: Willie Hamilton.
13 *Select Committee on the Civil List,* p.24.
14 *Daily Mirror,* 3 December 1971.
15 P. Ziegler, *Crown and People* (1978), p.143.
16 Crossman, *Diaries,* Vol.III, p.442.
17 Castle, *The Castle Diaries, Vol.II, 1974–76,* p.310.
18 *Private Eye,* 21 February 1975.
19 King, *The Cecil King Diary, 1970–74* (1977), p.295.
20 J. Campbell, *Edward Heath* (1993), p.494.
21 Interview: Sir Shridath (Sonny) Ramphal.
22 Interview: Sir Shridath (Sonny) Ramphal.
23 *Australian,* 12 November 1975.

24 Interview: Malcolm Fraser.
25 Interview: Malcolm Fraser.
26 P. Whitehead, *The Writing on the Wall* (1985), p.110.
27 D. Healey, *The Time of My Life* (1989), p.369.
28 Whitehead, *Writing on the Wall*, p.114.
29 B. Pimlott, *Harold Wilson* (1992), p.675.
30 Parker, *The Queen*, p.224.
31 Castle, *Diaries 1974–76*, p.671.
32 Interview: Willie Hamilton.
33 Interview: Alan Clark.
34 Warwick, *Princess Margaret*, p.143.
35 N. Dempster, *HRH The Princess Margaret* (1981), p.97.
36 *News of the World*, 21 March 1976.
37 Dempster, *Princess Margaret*, p.127.
38 Hamilton, *My Queen and I*, p.182.
39 Ziegler, *Crown and People*, p.143.
40 *Sunday People*, 26 March 1977.
41 *Director*, 18 January 1977.
42 Reply to the Loyal Address of both Houses, Westminster Hall, 4 May 1977.
43 Whitehead, *Writing on the Wall*, pp.296–7.
44 Kenneth O. Morgan, 'The Crown and Politics', in *New Statesman*, 3 June 1977, p.739.
45 J. Savage, *England's Dreaming* (1991), p.352.
46 D. Cannadine, 'The Context, Performance and Meaning of Ritual', p.160.
47 Interview: Countess Mountbatten.

Chapter 10

1 M. Thatcher, *The Downing Street Years*, (1993), p.18.
2 H. Young, *One of Us* (1989), p.460.
3 Wright, *Spycatcher*, p.223.
4 Interview: Alan Clark.
5 Interview: Sir Shridath (Sonny) Ramphal.
6 Lord Carrington, *Reflect on Things Past* (1988), p.277.
7 *Times of Zambia*, 1 August 1979.
8 Interview: Malcolm Fraser.
9 Interview: Sir Shridath (Sonny) Ramphal.
10 A. Verrier, *The Road to Zimbabwe* (1986), p.250.
11 Interview: Michael Shea.
12 A. Morrow, *The Queen* (1983), p.201.
13 Interview: David Carradine.
14 Interview: Anthony Holden.
15 Ziegler, *Mountbatten*, p.687.
16 Interview: Countess Mountbatten.
17 Interview: Barbara Cartland.

18 Young, *One of Us*, p.552.
19 Interview: James Whitaker.
20 Interview: Penny Junor.
21 Interview: Bob Edwards.
22 Interview: Barbara Cartland.
23 Interview: Elizabeth Emanuel.
24 J. Whitaker, *Diana v. Charles* (1993), p.118.
25 Interview: Lord Charteris.
26 Interview: Michael Fagan.
27 Interview: Rt Rev. Michael Mann.
28 Interview: Rt Rev. Michael Mann.
29 M. Hastings and S. Jenkins, *Battle for the Falklands* (1983), p.228.
30 Parker, *The Queen*, p.293
31 Interview: Alan Clark.
32 Hall, *Royal Fortune*, p.146.
33 Young, *One of Us*, p.280.
34 Interview: David Cannadine.
35 Young, *One of Us*, p.356.
36 *The Thatcher Factor 1: She Knew She Was Right*, Channel 4 TV, April 1989.
37 Interview: Alan Clark.
38 A. Sampson, *The Changing Anatomy of Britain* (1982), p.6.
39 Thatcher, *Downing Street Years*, p.331.
40 Interview: Sir Shridath (Sonny) Ramphal.
41 Thatcher, *Downing Street Years*, p.332.
42 Interview: Sir Shridath (Sonny) Ramphal.
43 Parker, *The Queen*, p.305.
44 Interview: Sir Shridath (Sonny) Ramphal.
45 Interview: Alan Clark.
46 Interview: Bob Hawke.
47 Interview: Sir Shridath (Sonny) Ramphal.
48 *Sunday Times*, 20 July 1986.
49 Interview: Andrew Neil.
50 Private information.
51 Interview: Michael Shea.
52 Letter in the *Times*, 28 July 1986.
53 Young, *One of Us*, p.493.
54 Interview: Anthony Holden.
55 Interview: Anthony Holden.
56 Private information.
57 *Manchester Evening News*, 23 October 1985.
58 Interview: Maxwell Hutchinson.
59 Interview: Maxwell Hutchinson.
60 Interview: Nicholas Soames MP.
61 Interview with Prince Charles in the *Australian*, January 1994.
62 Interview: Bob Hawke.
63 *Panorama*, BBC TV, 4 April 1988.

Chapter 11

1 V. Woolf, *The Moment and Other Essays* (1947), p.187.
2 Interview: Lord Charteris.
3 Interview: Susan Crosland.
4 Interview: Ian Hislop.
5 Interview: Andrew Morton.
6 Interview: Rt Rev. Michael Mann.
7 Interview: Penny Junor.
8 P. Junor, *Charles and Diana: Portrait of a Marriage* (1991), p.7.
9 Whitaker, *Diana vs. Charles,* p.162.
10 Electress Sophia of Hanover, *Memoir* (1888), p.3.
11 Seward, *Royal Children* (1993), p.224.
12 Interview: John Grigg.
13 Interview: Andrew Neil.
14 *Sunday Times,* 10 February 1991.
15 C. Hutchins and P. Thompson, *Fergie Confidential* (1993), p.342.
16 Interview: Dr June Patterson Brown.
17 Interview: John Grigg.
18 Interview: Anthony Holden.
19 A. Holden, *The Tarnished Crown* (1993), p.234.
20 A. Clark, *Diaries* (1993), p.235.
21 Interview: Alan Clark.
22 Interview: Prof. Anthony Clare.
23 Interview: Andrew Morton.
24 Interview: Andrew Neil.
25 Lady Elizabeth Cavendish is a member of the PCC.
26 *Daily Express,* 13 July 1982.
27 Interview: Nicholas Soames MP.
28 Interview: Penny Junor.
29 E. Longford, *Royal Throne* (1993), p.64.
30 Interview: Richard Kay.
31 Interview: Alan Clark.
32 Hall, *Royal Fortune,* p.227.
33 *Daily Mail,* 16 September 1992.
34 A poll in *The Independent on Sunday,* 24 February 1981, had 79 per cent in favour.
35 Interview: Anthony Holden.
36 Interview: Sir Edward Ford.
37 Longford, *Royal Throne,* p.143.
38 Interview: Countess Mountbatten.
39 Longford, *Royal Throne,* p.147.
40 Interview: Lord Harewood.
41 Interview: Lord Charteris.
42 In fact she travelled on the inaugural Inter City 225 to Edinburgh, and was seen so doing in *Elizabeth R,* BBC TV, 1992.
43 Interview: Anthony Holden.

Chapter 12

1 Interview: Sir Edward Heath.
2 N. Dempster and P. Evans, *Behind Palace Doors* (1993), p.10.
3 *Sun,* 19 January 1993.
4 *Daily Telegraph,* 9 February 1993.
5 Archbishop of Canterbury in *Times*, 1 February 1993.
6 Interview: Ven. George Austin.
7 Interview: Nicholas Soames MP.
8 Interview: Lady Elizabeth Cavendish.
9 Interview with Cyril Reenan for *Storyline,* Thames Twenty Television, 1993.
10 *Four Corners,* ABC, 1 March 1993.
11 Interview: Anthony Holden.
12 J. Le Carré, 'Don't Trust Carruthers', in *Daily Telegraph*, 20 January 1993.
13 Interview: Andrew Neil.
14 Interview: Anthony Holden.
15 *Spectator*, 20 November 1993.
16 *Daily Mail,* 21 August 1993.
17 *Sunday Express,* 27 February 1994.
18 Interview: Alan Clark.
19 Interview: Andrew Neil.
20 Interview: Malcolm Turnbull.
21 Interview: Thomas Keneally.
22 Interview: Bob Hawke.
23 Interview: Suzy Menkes.
24 Interview: Prof. Anthony Clare.
25 Interview: Lady Pamela Hicks.
26 Interview: Flora Maxwell-Stuart, the Lady of Traquair.
27 Opinion poll for BBC Wales, 2 March 1994.
28 A.N. Wilson, *The Rise and Fall of the House of Windsor* (1993), p.198.
29 Benn, *Diaries*, IV, p.599.
30 Interview: Tony Benn.
31 Sir Sidney Lee, *The Governance of England* (1904), p.12, quoted by Prof. Peter Hennessy in an Inaugural Lecture, 'Searching for the Great Ghost', at Queen Mary and Westfield College, University of London, 1 February 1994.
32 Hennessy, 'Great Ghost', p.15.
33 S. Haseler, *The End of the House of Windsor* (1993), pp.160–1.
34 *Elizabeth R.* BBC TV 1992.
35 Interview: David Cannadine.
36 Interview: Lord Charteris.

Index

Act of Settlement 249
Adeane, Sir Michael 145, 148, 162–3, 164, 165, 178, 194
Admirality Arch 4
Ahrends, Peter 213
Airlie, Countess of 26
Airlie, Lord 124
Albany, Duke of 19
Albert, Prince *see* George VI
Albert, Prince Consort of England 6–7, 132
Albert, Prince of Schleswig-Holstein 19
Alexandra, Princess 168, 178
Alexandra, Queen 8, 31
  as Princess of Wales 1, 2
Allende, Salvador 176–7
Altrincham, Lord 153, *see also* Grigg, John
Amanullah, King of Afghanistan 54
Amin, Idi 183
Amis, Kingsley 152
Andrew, Prince (Duke of York) 152, 220, 234
  created Duke of York 218
  Falklands War 202–3
  marriage 133, 215, 225
Andrew, Prince of Greece 125
Anne, Princess (Princess Royal) 143, 182, 187, 191, 220, 221
  first marriage 133, 181–2, 221
  Save The Children Fund 221
  second marriage 221, 241
Annigoni, Pietro
  portrait of Elizabeth II 151
Anson, Charles 224–5
Argyll, Duke of 153, 159
Armstrong, Sir Robert 193, 205
Armstrong, Sir William 184
Armstrong-Jones, Anthony *see* Snowdon, Anthony Armstrong-Jones, 1st Earl of
Arnold, Harry 242
Asquith Herbert Henry 13, 19, 25, 45
Asquith, Margot 29
Athlone, Earl of 19
Athlone, Princess Alice of 125
Attlee, Clement 88, 119–20, 140
August Wilhelm, Prince of Prussia 60
Austin, Ven. George 240–1

Australia 183–4, 214, 246–7, 253

Badminton House 113
Bagehot, Walter 3–4, 28, 34, 41, 43, 56, 67
Baker, James 231
Baldwin, Stanley 46, 50, 51, 55, 56, 70–1, 72, 77, 78, 80, 81, 84, 85, 90, 104
Balfour, Arthur 20, 46
Balfour Declaration 15
Balmoral Castle 7, 84, 91, 97, 104
Banda, Dr Hastings 251
Baring, Helen 40
Barnett, Joel 179
Baron (Baron Nahum) 159–60
Bartholemew, Carolyn 228
Barucci, Giulia 2
Battenberg, Prince Alexander of 19
Battenberg, Prince Louis Alexander of *see* Mountbatten, Prince Louis Alexander
Battenberg, Princess Alice of 125
Beaton, Cecil 62, 90
Beatrice, Princess 219
Beaverbrook, Lord 77, 82, 83, 84, 95, 110, 116
Bedaux, Charles 98, 101, 103
Beerbohm, Max 11
Benn, Tony 85, 121, 161, 167, 176, 250–1
Bennett, Alan
A Question of Attribution 164
Bentinck, Lord George 132
Besant, Annie 37
Betjeman, John 65
Bevan, Aneurin 87
Bevin, Ernest 120
Bishop, Maurice 207
Bismarck, Otto von 7, 71
Blunt, Anthony 116, 158, 164–6, 193–4
Boothroyd, Basil 132
Bowes-Lyon, Lady Elizabeth –see Elizabeth, Queen Consort
Boyle, Andrew
The Climate of Treason 193
Brabourne, Lord 171
Branson, Richard 245
Brighton bombing 205
Britannia, royal yacht 144, 203–4, 236, 254
British Broadcasting Corporation (BBC) 91, 95
British Empire Exhibition, Wembley 49–50, 94
British Gazette 51
Broadlands 126
Brooke, Henry 165
Brooke, Peter 234
Brownlow, Lord 83, 96, 98
Bryan, Johnny 229
Buccleuch, Duke of 52
Buchan, John 46
Buchan-Hepburn, Patrick 132
Buckingham Palace 4, 20, 21, 25–6, 52, 55, 62, 67, 69, 72, 83, 93, 105, 112
bombing of 109, 111, 112
break-ins 202
Budgie the Helicopter 219
bugging of Royal family 205, 222, 229–31, 239–43
Bulganin, Nikolai 143
Bullitt, William 102
Burgess, Guy 158
Business in the Community (BiC) 212, 225
Butler, R.A. 89, 133, 135, 148–9, 161–3, 170

Caernarvon Castle, Prince of Wales's investiture 170, 171–2
Caesar (Edward VII's dog) 5
Calder, Ritchie 93
Callaghan, James 171, 186, 187, 189, 191
Cambridge, Marquess of 19
Canada 176
Cannadine, David 89, 191, 197, 204, 235, 253
Carisbrooke, Lord 8, 19
Carr, Sir William 159
Carrington, Lord 195
Cartland, Barbara 60–1, 67, 74, 100, 198, 201

Castle, Barbara 166, 175
Cavendish, Lady Elizabeth 139, 140, 151–2
Cawston, Dick 171
Cenotaph 27
Chamberlain, Neville 56, 104, 105, 110, 120
Channon, Sir Henry (Chips) 29, 41, 73, 77, 79, 90, 99, 121
Charles, Prince of Wales 171, 184, 210, 225–6
  alternative medicine, support of 213
  architecture, views on 213–14, 225
  Business in the Community 212, 225
  and Camilla Parker-Bowles 1, 199, 221–3, 227–8, 239–43
  Camillagate tapes 239–43
  character 143–4, 197–8, 212–13
  childhood 143–4, 197–8
  children 223
  education 144, 169–70, 171–2
  Inner City Aid 214–15, 225
  investiture 170, 171–2
  Klosters skiing tragedy 221
  marriage 197–202, 212, 221–4, 227–9, 233
  and Mountbatten 192, 198
  press coverage 213, 239–46
  rehabilitation 245–7
  role 214–15
  separation 236
  succession 240–3, 249–50, 254
  Sydney shooting 246
  Windsor Conference 212
Charteris, Lord 130, 133, 134, 135, 154, 165, 166, 169, 201, 219, 247, 254
Checketts, David 170
Christian, Prince of Schleswig-Holstein 14
Christmas broadcasts 58, 100, 142, 155
Church of England 98, 204, 240–1, 249
Churchill, Sir Winston 25, 50, 52, 56, 77, 83, 84, 85, 100, 109, 110–11, 114, 115, 130, 131, 134, 136, 137, 156
Civil List 56, 57, 69, 135, 177–81, 233–6
  Duke of Windsor excluded from 97
Clare, Anthony 226
Clarence, Prince Edward, Duke of 8–9
Clarence House 120, 131, 132
Clark, Alan 186, 194, 203, 206, 208, 211, 226, 231, 246
Clark, Kenneth 47, 105
Cobbold, Lord 178, 179, 180
Cole, G.D.H. 53
Colville, Lady Cynthia 129
Colville, Jock 110
Colville, John, 130, 131, 132, 134, 139
Colville, Commander Richard 145, 170
Common Market *see* European Community
Commonwealth 121–2, 127, 146, 155–8, 182–3, 251
  Conference 182–3, 194–6, 208–9
  Heads of Government Meeting, New Delhi 207–8
  Prince Philip's attitude towards 176
  US invasion of Grenada 207
Connor, Bill 154
Conservative Party, leadership elections 163–4
Cook, A.J. 50
Cooper, Lady Diana 74
Cooper, Duff 110
Cornwall, Duchy of 69
coronations
  Edward VII 5
  Elizabeth II 135–7
  George V 7
  George VI 91–4
Correa, Charles 213
Courcy, Kenneth de 119
court and entourage 155
Coward, Noël 85, 139–40

Crawford, Lord 105
Crawford, Marion (Crawfie) 138
Craxton, Anthony 155
Crewe, Lord 54
Cripps, Sir Stafford, 54, 120, 123
Crosland, Anthony 166
Crosland, Susan 219
Crossman, Richard 136, 143, 160, 166, 167, 177, 181
Cumberland, Duke of 19
Cunard, Emerald 90, 96
Curzon, Alexandra 39
Curzon, Lord 24, 39, 46

Daily Express 83
Daily Herald 49
Daily Mirror 154, 159, 176, 179–80, 210, 224, 229, 233
Daily News 15
Daily Star 224
Daily Telegraph 82
Daily Worker 77
Daladier, Edouard 104
Dalton, Hugh 120
Davidson, J.C.C. 47
Dawson, Geoffrey 76, 79, 80, 81, 95
Dawson of Penn, Lord 64–5
De Freitas, Geoffrey 157
De Gaulle, Général Charles 158
De Manio, Jack 172
debutantes, presentation at court 154
Delamere, Lady 52
Denning Report 159, 160
Depression, the 56–9
Derby, Lord 28
Detroit News 103
Devonshire, Duchess of 134
Diana: Her True Story 227–9, 244
Dilhorne, Lord 161, 162
Dimbleby, Jonathan 245
Dimbleby, Richard 136, 152
Disraeli, Benjamin 2, 6, 132
Dobbs, Michael
  To Play the King 243–4
Douglas-Home, Sir Alec 161–4
Dudley, 3rd Earl of 10
Dudley Ward, Freda 34, 35, 37, 60
Duncan, Andrew 141
Durham, 3rd Earl of 3

Eccles, David 136
Ecila (Edward VII's horse) 10
Economist 210
Edelman, Maurice 143
Eden, Sir Anthony 54, 71, 78, 123, 134, 140, 143
  Suez crisis 147–9
Edinburgh, Alfred, Duke of 217
Edinburgh, Prince Philip, Duke of 130, 131–2, 139, 175–7, 189, 202, 234
  charitable causes 142, 166
  education 125
  as father 143–4, 197–8
  position as husband of Queen 131–3, 141–2
  Profumo affair 159–60
  wedding 126
Edward VII
  accession 2
  clothes 4
  coronation 5
  education 8
  Entente Cordiale 6
  as father 10
  funeral 5–6, 7
  as Prince of Wales 1–2, 28
  wedding 41
Edward VIII 31, 50*ff*, 167
  abdication 82–6
  accession 65
  ambassadorial role 35–7
  character 33–5, 37–8
  in East Africa 51–2
  education 32–3
  golden handshake 84–5
  as monarch 67–86
  Nahlin cruise 73–4
  as Prince of Wales 33–8, 50–4
  pro-German leanings, 60, 69–71, 102–3, 109, 164–5
  South Wales visit 79–80
  tax exemption 57
  and Wallis Simpson 60–2, 65, 67, 70–86

World War I 33–4
see also Windsor, Duke of
Edward, Prince 152, 220
Edwards, Bob 200
Eisenhower, Dwight D. 114
Elizabeth II 129*ff*
accession 129–30
annus horribilis speech 235
children 152
coronation 135–7
court and entourage 155
foreign tours 134, 155, 156–7, 182, 189, 194–7
Jubilee 188–91
marriage 126, 142–6
shots fired at 197
Elizabeth, Princess 115
Auxiliary Territorial Service (ATS) 123–4
birth 123
character 124
education 123–4
engagement 126
twenty-first birthday broadcast 127
wedding 126
see also Elizabeth II
Elizabeth, Queen Consort 40–1, 89–90, 104–5
wedding 40–1
see also Elizabeth, Queen, The Queen Mother
Elizabeth, Queen, The Queen Mother 99–100, 131, 132, 133, 200, 201, 231, 233, 254
Civil List 178
and Duke and Duchess of Windsor 99, 118, 168–9
political views 166
see also Elizabeth, Queen Consort
Elizabeth R 226–7, 231–2, 247
Elveden 57
Empire's Homage to the Throne, The 92
Encounter 154
Entente Cordiale 6, 104
Ernest Augustus, Prince 131
Esher, Lord 23, 25, 43
European Community
British applications for membership 158, 182
effect of British membership 251–3

Fagan, Michael 202
Falklands War 202–4
Ferdinand, King of Bulgaria 5, 20
Ferguson, Ronald 218
Ferguson, Sarah *see* York, Sarah, Duchess of
Fermoy, Lady 199
Fiji 251
Finch-Hatton, Denys 52
Fisher, Admiral 31
Fisher, Archbishop 136, 141
Foot, Michael 204
Forbes, Alastair 122
Ford, Sir Edward 129, 154, 155, 157, 235
Forster, E.M. 29
Fort Belvedere 62, 69, 70, 72, 78, 85, 97
Forwood, Sir Dudley 83, 96, 101
Franz Ferdinand, Archduke of Austria 5, 20
Fraser, Malcolm 183–4, 195
Frederick, Crown Prince of Prussia 7
Furness, Lady 60

Gaitskell, Hugh 120–1, 134, 140, 159
Galbraith, Tam 158
Gandhi, Indira 207
Gandhi, Mahatma 55, 72, 121
Gandhi, Rajiv 208
GCHQ 243
ban on trade union membership 204–5
General Strike 50–1
Genoa Conference 45
George V 6, 7*ff*
"Balmorality" 11
character 8, 88–9
children 27–8, 32–3, 59–60
coronation 7
death and funeral 64–5, 68–9

hobbies 9–10
Indian Durbar 12
and Ireland 43–4
and Kaiser Wilhelm II 7–8
and Lloyd George 44–6
Silver Jubilee 63–4
will 69
George VI 31, 39–41, 63, 84, 87*ff*
accession 87–9
character 33, 88–9, 100
children 123
coronation 91–4
death 127, 129–30
education 32–3, 39
foreign tours 49, 106, 114, 120, 122, 126
Pig Club 112
wedding 40–1
George, Prince *see* Kent, George, Duke of
Gibbon, Edward 38
Gibbs, Philip 68
Gissing, George 3
Glamis Castle 40
Gloucester, Henry, Duke of 31, 33, 39, 51, 52, 87, 130
Gloucester, Richard, Duke of 250
Glücksburg family 132
Goering, Hermann 102
Gordonstoun school 125, 144, 169–70, 223
Gore, John 8
Govan Yard, Glasgow 248
Graves, Robert 137
Grenada, US invasion 207
Grigg, Edward 153
Grigg, John 141–2, 153–4, 89, 155, 224, 225, *see also* Altrincham, Lord
Gulf War 224
Gunther, John 77

Hackney, Rod 213, 214, 225
Hahn, Kurt 125
Haig, General Sir Douglas 15, 45
Haile Selassie, Emperor of Ethiopia 71
Hailsham, Lord 147, 158, 161, 162–3
Haines, Joe 185
Halifax, Lord 89, 110, 113, 117, 118
Hall, Philip 135, 178, 203–4
Royal Fortune 232
Hall, Stuart 220
Halsey, Admiral 62–3
Hamilton, Willie 178, 179, 180, 186, 187
Hardie, Keir 7
Hardinge, Lord 28
Hardinge, Major Alexander 71, 80, 81, 99, 114–15
Harewood, Earl of 29, 168, 235
Harmsworth, Esmond 82
Harry, Prince 223
Hartnell, Norman 90, 113, 126
Harvey, Oliver 115
Haseler, Professor Stephen 252
Hassan II, King of Morocco 196–7
Hawke, Bob 208, 214, 246
Hearst press 71
Heath, Sir Edward 148, 181, 182, 183, 184–5, 231, 239
Helena, Princess 14
Hello, York photographs 219
Hennessy, Professor 252
Henry, Prince of Prussia 13
Henson, Hensley 98
Herald 24
hereditary titles 181
reintroduction 218
Heseltine, Bill 155, 170, 171
Heseltine, Sir William 211
Hicks, Lady Pamela 119, 247
Highgrove House 198–9, 222
Hirohito, Emperor of Japan 37, 105
Hitler, Adolf 60, 70, 71, 101, 102, 103, 105, 106, 110, 117
Hoesch, Leopold von 70
Hogg, Quintin *see* Hailsham, Lord
Holden, Anthony 1, 211–12, 225, 234

Home, Lord *see* Douglas-Home, Sir Alec
honours system 5, 120, 181, 218
Hore, Belisha, Leslie 105
Houghton, Douglas 179
House, Colonel 44
House of Lords, attempted reform 181
Hudson, Lady 31
Hughes, Emrys 167
Hurd, Douglas 196–7
Hutchinson, Maxwell 213–14

Ingham, Bernard 205, 208
Inner City Aid 214–15, 225
International Monetary Fund Crisis 185
Invergordon mutiny 56
Irish Republican Army (IRA) 192, 205
Ironsi, Major 155
Ismay, General 123
It's a Royal Knockout 220–1
Ivanov, Evgeny 159
Iveagh, Lord 57

James, Clive 244
Jardine, Rev. J.A. 98
Jenkins, Roy 167, 180
John, Prince 31
Johnson, Paul 179
Jones, Hywel 170, 172
Jones, Thomas 78
Junor, Penny 200, 223, 229

Kant, Immanuel 24
Kaunda, Kenneth 157, 195
Keating, Paul 246, 251
Keay, Douglas 168
Keeler, Christine 158–9
Keneally, Thomas 246
Kennedy, John F. 157
Kennedy, Joseph 112
Kent, Duchess of 100, 241
Kent, George, Duke of 31, 33, 39, 59, 87
Kent, Prince Michael of 192
Kent, Princess Michael of 188
Keppel, Alice 10
Kerr, Sir John 183–4
Khrushchev, Nikita 143
Kilmuir, Lord 148, 158
King, Cecil 159–60, 176, 182
King, Mackenzie 106
Kipling, Rudyard 19, 58–9
Kitson, Michael 165
Knatchbull, Amanda 198
Korda, Alexander 137

Labour Party 23–4, 88, 97, 119–21
Lacey, Robert 147
Lamont, Norman 233
Lancaster, Duchy of 57
Lancaster House Conference 196
Lang, Archbishop of Canterbury 80, 94, 95
Langtry, Lillie 28
Lansbury, George 47, 80
Lascelles, Alan 38, 51, 53, 72, 74, 99, 115, 118, 130, 131, 132, 139
Lascelles, Henry, Viscount 40
Laski, Harold 56, 88, 103
Laurence, Tim 221
Law, Andrew Bonar 46
Le Carré, John 243
League of Nations 71
Lenin, Vladimir Ilyich 45
Leopold III, King of Belgium 113
Libya, US air-raid 210
Lightbody, Nurse 143
Lindsay, Major Hugh 221
Lindsay-Hogg, Lucy 187
Litvinov, Maxim 70
Llewellyn, Roddy 187, 188
Lloyd, Selwyn 158
Lloyd George, David 13, 15, 16, 20, 24, 25, 26, 35, 38, 40, 44–6, 56, 93
Longford, Lady 235, 236
Lord Chamberlain, office of 180
Lutyens, Sir Edwin 12

Maastricht Treaty 251–2
MacDonald, James Ramsay 47–9, 55–6, 120

Macgregor, Lord 227
Mackenzie, Kelvin 240
Maclean, Donald 158
Maclean, Veronica 124
Macleod, Iain 161, 162, 163
Macmillan, Harold 81, 115, 133, 134, 155, 156–8, 160–3
  Profumo affair 158–60
  Suez crisis 148–9
McNally, Paddy 218
Magnus, Philip 4
Major, John 233, 236, 252
Mall, London 4
Manchester Evening News 213
Mann, Michael 202, 220
Margaret, Princess 115, 139, 166, 178, 180
  birth 123
  character 124–5
  divorce 186–7
  education 123–4
  marriage 141, 151–2
  and Peter Townsend 137–41
  press treatment of 187–8
  and Roddy Llewellyn 186–7, 188
Marie, Queen of Roumania 217
Marie-Astrid, Princess of Luxembourg 199
Marina, Princess 59
Markham, Beryl 52
Martin, Kingsley 91
Mary, Princess Royal, 31, 33, 40, 99
Mary, Queen 9, 27, 110, 113–14, 123, 129, 131
  character 28–31
  children 31–3
  as collector 30–1
  death 135
  and Wallis Simpson 81–2, 99, 118
Mary of Teck, Princess *see* Mary, Queen
Mass Observation surveys 93, 111
Maudling, Reginald 162
Maxton, James 88
media coverage of the monarchy 17–18, 68, 74, 75–8, 90–1, 152–4, 170–3, 175–7, 177, 182, 186–8, 199–201, 212, 219–25, 227–31
  Camillagate tapes 239–42
  Edward VIII's abdication 82–3
  monarchy and Thatcher government 209–11
  Squidgygate tapes 230, 239, 242–3
  see also television broadcasts
Meet the Press, Prince Philip's appearance on 177
Menkes, Suzy 30, 247
Mensdorff, Count 13
Menzies, Sir Robert 134, 146, 147, 155
Metcalfe, Fruity 96, 98
Milford Haven, 1st Marquess of *see* Mountbatten, Prince Louis Alexander
Milford Haven, David 144–5
miners' strike (1974) 184–5
miners' strike (1984) 205
Mitterand, Francois 206
monarchy
  economic cost 236
  modernising changes 154–5
  press criticisms of 152–4, 179–80, 182, 187–8, 212–15, 219–25, 227–31, 239–43
  public's attitude towards 20–1, 73, 78, 84, 88, 93, 111–12, 152–3, 215, 219–26, 240
  royal family, image of 28, 36
  sovereign's tax-free status 97
  tax exemption 57, 135, 178–9, 232–6
Monckton, Walter 74, 78, 81, 84, 98
Montague-Douglas-Scott, Lady Alice 52
Morning Post 94
Morrison, Herbert 103
Morshead, Sir Owen 164
Morton, Andrew 200, 220, 222
  Diana: Her True Story 277–9, 244
Mosley, Diana 72
Mosley, Sir Oswald 72
Mother Teresa 244

Mount Temple, Lord 104
Mountbatten, Prince Louis Alexander 14, 19
Mountbatten of Burma, Louis Mountbatten, 1st Earl 14, 16, 38, 121, 124, 125, 131, 133, 136, 169, 170, 176, 198
assassination and funeral 192
Suez crisis 146–8
televised autobiography 170–1
Mountbatten, Countess 192, 198, 235
Mountbatten-Windsor surname 131, 133
Movietone newsreels 91
Mugabe, Robert 196
Muggeridge, Malcolm 48, 152–3, 154
Murdoch, Rupert 212, 239
Mussolini, Benito 71, 73, 105
Muzorewa, Bishop 194

Nahum, Baron 144–5
Nairn, Tom 173
Namibia 251
Nasser, Gamel Abdel 146–8
National and English Review 153
National Enquirer 230
National Gallery 213
Neave, Airey 192
Nehru, Jawaharlal 147, 156
Neil, Andrew 210, 224, 227, 243
Neilson, Nigel 170
New Statesman 77, 91, 152, 190–1
New York Times 63
News of the World 187, 201–2
Newspaper Proprieters' Association 77
Nicholas II, Tsar 14, 15–16
Nicolson, Harold 43, 64, 107
Nixon, Richard M. 171
Nkrumah, Kwame 156–7
Norfolk, 16th Duke 135–6
Norfolk, Duke of 94
Norgrove, Janet 242
Northcliffe, Lord 76
Northern Ireland 43–4, 188, 190, 192, 197, 231

Obote, Milton 183
Order of the Garter 120
Order of Merit 5
Osborne, John 154

Page, Walter Hines 11
Paglia, Camille 244
Palmer-Tomkinson, Patti 221
Paris-Soir 78
Parker, Dorothy 217
Parker, Eileen 145
Parker, Mike 130, 145
Parker, Peter 175
Parker-Bowles, Brigadier Andrew 222
Parker-Bowles, Camilla 1, 199, 200, 221–3, 227–8, 239–43
Paul, Prince of Yugoslavia 110, 135
Peace Day 26
Peake, Charles 118
People 137–8
Philby, Harold (Kim) 158, 164
Philip, Prince *see* Edinburgh, Prince Philip, Duke of
Phillips, Captain Mark 181–2, 221
Polan, Brenda 206
Ponsonby, Arthur 13, 32
Ponsonby, Sir Frederick 34, 93
Post, Laurens van der 2
Pound, Ezra 21
Powell, Charles 208
Powell, J. Enoch 67, 114, 132, 146, 163, 184
Preston, Kiki 59
Princess Royal (Anne) *see* Anne, Princess
Princess Royal (Mary) *see* Mary, Princess Royal
Princess Royal (Victoria) *see* Victoria, Princess Royal
Private Eye 180, 181, 188, 219–20, 229, 231
Profumo, John 158–60
Punch 70

Raffray, Mary 75
Ramphal, Sonny 183, 194, 209
Reagan, Ronald 207, 231

Reenan, Cyril 242
Reith, Sir John 58, 80, 91, 112
republicanism 250–3
Reynolds' News 41, 152
Rhodesia 157–8, 176, 194–6
Ribbentrop, Joachim von 70–1, 84, 102, 117
Riddell, Lord 17
Robinson, Mary 250
Rocco, Fiammetta 145
Rockefeller, John D. 103
Roosevelt, Theodore 5–6, 94, 102, 106, 107, 110
Rothermere, Lord 82
Rothschild, Baron de 96
Rothschild, Baroness 87
Royal Ascot 27
Royal Family 171, 172, 175, 182
Royal Flight, 236, 254
Royal Fortune 232
Royal Marriages Act 168, 249
Royal Maundy service 155
Royal Naval College, Dartmouth 32, 39, 125
Royal Naval College, Osborne 32
Royal Navy 125
Royal Train 236, 254
Runcie, Robert, Archbishop of Canterbury 204
Runciman, Sir Steven 31, 58, 71, 105
Russian Revolution 15–16

Saddam Hussein 224, 231
St George's Chapel, Windsor 14, 18, 69
St John of Fawlsey, Lord 240
St Paul's Cathedral 63
Salisbury, 4th Marquess of 87
Salisbury, 5th Marquis 134, 146, 148, 158
Sandringham 9, 31, 64, 84, 91, 97, 127
Sandys, Duncan 156
Santa Cruz, Lucia 170
Save The Children Fund 221
Saxe-Coburg, Charles, Duke of 70, 101, 125
Scargill, Arthur 205
Scoon, Sir Paul 207
Scott, Selina 228
Scottish nationalism 188, 189–90, 249
Secombe, Harry 172
Secular Review 7
Sex Pistols 91
Shand Kydd, Frances 199, 200
Shea, Michael 196, 201, 210
Sheean, Vincent 79
Shils, Edward 137
Simpson, Ernest 60, 75
Simpson, Wallis 34, 60–2, 65, 67, 70–1, 72–86, 98
see also Windsor, Duchess of
Sims, Charles 50
Sitwell, Osbert 96
Sixty Glorious Years 91
Skardon, William 164
Slim, Sir William 146
Smith, Ian 157, 194
Snagge, John 130
Snowden, Ethel 48
Snowden, Philip 49, 56
Snowdon, Anthony Armstrong-Jones, 1st Earl of 151–2, 171, 172, 178, 186, 187, 188
Soames, Sir Christopher 169, 196
Soames, Nicholas 214, 229, 241
South Africa 156, 208–9, 251
Soviet Union 49
Spanish Civil War 78
Spectator 163
Spencer, 8th Earl 199, 201
Spencer, Lady Diana *see* Wales, Princess of
Spencer, Raine 199, 201
Sphere 54
Spitting Image 224, 231
Spitzy, Reinhard 70, 100, 101
Squidgygate tapes 230, 239, 242–3
Stamfordham, Lord 13, 16, 17–18, 36, 46
Stansgate, Lord 121
Stark, Koo 218
State Opening of Parliament 4, 11, 25, 55, 78–9

Stead, W.T. 1
Stephen, Sir Ninian 214
Strathmore, 14th Earl of 40
Stuart, James 134
Stuart dynasty 249
Suez crisis 146–9
Suffragettes 43
Sun 210, 224, 230–1, 240, 242
Sunday Mirror 200, 240
Sunday Pictorial 145
Sunday Times 209–11, 224–5, 228, 246

tax status of monarchy 57, 135, 178–9, 232–6
Taylor, A.J.P. 43, 112
Tebbit, Norman 215
Teck, Prince Alexander of 19
Teck, Duke of 19, 68
television broadcasts
  Christmas broadcasts 142, 155
  Elizabeth II's coronation 136
  Elizabeth R 226–7, 231–2, 247
  It's a Royal Knockout 220–1
  Prince of Wales' wedding 201
  Princess Margaret's wedding 152
  Royal Family 171, 172, 175, 182
  To Play the King 243–4
Temple, Frederick, Archbishop of Canterbury 4, 5
Templer, General 147
Thatcher, Margaret 189, 191–2, 193–6, 197, 199, 202–12, 214, 218, 232
  Brighton bombing 205
  Falklands War 202–4
  miners' strike 205
  and South Africa 208–9
  US invasion of Grenada 207–8
Thomas, George 171
Thomas, Sir Godfrey 36, 53
Thomas, Jimmy 48, 56
Thomas Cook travel company 92
Thorne, Will 16
Thorpe, Jeremy 185
three-day week 184
Thursday Club 144–5, 159
Timbertop school 169–70
Times 17, 18, 19, 27, 64, 76, 82, 83, 91, 92, 94, 95, 140, 188
Titles Deprivation Act 19
Tonga, Queen of 137
Townsend, Group Captain Peter 40, 115, 122, 134, 137–41
Treaty of Versailles 44
Treetops, Kenya 129
Trotsky, Leon 45
Trudeau, Pierre 183
Tuckwell, Patricia 168
Turnbull, Malcolm 246–7
Two Minutes' Silence 26

Unknown Warrior, funeral of 27

Vansittart, Sir Robert 91
Vassall, John 158
Verwoerd, Dr Hendrik Freusch 156
Victoria, Princess 64
Victoria, Princess Royal 7
Victoria, Queen 2–3, 6, 76, 91
Victoria the Great 91
Victoria Memorial 4
Victory Day 26
Victory in Europe Day 115
Von Reibnitz, Marie-Christine *see* Kent, Princess Michael of

Wade, Virginia 191
Wales, Charles, Prince of *see* Charles, Prince of Wales
Wales, Edward, Prince of *see* Edward VII: Edward VIII
Wales, Princess of (Alexandra) 1, 2
Wales, Princess of (Diana) 2, 197–202, 218–19, 236–7, 244–5, 254
  character 199–200, 202
  children 223
  Diana: Her True Story 227–9, 244
  eating disorders 201, 227
  health club photographs 245
  marriage 197, 221–4, 227–9, 233
  press coverage of 199–202
  separation 236

Squidgygate tapes 230, 239, 242–3
suicide attempts 227
Wallace, Billy 139–40
Ward, Dr Stephen 159–60, 165
Warwick, Lady Brooke, Countess of 2
Warwick, Christopher 186
Washington Daily News 182
Waugh, Evelyn 83
Webb, Beatrice 48
Wedgwood Benn, Anthony *see* Benn, Tony
Wellesley, Jane 198
Wellington, Duke of 92
Wells, H.G. 17–18
Welsh nationalism 188, 189–90, 249–50
Wenner-Gren, Axel 117
Westminster Abbey 27, 41, 92, 126
Whitaker, James 199–200
Whitelaw, William 202
Whitlam, Gough 183–4, 189
Wigram, Lord 20, 45, 56, 72, 91, 99
Wilhelm II, Kaiser of Germany 4, 5, 6, 7, 8, 14, 20, 24–5, 64
William, Prince 202, 223
William Prince (son of the Kaiser) 69
Wilson, A.N. 140, 250
Wilson, Harold 162, 166–7, 170, 171, 177, 180, 181 185–6
Wilson, Sir Arnold 88
Wilson, Woodrow 11, 25, 44
Windsor, Duke of 96–104, 130, 137, 167–9, 182
abdication broadcast 85
biography 116–17
death 169
Elizabeth II's attitude towards 135
excluded from Civil List 97
Governor of the Bahamas 109, 115, 117, 118
in Paris 118–19
pro-Nazi leanings 101–3, 109
public's attitude towards 100, 101
Queen Mary's funeral 135
Verdun peace broadcast 106
World War II 115–17
see also Edward VIII
Windsor, Duchess of 90, 96–104, 118–19, 131, 168–9, 169
jewellery 61, 72, 79, 169
title refused to 98–9
wedding 98
see also Simpson, Wallis
Windsor Castle 18–19, 55, 72, 83, 85, 91, 123
fire 233–4
Windsor surname 18–19, 131, 133
Woolf, Virginia 217
World War I 13–21
World War II 109–15
World Telegram 76
Wright, Peter 164, 194
Wyatt, Steve 224

York, Albert, Duke of *see* George VI
York, Andrew, Duke of *see* Andrew, Prince
York, Elizabeth, Duchess of *see* Elizabeth, Queen Consort
York, Sarah, Duchess of 74, 219–20, 224–5
marriage 215, 218, 225, 229
York Cottage, Sandringham 9, 31
Yorkshire Post 82
Young, Hugo 211
Young, Michael 137

Ziegler, Philip 76, 116, 117, 164, 187, 190
Zimbabwe *see* Rhodesia